SPITFIRE PEOPLE

To Helen

SPITFIRE PEOPLE

The men and women who made the Spitfire *the* aviation icon

With many best wishes

EVRO
PUBLISHING

PAUL BEAVER
FOREWORD BY CAPTAIN ERIC BROWN CBE DSC AFC

Published in June 2015

ISBN 978-1-9105050-5-2

Published by Evro Publishing
Westrow House, Holwell, Sherborne, Dorset DT9 5LF

Printed and bound in China by 1010 Printing International Ltd

Every effort has been made to trace and acknowledge holders of copyright
in photographs and to obtain their permission for the use of photographs.
The publisher apologises for any errors or omissions in the credits
given throughout this book and would be grateful to be notified of any
corrections that should be incorporated in future reprints or editions.

Designed by Richard Parsons
Edited by Mark Hughes

www.evropublishing.com

CONTENTS

FOREWORD
CAPTAIN ERIC MELROSE BROWN

When my old friend Paul Beaver asked me to write a foreword for his new book on the Spitfire, my first thought was 'what can possibly be left to say', but I am delighted to say Paul has found a subject that few have researched – the people who made the Spitfire *the* aviation icon.

No icon of the 20th century is more recognisable than the Spitfire yet few know the names of the people behind the design, the development, the testing and the operations, nor the challenges to produce the first of these magnificent fighter aeroplanes.

In my early service career, I had the privilege of meeting many of the people highlighted in this book. I worked with them on the development of the Seafire from the Hooked Spitfire, and on the challenges of high-speed flight as we neared the sound barrier.

As Paul records, I flew nearly every mark of Seafire and many of the numerous Spitfire variants that were produced.

I grew to love the later marks with their uprated Merlin engines or thunderous Griffons. I tested the fighters against the then enemy's machines as well as those of our Allies. Each time, Mitchell's machine showed its worth.

I marvelled at the skill of men at Supermarine like Joe Smith, Alan Clifton and, most of all, Jeffrey Quill.

I enjoyed testing the new variants as they were produced at Southampton, Salisbury, Trowbridge or Castle Bromwich. The Seafires, of course, came off the lines at Hamble and Yeovil where Folland, Aviation Training Services and Westland's people worked all hours so that the Fleet could be defended from air attack.

It has not been possible for Paul to list everyone in his book, which is a timeless and significant tribute to both those included and all those not mentioned by name but to whom we all owe so much.

I am delighted to be associated with this book, which I believe is the first comprehensive compilation of the people, places, politics and means of production of the Spitfire. It is a significant achievement.

Captain Eric Melrose Brown CBE DSC AFC FRAeS Royal Navy
Copthorne
January 2015

Captain Eric Brown is a national treasure. Not only is he the most decorated aviator in the Fleet Air Arm but he is a Guinness World Record holder for types flown and carrier deck landings completed. Since leaving the Royal Navy, he has lectured and advised tirelessly on naval aviation and the need for continued technological advance in aviation. Eric has flown more Spitfire variants than any man alive. FNHT

INTRODUCTION

There have been more books on the Spitfire than on any other aeroplane type. That is not surprising as the Spitfire is arguably the greatest aviation icon of all. It not only saved a nation and its allies, but it also set the standard against which all other types are judged.

This book takes the story forward into areas that have rarely been examined. It looks at the people who designed, built and flew the Spitfire. It explores the contribution of great designers and shop-floor workers, politicians and pilots, backers and detractors. It is the book I have wanted to read for 40 years but could never find.

It will, of course, be controversial. Not because controversy was my aim when I set out on my research, but because my conclusions sometimes differ from the established view. I question, for example, whether Reginald Mitchell deserves all the credit for the Spitfire when his initial work was flawed and his team were the people who shaped his grand design into a working product. I have also examined the role played by politicians in the mid-1930s when Britain needed to rearm and found that Neville Chamberlain, so long the villain of the peace (as it were), was actually the Cabinet Minister who pushed through funding for the Spitfire (and Hurricane) against the advice of others who preferred to see the production of more bombers. Chamberlain was a Spitfire Person and deserves his place in this story.

When it comes to production, which takes up a significant proportion of this book because that is where much of the untold story lies, it is clear that plans were laid early on for the dispersed assembly sites of Salisbury, Trowbridge, Reading and Newbury, that engine plants were planned as far north as Scotland, and that Castle Bromwich, despite what local newspapers in Birmingham might have us believe, was not a great development centre but just a good 'build-to-print' facility which, like the others, had its teething problems.

Before sitting down to draft the first chapters, I took two important decisions. The first was to spend time at the Solent Sky Museum in Southampton where there are unpublished records of Supermarine, Folland and other aviation companies of the South Coast. The second was to talk to my old friend Captain Eric ('Winkle') Brown to make sure that I had the context right. He kindly agreed to write the foreword, for which I am honoured and hugely grateful. He is a true national treasure, just like the Spitfire.

As much of the published work about the Spitfire has retreaded previous work, complete with the errors generated by censorship, official biases and personal prejudice in the period immediately after the war, I have used original source material at Solent Sky and elsewhere,

Paul Beaver is passionate about aviation in general and Spitfires in particular. He lectures frequently and widely, bringing his contemporary expertise on procurement and development to historical subjects. His key endeavour is to find ways of bringing young people into aviation to share the delights of 100 years of manned flight. John Goodman

including my own interview notes from 30 years of private study. There have been notable exceptions to those who retread, including the seminal works of Dr Alfred Price and the late Ray Sturtivant, to whom I owe much in my early enthusiasm for writing in the late 1970s and early 1980s before joining Jane's Information Group.

We have been blessed with details of almost every contact in aerial fighting made by a Spitfire. Through the Osprey publishing series on air aces, we know about the heroes of the air, but historians nowadays have increasingly come to realise that the Spitfire's iconic position is due to much more. I have always been struck by the late Group Captain Douglas

Bader's view that 'the British people won the Battle of Britain' and have extrapolated this thesis to look at the men and women who made the Spitfire in every possible definition of the term 'made'.

Travelling the country giving lectures on the Spitfire, the Battle of Britain, Assault Glider Operations and other facets of aviation history that attract me – particularly the late 1930s and the early years of the Second World War – I have been struck by the number of people who come up after a talk to tell me about a personal connection with the Spitfire: 'My mother was a wing-riveter'; 'My father worked on the 100-octane fuel at Ellesmere Port'; 'My grandmother made Spitfire gun sights in a back street of Southampton'; 'My father was the third man to fly the Spitfire prototype'.

I have tried to be loyal to these informants in the text of the book and credited them where I can. The wonderful thing about speaking to groups of non-experts is that the questions asked are often so basic and genuine that the speaker has to think and sometimes even say, 'That's interesting, I don't know, but I will do some research and come back to you.' So it was with the story of Wiltshire's Presentational Spitfires that has resulted in new evidence being uncovered of community spirit, generosity and not a little grandstanding.

'How much did a Spitfire cost?' has been asked frequently and is as difficult to quantify as such questions are nowadays, as when a modern reporter wants to know how much a piece of military hardware cost the taxpayer so that a headline can be constructed about '£x million jet crashes' or some such. It is almost impossible to be certain, accurate or correct.

My initial research into costs, part of a theme running through this book, was spurred on by an article in a Ministry of Defence publication claiming that the Ministry of Aircraft Production (a forerunner of the Defence Equipment & Support that provides today's military equipment and services to the armed forces) held the cost to the taxpayer of a Spitfire at £5,000 throughout the war. I realised, from my own work as a Parliamentary Advisor on defence matters in the House of Commons, that this was mistaken at best and perhaps even disingenuous. Research at the Royal Air Force Museum shows the MoD's assertion to have been rubbish.

What it did, however, was awaken my sceptical instincts that had been dormant for 20 years since I stepped down from running *Jane's Defence Weekly*. I had to find out. The answer – and proof of the misunderstanding of costs and payments that must have led to the MoD's assertion – is that the nominal presentational gift price was £5,000. This was not the cost to the taxpayer.

After that, this book gestated very quickly. Research for a lecture to the Army Flying Association at Middle Wallop, itself a Battle of Britain Spitfire station, was followed by an invitation from my old friend James Holland to speak at the Chalke Valley History Festival in 2014. The thesis at the centre of the talk was that people, politics and places of production influenced the creation of the iconic status of the Spitfire as much as the brave – truly gallant in many cases – exploits of the air and ground crews. In fact, the Spitfire is quintessentially British in its gestation, development, production and rapid introduction to service. It nearly did not make it and might even have been replaced as early as 1942 by the twin-engined

Probably the best autobiography of a Battle of Britain Spitfire pilot, Geoffrey Wellum's First Light *should be a set text in our schools. Geoffrey's self-effacing charm and wit have inspired many, and his continued work for charity is tireless, both for fly2help (where he is a patron) and the Battle of Britain Fighter Association (where he is vice-chairman).*

John Goodman

Westland Whirlwind had it not been for the skill and tenacity of Joe Smith, who eventually replaced R.J. Mitchell as chief designer of Vickers Supermarine. But how many people have heard of Joe Smith? Or Alf Faddy? Or Alan Clifton? During my research I found many people who deserve more and better attention.

I hope, too, that this book will have uncovered new ground and paid appropriate homage to those who toiled and risked much to bring the Spitfire to the service of the nation. It did win the Battle of Britain, if not in sheer numbers of enemy aircraft destroyed, then certainly in terms of public morale. The Ministry of Aircraft Production's 'Spitfire Fund', attributed to Lord Beaverbrook's entrepreneurial skills and thirst for publicity, was never joined by a 'Hurricane Fund' or a 'Blenheim Fund' – both good aircraft in their time but without the public acceptance of the Spitfire. The old adage that Luftwaffe pilots often claimed to have been shot down by a Spitfire rather than a Hurricane rings true in this connection.

With the help of the Battle of Britain Fighter Association historian, Geoff Simpson, I can confirm that the first Spitfire ace was Bob Stanford Tuck – and he achieved that distinction

Experiencing the Spitfire is every schoolboy's dream – or should be. For the author, completing a 'victory roll' over a Dutch airfield has been part of that dream. Thinking about his Spitfire flying relative to the run-up to the Battle of Britain anniversary, he realised that he had just enough Spitfire 'time' to have been sent into action in the seminal conflict and probably would not have returned from a first sortie. Author's collection

before the official start of the Battle of Britain on 10 July 1940. Geoff is always willing to lend a hand and give advice, especially about people. His recent works on the BBFA and the complete listing of all Battle of Britain aircrew are must-haves for any self-respecting historian of Second World War aviation.

I think Geoff supports my view, as many historians do, that the battle that is widely regarded as the nation's – and the Spitfire's – finest hour started over the French countryside rather than the fields of Kent. For his mighty tome *The Battle of Britain*, published in 2010 to coincide with the 70th anniversary year, James Holland used the subtitle 'five months that changed history', taking May as the starting date. I wholeheartedly concur: the Battle of France and Dunkirk gave valuable lessons to Fighter Command and both Hugh Dowding and Keith Park learned them.

James Holland is the director and co-founder of the Chalke Valley History Festival and it was there that Eric Verdon-Roe heard my talk. He is the grandson of a great name in British aviation history, A.V. Roe, whose company built the Lancaster and the Vulcan. Afterwards, over lunch on a beautiful sunny afternoon in the Wiltshire countryside, we hatched the idea of a book that brings together all those people who actually made the Spitfire possible. Battle of Britain legend Geoffrey Wellum, who dined with us, readily agreed. So it is that *Spitfire People* is the first aviation title of Eric's new publishing house, Evro Publishing, which in many ways is a successor to my first publisher, Patrick Stephens Limited.

The modern Spitfire world is a small place. Besides dozens of expert enthusiasts, I have been delighted to have the friendship and support of the heritage flying community as I have accumulated personal flying hours on the Spitfire. Chief among those influences are Matt Jones, MD of the Boultbee Flight Academy, Phill O'Dell, guru of Spitfire flyers and chief test pilot at Rolls-Royce, Squadron Leader Andy Millikin of the Battle of Britain Memorial Flight, and Alfie Southwell, a sometime business partner and commercial genius with whom, one day, I am sure I will own a Spitfire. No serious historian should go anywhere near the subject without touching base with Seb Cox, who runs the Air Historical Branch of the Royal Air Force, and I have listened to his wise words on more than one occasion.

Sources were developed and consulted, including my own notes from interviews with veterans as well as the resources of the Solent Sky Museum, where Squadron Leader Alan Jones, his son Andy (a trustee) and the backroom boys, especially former aeronautical engineer Dave Gash, have been so helpful. Other museums at Hendon, Yeovilton and Middle Wallop have curators and keepers who have been free with time and advice.

The RAF Museum's Peter Devitt is a whizz on the other nationalities in the Royal Air Force and is keen as mustard to help researchers. No 609's Association gave valuable insight and connections, as did the Sikorski Institute; where would we be without such people? For tracing photos of Norwegian pilots, I am grateful to the Cato Guhnfeldt Collection.

I have also been immeasurably helped by many others: Clare Walker, whose knowledge of the Air Transport Auxiliary is unsurpassed; Wing Commander John Davis, the former Boscombe Down test pilot who took a red pen to the early drafts; Air Commodore Jane Middleton, RAuxAF for her counsel on balance; Jon Freeman, the artist; John Goodman, the photographer; Jack Beaver, my spotter of a son on Spitfire mark numbers; and, of course, my darling wife, Cate Pye, whose valuable help included bringing her process-engineering knowledge to bear when proof-reading.

In the end, of course, it is my interpretation of the facts and my views that make up this book, so any errors or misjudgements are my fault. Despite the best efforts of my inestimable editor Mark Hughes, there will be bones of contention and there are bound to be errors and omissions. Please let me know.

In conclusion, I hope I have identified a series of individuals who put their talents at the service of the nation and, very often, put their careers on the line too. There will be more people out there who need to be recognised and perhaps we will do that in due course. For now, here are the 50 or so people who made the Spitfire *the* aviation icon.

Paul Beaver
Goodworth Clatford
March 2015

CHAPTER 1
THE GREAT MINDS

Creating a new generation of fighting machine takes time and effort. It takes funding and technological breakthrough in both materials and applications. And it takes luck. Chance, it is said, favours the prepared mind, and there were colossal minds ready and waiting. The contribution of five of them is examined in this chapter.

If all great projects have the need for great figures to make them happen, then many of the most successful projects in the first half of the 20th century seem to have had input from one man – Winston Spencer Churchill. Although he did not directly contribute to the Spitfire's creation, he certainly understood the need for the technology of rearmament as it became clear that Germany had transgressed the Treaty of Versailles and was itself rearming. Having set the conditions through political persuasion, it was up to others to create the fighter that would become the greatest aviation icon ever.

Keen on flying from its earliest days, Churchill took more than 100 flying lessons before the First World War and was instrumental in the formation of the Royal Naval Air Service, which in 1918 became the Royal Air Force. The RNAS resurfaced as the Fleet Air Arm in 1937 as a result of the Inskip Report, which also saw emphasis placed on the Spitfire. As First Lord of the Admiralty for the second time, Churchill pushed for more and better naval aircraft and this eventually led to the Seafire being brought into service.

To bring the Spitfire into being required the talent of many people. The need was obvious and the technology to achieve that need had started to become available. It is tempting, as so many authors and commentators have done, to credit one man with the design of the Spitfire, especially its magical wing. This chapter shows that the one man previously singled out, Reginald Mitchell, the chief designer of Vickers (Supermarine) Ltd, was really the conductor of the orchestra of talents that created the Spitfire.

Mitchell sadly died before the Spitfire was taken into production but he did see the first flight and attended some of the progress meetings afterwards. Perhaps history has chosen to eulogise him because of his early death and because of his talent with seaplanes and flying boats. So much more could have been expected of him had his life not been cut short.

This chapter shows that three other great engineering minds were also at least as worthy of praise as Mitchell. These were conductor-in-waiting Joe Smith, leader of the orchestra Alf Faddy and lead violinist Beverley Shenstone. They deserve to be right up there with the great names of British aviation. This chapter also reviews their contribution to the Spitfire.

A colossus on the stage of the 20th century, Winston Churchill was fascinated by science and technology throughout his long life at the centre of British politics and of world affairs. He also loved flying and is seen here at the controls of a Boeing Clipper returning from America in 1942. Churchill's grandson, Sir Nicholas Soames MP, has written, 'I can well imagine his glee when he found out that he could return from Christmas in the White House by flying boat.' Getty Images (Keystone)

Winston Spencer Churchill

Born 30 November 1874
Died 24 January 1965
Parliamentarian, 1900–64
Prime Minister, 1940–45 and 1951–55

Winston Churchill embraced all aspects of technology, especially aviation and aeroplanes, before the First World War. His credentials included forming the Royal Naval Air Service, sending the Naval Wing to France to support the British Expeditionary Force and giving aircraft production a Ministerial helping hand in the First World War.

Churchill's relationship with the Spitfire can be traced back to 1933 and his deliberate campaign to persuade his political colleagues that the Germans were rearming and embracing new technologies, especially in aviation – and that the United Kingdom was falling seriously far behind.

During his 'voice from the wilderness' period of trying to influence British Government policy to dispense with the Ten-Year Rule of restricted spending on national defence for the decade ahead, he was well advised by friends in the aircraft industry and even in the Royal Air Force. Ironically, it was Churchill, as Chancellor of the Exchequer, whose policy had led to the Ten-Year Rule with his insistence in 1919 that the Committee of Imperial Defence should consider the likelihood of a major war and, if there were no war clouds on the horizon, then a moratorium on spending would exist for 10 years – it became a rolling stagnation in defence spending.

In the 1920s, there were savage cuts in defence spending and both the Royal Navy and the British Army nearly succeeded in destroying the Royal Air Force. The Air Council, however, had an ally in Churchill, who had told Lord Trenchard – the father of the Royal Air Force – as far back as October 1925 that he supported a separate, but not necessarily independent, air force. The Royal Air Force survived.

In true Conservative thinking of the time, Churchill liked the idea of examining new technology to see if existing techniques and capabilities could be better achieved by another, perhaps cheaper, means, such as air policing of Iraq and even maritime policing of the Arabian Gulf by means of flying boats rather than warships. Yet, the Ten-Year Rule severely hampered technological development and reduced the Royal Navy and the British Army to maintaining their mass without looking at future equipment.

The Royal Air Force, although still hampered by its Trenchard doctrine centred on strategic long-range bombers, did invest in research and development. In fact the Air Ministry spent more than the Admiralty or the War Office by proportion and amount, which is why development of what was later called radar and ground-to-air communications improved dramatically. Churchill was supportive of this kind of thinking that, elsewhere in Europe, was found only in Germany.

It is ironic to think now that the Royal Air Force won a significant victory that appears to contradict the very founding principles of the service as devised by Trenchard and

Research in the archives of Churchill College, Cambridge, has shown that Winston Churchill took more than 100 flying lessons before the First World War but did not qualify. On 16 April 1939 he was appointed Honorary Air Commodore of No 615 (County of Surrey) Squadron, Auxiliary Air Force and taken flying in a Hawker Hector for his 'honorary wings'. The squadron was flying the fighter from RAF Kenley in Surrey; coincidentally the air station was close to Chartwell, Churchill's home. Rex Features (Associated Newspapers)

The year 1940 was the nation's finest hour and probably Churchill's too. That summer, all thoughts were on the possibility of invasion by Germany from Occupied Europe and the Prime Minister was tireless in ensuring that Britain was defended. He is seen here on the South Coast with Lieutenant General Sir Bertie Fisher, CinC Southern Command and himself a former army aviator. Rex Features (Everett Collection)

perpetuated by Sir John Salmond, Sir Cyril Newall and that generation. The Battle of Britain was a major achievement and it proved that bombers would not always get through and that control of the air was vital. It still is today.

Out of power for much of the time, Churchill worked hard to influence events from the sidelines. The head of the British government's Industrial Intelligence Centre, Desmond Morton, a friend and devotee for 20 years, informally and quite unofficially advised him, and such 'classified' information was vital to Churchill's thinking and rhetoric.

Other informants and supporters of Churchill's stance for rearmament included serving officers who risked career and liberty to help the campaign to rearm Britain. During this time Churchill kept his sources secure but it is now known that Wing Commander Peter Warburton MBE and Group Captain Francis Don, the British Air Attaché in Berlin, either directly or, more probably, indirectly supplied to Churchill detailed intelligence (not just information but analysis too) that he was able to utilise in his speeches and newspaper articles.

Warburton had been promoted to Wing Commander in December 1935 in the half-yearly appointments that saw several other significant players in the Spitfire story mentioned: Trafford Leigh-Mallory became an Air Commodore and Jeffrey Quill's retirement to the Reserve was noted.

Don's appreciation of the Luftwaffe's strength – 300 combat aircraft in 1936 – seems more accurate than that of his American counterpart who suggested to Washington that Germany possessed more than 1,000 combat aircraft at the time. But those 300 modern fighters and bombers gave Germany a technological advantage over Britain and France, at least for a while.

Two relatively junior officers also shared information with Churchill. In 1936 Squadron Leader Herbert Rowley, a test pilot from RAF Martlesham Heath, and Flight Lieutenant Richard Atcherley, a counterpart from the Royal Aircraft Establishment at Farnborough, flew a private aeroplane to Berlin as part of a 10-day tour. In Germany they were shown the latest treasures of the fast-developing Luftwaffe, including the Heinkel He 111 bomber and the Junkers design bureau. Their detailed report was shelved in the Air Ministry but a copy did find its way to Churchill at Chartwell, and he made good use of it.

Rowley, a veteran ace of the Royal Naval Air Service, who retired as an Air Commodore in 1944, was particularly taken by the capabilities of the bombers he had seen and may have identified the wrong lessons about those capabilities. Churchill, on hearing about the intrepid airmen's adventures, understood the mass-production issue and almost his first action on moving into Downing Street was to appoint Lord Beaverbrook to take over a new Ministry for Aircraft Production, where the Spitfire would be top of the agenda.

The younger 'Batchy' Atcherley was a flying legend already. He joined the Royal Air Force through Cranwell in 1922, he was a Central Flying School graduate, and he was a member of the Schneider Trophy-winning High Speed Flight from 1929. He looked at the Heinkel and Junkers bombers from another angle – as a threat to be countered by high-performance fighters rather than terror weapons that would always 'get through'. Atcherley's career would be centred on fighter aircraft and during the Second World War he commanded RAF Drem and RAF Kenley, as well as leading the Royal Air Force on the ill-fated Norway campaign and learning to use the Spitfire in the Mediterranean theatre of operations under Air Marshal Sir Arthur 'Mary' Coningham. He left the Royal Air Force as an Air Marshal with KCB, CB, AFC* and the Norwegian war medal.

Churchill also received the benefit of industrial advice from captains of industry. Bristol Aeroplane Company chief engineer Roy Fedden twice went to Germany in 1937 to report back on industrial developments, and his equally worrying conclusions were shelved as he did not say what the Air Council wanted to hear. Churchill, however, duly received a copy of the report.

The main conduit for the intelligence was Wing Commander David Torr Anderson DFC, who had been promoted in July 1936, sharing the same *London Gazette* entry with Ralph

Sorley, another key Spitfire supporter and armaments expert, who also contributed to the Spitfire in his own way. Torr Anderson was also close to Lord Addison, a Labour peer who detested appeasers and, although not a Churchill ally, ensured that the Labour Party took the defence of the realm seriously. Torr Anderson was to become personal assistant and air advisor to Lord Beaverbrook at the Ministry of Aircraft Production in the rank of Group Captain in 1940 before retiring due to ill health in 1942. To such people who risked their reputation for the good of the country, we owe as great a debt as to others who came face to face with the enemy.

London was the largest city in the world after the First World War and, by late 1937, Churchill considered it highly vulnerable, especially with the Luftwaffe now larger and better equipped than the Royal Air Force. Churchill was keen to see London's air defences improved with more day fighter squadrons and also by harnessing the new sciences: voice communications by radio, radio direction finding and transponder technology, the latter known as IFF (Identification, Friend or Foe) and something that Churchill is believed to have been been told about. Furthermore, his relationship with the oil industry brought him knowledge of the potential of higher-octane fuels.

Churchill was no scientist but he was able to grasp the potential that science brought. He also learned some doubtful science from his friend Lord Cherwell (Sir Frederick Lindemann), who was a pilot of no mean ability but often flawed in his advice. It is fortunate that Lindemann was not influential in the development of fighter defences before the Dowding system was implemented.

It is not clear when Churchill first saw a Spitfire nor when he first became its advocate. There are no photographs of the great leader with a Spitfire before he reached 10 Downing Street but it seems likely that he had conversations in 1936 with industry leaders and other advisors about the new Supermarine fighter.

At first Churchill thought that having too many fighters with forward-firing machine guns would make our forces vulnerable to an enemy attacking from behind. He is known to have been briefed on, and to have supported, Air Ministry Specification F9/35 for a two-seat day/night fighter with a rear turret and capable of 290mph at 15,000ft; the rear turret would not be supplemented by forward-firing guns. There was a body of opinion in the upper reaches of the Air Ministry (among people who had served in the First World War) and the scientific community that a modern version of the two-seat Bristol fighter of the period 1917–24 was needed but they conveniently forgot that most of the Bristol's kills were gained by the pilot, not the air-gunner. The Boulton Paul Defiant won Specification F9/35 and was much praised for its 'powerful guns' and Merlin engine, but it proved to be a costly failure. Interestingly, Supermarine entered the fray with Type 305, a two-seat Spitfire, and perhaps fortuitously did not win.

When war came in September 1939, Churchill was a true advocate of defensive air power and the air defence of Britain through the Dowding system. Churchill even went into print about the inability of the enemy bomber to reach its target, an opinion that differed sharply from his position a decade earlier. It might well be that the Spitfire played a part in this

One of the few photographs to survive of Churchill and the Spitfire, this picture was taken on 7 July 1941 at RAF Biggin Hill when the Prime Minister was inspecting cannon-armed Spitfires of No 609 Squadron. The Spitfire People with Churchill in this view are, from left, Group Captain Philip Barwell (Station Commander), Air Marshal Sholto Douglas (CinC Fighter Command), Wing Commander 'Sailor' Malan and Jock Colville (private secretary). No 609 Squadron Association

change of emphasis. Churchill would have seen the media coverage from the first previews in May 1939 and may even have been shown reports by Torr Anderson and others.

Having been brought back into Government on 3 September 1939, as First Lord of the Admiralty (the political head of the Royal Navy, not to be confused with the First Sea Lord, who was the professional head), Churchill was keen to ensure that the naval forces were re-equipped. Ironically for a man who is credited with the formation of the Royal Naval Air Service in time for action in the First World War, Churchill seems to have been persuaded against a 'navalised' Spitfire even after successful trials of a hooked version in November 1939. Having already dismissed Fairey Aviation's proposal for a folding-wing Spitfire with an arrestor hook for deck landings, Churchill inexplicably cancelled the development and production of 50 folding-wing Spitfires in favour of the slower, heavier and less effective Fairey Fulmar heavy reconnaissance fighter. Instead, the Admiralty would order American Wildcats – initially called the Martlet – and allow the Spitfire to be built solely for Fighter

Command. In the event, this was good for the Battle of Britain but reduced the effectiveness of the Fleet Air Arm until late 1942, when the first Seafires appeared.

For all of the briefings that Churchill had received from well-meaning aviators in the Air Ministry, he was still a decided amateur concerning the operational or tactical use of air power, and, like so many of his generation with direct experience of the First World War, he believed that air forces would behave the same way as ground forces, but more quickly. Leaving aside the Norwegian adventure of April/May 1940 that hastened the end of the Chamberlain administration, Churchill was at first supportive of sending more fighters to shore up the French, even wanting the latest Spitfires there. Luckily, he listened to Dowding and the valuable assets were not wasted on French bases, which were vulnerable to air attack because of the lack of early-warning technology. Spitfires did, of course, operate over France from 10 May onwards but were not based there.

In his persistent and sadly doomed efforts to keep France in the war and help the country's morale, Churchill travelled to France several times after the German invasion and before capitulation. He understood the need for air escort and on these flights three Spitfires always accompanied his de Havilland Flamingo. The first such flight was to Paris Le Bourget using early production Mk I Spitfires – with the fixed, wooden, two-blade airscrew – from Biggin Hill's No 92 Squadron, with Flight Lieutenant Bob Stanford Tuck as the escort commander. Churchill's later flights, also to Dunkirk as well as further south to Orléans and Tours, were escorted by No 609 Squadron, an Auxiliary Air Force unit based at RAF Middle Wallop that was equipped with newer Mk Is fitted with the de Havilland-designed two-pitch (fine and coarse) three-blade propeller hub, which dramatically increased the rate of climb. These flights passed off without engaging the enemy, although Churchill described in his book *The Second World War* how, on the return from his last trip, in June 1940 just before the capitulation, he and his fellow passengers saw Messerschmitt Bf 109s in the distance and a Spitfire screened the vulnerable Flamingo from the potential threat. The Germans had no radar coverage, luckily, and on this occasion the British formation was not spotted.

The Prime Minister did grasp the role played by the Spitfires of No 11 Group, operating at range from their bases in Kent and Sussex over the Dunkirk beachhead. He understood that they were outside radar coverage and therefore needed to operate standing patrols, which limited the Spitfires' time over France and Belgium. It was at this time that he started to draft the famous speech that created the 'Few' as popular shorthand for the pilots of Fighter Command.

The Battle of France cost Fighter Command dearly with the loss of around 400 fighters, mainly Hurricanes, but a good proportion of Spitfires were destroyed and some even captured. Dowding, with Churchill's support, ensured that the losses of fighter aircraft were as low as possible. On 19 May the Prime Minister directed that no more fighters were to be deployed to France – or anywhere else. Dowding was delighted (but probably did not show it) and, interestingly, he was supported by the Chief of the Air Staff, Sir Cyril Newall.

Over Dunkirk, Fighter Command did, at times, achieve air superiority, according to German war diaries, but the 'Tommies' on the ground did not see it, leading to arguments

*Winston Churchill, often accompanied by Clementine, visited the infrastructure of the
nation's war effort as often as his official duties in London allowed. On 28 September 1941
he visited the Castle Bromwich Aircraft Factory and is seen here with one of the riveters
working on a Spitfire Mk V before watching pilot Alex Henshaw give a display.* Getty Images

between the Air Ministry and the War Office that Churchill had to quash. Churchill also had to defuse continued attempts by the 'Trenchardists' to remove Dowding from Fighter Command just as the fight moved across the Channel to the skies over England and Scotland, and he backed Dowding at least six times in the summer of 1940. There was a decided personality clash between Dowding and the Secretary of State for Air, Sir Archibald Sinclair, which is so well portrayed as just breaking the surface in Guy Hamilton's film *Battle of Britain*.

Churchill was also a great admirer of the New Zealand-born master tactician, Keith Park. The now-famous occasion on 15 September 1940 when Mr and Mrs Churchill visited RAF Uxbridge, the Group Headquarters just to the west of London, also features in the film *Battle of Britain*. Today, this date is celebrated as Battle of Britain Day and after the war Churchill frequently commented about that visit, although at the time victory was far from certain. History does not record Park's view of having his ultimate boss in the visitors' gallery when he needed to marshal his thoughts and react to the largest concentration of attacking German formations – today it would be called 'a maximum effort'.

Both Park and Dowding had gone when Trafford Leigh-Mallory and Sholto Douglas took to the offensive over northern France and Belgium, losing more pilots and fighters on Circuses (day-time bomber attacks with fighter escorts) and Rhubarbs (opportunistic attacks made when taking advantage of low cloud and poor visibility), as well as other tactical air operations, than were lost in the Battle of the Britain. Churchill certainly supported taking the battle to the enemy but by then was too tied up with defeats around the Empire to spend much time considering cross-Channel operations.

The Prime Minister, however, was not so occupied with the affairs of Empire and trying to bring America into the war that he forgot about the Spitfire. Once the giant Castle Bromwich Aircraft Factory was in production, he visited in September 1941 to witness the scale of the endeavour and the skills of the civilian chief test pilot there, Alex Henshaw. In his autobiography *Sigh for a Merlin*, Henshaw recalls that Mrs Churchill visited the Spitfire factory several times before bringing the Prime Minister to see the production facilities and watch a Spitfire display, which included a Henshaw speciality of inverted pass in a Spitfire Mk V. Churchill was impressed and asked for a private *tête-à-tête* with Henshaw. Apparently the Prime Minister talked about flying and asked numerous questions about the Spitfire's performance, but Henshaw seems to have been almost overawed by the conversation and in his account found it difficult to recall the details.

After that time Churchill appears to have become more concerned with heavy bombers than fighters. Operations in the Mediterranean and Far East were centre stage as well as the war against the U-boats in the North Atlantic. The Prime Minister did push to have Spitfires and experienced pilots sent to Malta and later shipped to India, but his attention after the US entered the war was very much on grand strategy rather than operations or tactics; this did not stop him from 'meddling', as some saw it, but not down to unit level.

Perhaps the final link between Churchill and the Spitfire is the Davidoff range of cigars bearing both names!

Reginald Mitchell CBE FRAeS

Born 20 May 1895
Died 11 June 1937
Chief designer, Supermarine, 1924–36

Reginald Mitchell has gone down in history as one of the greatest aeroplane designers. His high-speed seaplanes won the Schneider Trophy and his biplane flying boats and amphibians were still in production in 1940. It is for the Spitfire, however, that he is best known, and yet he died before it entered production or service.

Mitchell was a blank-sheet-of-paper designer. He designed to the required specification and used his team of dedicated and talented people to work around problems and create solutions that brought together the best elements into a single entity. His first ideas for a monoplane fighter were very ineffective and yet his penultimate fighter design turned out to be a world-beater; 'penultimate' because Mitchell may have already been working on a two-seat Spitfire, the Type 305 with a gun turret, as a replacement for the Mk II, to

Reginald Mitchell started with trains and ended his career with high-speed flying boats and a revolutionary bomber aircraft design. In between, there were more than 20 other designs, with the Spitfire centre stage. Sadly, R.J. died before the Spitfire was ready for production and so his influence was very much in the initial concept. His work on the racing seaplanes that won the Schneider Trophy should be equally highly regarded. Solent Sky

Probably most comfortable with seaplanes and flying boats, Mitchell enjoyed the hands-on approach that his role as chief designer at Supermarine afforded. Here he is pictured (second from right) with Hubert Scott-Paine (right), the then owner of Supermarine, discussing the Supermarine Sea Lion II, an early Schneider Trophy contender. Solent Sky

enter service in 1941. In addition, Mitchell sketched several innovative twin-engine fighter designs, including one with six cannon.

Mitchell – known as 'Mitch' only to the Royal Air Force and otherwise as 'RJ' to his contemporaries – was certainly still working on a four-engine bomber, a new fighter and developing amphibians when his cancer finally forced him into bed. His brain was still active until the end. In 16 years with Supermarine, he led the design teams on 24 different aeroplane projects.

The Schneider Trophy certainly played an important part in the development of airframes, systems and engines, but it is doubtful that there is any direct line to be drawn between Supermarine's Schneider designs, even the Royal Air Force High Speed Flight's winning S6 series, and the Spitfire.

Mitchell was influenced by the success of his racing seaplanes, however, with their use of an in-line engine and small frontal area to reduce drag. The Supermarine S4, which first flew on 24 August 1925, was designed to compete in that year's Schneider race and Mitchell, having seen other competitors, used a clean monoplane design, Supermarine's first, and laid the foundation for a fuselage of small frontal area. Although originally conceived to be of all-wood construction, in practice the S4 had a revolutionary wood/metal monocoque fuselage to which the unbraced cantilever wing was attached, the whole design representing a huge leap forward in aerodynamics and technology. Power came from a Napier Lion VII engine that developed 680hp at sea level.

Before the 1925 Schneider Trophy, held in America at Chesapeake Bay, the S4 was trialled at 226.75mph, a world record, but during practice a wing vibration caused it to crash, nearly killing pilot Henri Biard and leaving American pilot Jimmy Doolittle to win the race the following day. Undaunted, Mitchell set to work on the S5, which was even more advanced, using a metal stressed skin for the fuselage and increased wing bracing in order to prevent the vibration problem.

The Italian victory with a sleek Macchi M39 monoplane in the 1926 Schneider Trophy (the High Speed Flight did not take part that year) must have given Mitchell the reassurance to continue with the monoplane, and indeed S5s came first and second in the 1927 race. During 1928, after the nations involved had agreed to wait until 1929 for the next contest, the highly experienced Flight Lieutenant Sam Kinkead sadly lost his life when his S5 flew into the Solent.

For the 1929 Schneider Trophy, Supermarine designed and built the sleek, streamlined and larger S6, a completely new design with a new engine from a different manufacturer, Rolls-Royce, then relatively new to the aero-engine business. The Rolls-Royce R-type engine developed 1,900hp, giving the aeroplane a top speed of 328mph.

Supermarine did not possess a wind tunnel and much of the work, including the all-important flutter tests, was carried out by trial and error, albeit with the experienced engineering knowledge of Mitchell's team. Mitchell kept a close eye on the Italians during the Schneider Trophy competition, admiring the streamlining of the Macchi floatplanes achieved by use of the Mach 2.2 wind tunnel funded by the Mussolini government. A few years later he applied the same care and interest – a 'hawk eye' as Captain Eric Brown says – into what the great German designers like Ernst Heinkel, Willy Messerschmitt and Kurt Tank (at Focke-Wulf) were doing, especially with their access to at least two supersonic wind tunnels, like the one at Peenemünde.

Mitchell was obviously convinced that the low-drag monoplane was the right way to go despite the fact that all fighter aircraft of the day were biplanes. The S6b won the Schneider Trophy outright in September 1931 and Mitchell became a household name, but his radical thinking might have been too much for the Air Ministry as the winning fighter of the F7/30 contest, issued by the Air Ministry just a month after the Schneider Trophy win, was the Gloster Gladiator radial-engine biplane – a safe choice for any bureaucrat because it was so similar to everything that had gone before. Supermarine's unsuccessful candidate for Specification F7/30, which required a fighter capable of at least 250mph and armed with four machine guns, was the Type 224.

With his design team now strengthened by new blood, men like Joe Smith and Alf Faddy, Mitchell was set on the streamlined monoplane even if the Type 224 did not attract

Early aviation partnerships between airframe designer and engine manufacturer were vital. Mitchell developed a great relationship with Henry Royce (1863–1933) that led to the development of the R-type racing engines for the Schneider Trophy aeroplanes and thence to the Merlin, which Royce sadly did not see come to fruition. Solent Sky

a contract, and development of a single-seat, monoplane fighter continued. By the time the Type 300 emerged in 1936, Mitchell was wedded to the low-wing, streamlined monoplane of all-metal, stressed-skin construction and powered by a development of the Schneider Trophy engine, a radical, glycol-cooled V12 engine called the PV-12. The Type 300 became the Spitfire and the PV-12 became the Merlin – an aeronautical marriage made in Heaven.

Just as Formula 1 motor racing influences the development of motor cars, so the Schneider Trophy influenced the design of fighter aircraft in France, Italy, the US and Great Britain. Macchi's wartime fighters, met by Spitfires over Malta and Curtiss P-40s, undoubtedly owed much to the Schneider Trophy races and the developments made in the pursuit of speed.

Reginald Mitchell, then, was the great coordinating genius but it was a team effort to design the Spitfire. He has been likened to the conductor of the orchestra with his various team members taking important parts. He was not, by all accounts, a details man and needed experts in wing design and stress techniques, especially in the latter case for the stressed skin first tried on the Type 224.

When it came to the Type 300, the wing designs conceived by Beverley Shenstone were mathematically proven but needed to be translated into drawings, which were prepared by Alan Clifton and Joe Smith. Mitchell wanted to have retractable undercarriage and room for eight Browning guns, so Clifton and Smith decided that a single spar wing, using the leading-edge 'D' section for bending and torsional stiffness, would work. Mitchell apparently commented, somewhat dismissively, 'I don't care what shape the wing is as long as it houses the wheels and the guns.'

Mitchell took his role and stature as chief designer seriously in another way. Supermarine contracted Mitchell for ten years from 1923 and he managed to turn his position into a directorship in 1927. When Vickers bought the company in 1928, it is said that part of the deal was a binding contract for Mitchell to remain in place in 1933 – which happened to be the year that his colon cancer was diagnosed.

In 1932 the New Year's Honours list included the award of Commander of the British Empire for him in recognition of his contribution to the Schneider Trophy win and the work of the High Speed Flight.

As a designer Mitchell was still working closely on flying boats and amphibians while as an engineer he was struggling with the demands of producing stressed-skin surfaces and controls. His concentration would not have been helped when Vickers sent the young assistant designer at Weybridge, Barnes Wallis, to Southampton, where Wallis proceeded to take over Mitchell's desk. There was also some rivalry between the two men in respect of bomber design: Wallis's Wellington flew shortly after the Spitfire and Mitchell was working on a high-speed, long-range bomber.

Interestingly, history records that Mitchell did not care for the name 'Spitfire'. When he heard of the Vickers Board's decision about the name, he is reported to have said, 'That's just the sort of damned silly name they would choose.' By then K5054, the prototype known by its serial number, had flown successfully in the hands of 'Mutt' Summers and the new fighter was on its way to being the great success we know today.

After the first flight of the Spitfire prototype, and knowing that he was terminally ill, Mitchell turned his focus to the Supermarine bomber project, known by its Air Ministry Specification as B12/36, and left the Spitfire to Joe Smith, Alf Faddy and Ernie Mansbridge. In fact, as early as 1935, Mitchell only turned up to occasional design meetings and then said very little, if anything, leaving the team to work through the production issues and the last-minute design changes. After his death, work on the B12/36 bomber design was abandoned, and in September 1940 the prototype was destroyed by Luftwaffe bombing.

Mitchell's other preferred projects were a high-speed flying boat, known as R1/36, and a follow-on fighter (to fulfil Air Ministry Specification F37/35) that was envisaged to have four cannon and be a replacement for the Spitfire. These projects included the Type 312, a single-seater powered by the Merlin E engine for which the Supermarine specification and general arrangement drawings were issued as early as 29 April 1936. Other ideas from Mitchell's fertile mind were the Type 313, with two Goshawk engines, and the later Type 327, for which a specification was issued at Supermarine in August 1938 for a six-cannon, twin-engine fighter looking remarkably similar to the Westland Whirlwind, except that the armament was situated in an enlarged elliptical wing. Mitchell kept a guiding hand on the prototype with regular meetings with the design, technical and test pilot teams.

Mitchell died on 11 June 1937, before the first production Spitfire had taken to the air. At the time only K5054 was in existence, such were the problems that Supermarine faced with 'productionisation' of the Spitfire.

Mitchell's greatest strength was his ability to build a team of talented people and have them make a significant contribution. In the case of the Spitfire, he and his team created an entirely new generation of aeroplane design with many engineering innovations, which, despite causing production headaches at first, led to a glorious outcome.

Joe Smith CBE

Born 25 May 1897
Died 20 February 1956
Deputy chief designer, Spitfire, 1935–39
Chief designer, Supermarine, 1941–46

History remembers R.J. Mitchell as the designer of the Spitfire and lauds his contribution to the victory of the Royal Air Force in the Battle of Britain. Yet, for many, it was the steadfast support given to Mitchell by Joe Smith and his subsequent redesign of the Spitfire that put it into production and kept it there for the whole of the Second World War – the only Allied aircraft to achieve such utility. Smith deserves just as much national recognition as Mitchell.

Smith virtually took over development of the Spitfire after Mitchell's cancer became prevalent in 1936 and oversaw the complex engineering drawings required for production and for the subsequent development of what became the supreme British fighter.

His talent was obvious from the time he left the Birmingham Municipal Technical School and was apprenticed to the Austin Motor Company at Longbridge, Birmingham in 1914. Smith joined the Royal Naval Volunteer Reserve that year and served on motor launches, including operational deployments to the Mediterranean and Malta.

On discharge from the RNVR, Smith returned to Longbridge to complete his apprenticeship and was appointed to the aeroplane department as a draughtsman. In 1919 the Austin Whippet was being made ready for flight testing as an inexpensive, single-seat private pilot's aeroplane and Smith was part of the design team. The Whippet attracted few customer orders and its lack of success caused Austin to withdraw from aviation and concentrate on motor cars. Keen to continue in aviation, Smith moved south to Supermarine in 1921 as one of the senior draughtsman in a new team being created by Mitchell to work on a variety of programmes and private ventures in seaplane and flying-boat development, and in 1926 Mitchell appointed him chief draughtsman This, of course, was the pioneering age of aviation.

The relatively unknown genius behind the Spitfire's production and development was Joe Smith. A quiet and unassuming man with a rare skill for designing 'by rubber rather than pencil' – in other words 'improving rather than dictating' a line. Just how much of the Spitfire was Smith rather than Mitchell is the stuff of debate. Royal Aeronautical Society (National Aerospace Library)/Mary Evans Picture Library

Supermarine's development as a company saw ownership changes but the core team remained in place. Besides Smith, Mitchell started to bring together others in a team that would be the cornerstone of the Schneider Trophy and future fighter design teams. The team stayed together when Supermarine was sold to Vickers (Aviation) in 1928 and the company's name officially changed to Supermarine Aviation Works (Vickers) Ltd, hence the common usage of Vickers Supermarine.

Workmates in the late 1920s and early 1930s described Smith as hard working and showing great interest in the work of all his subordinates, not just from the point of view of work ethic but also for encouragement to get the best out of the team.

As work on Air Ministry requirements replaced the development of flying boats at Supermarine, Smith became intimately involved in Air Ministry Specification F37/34, for which Supermarine developed the Type 300, as the Spitfire was first known. Smith was one of those consulted on the name for the new fighter after the Vickers chairman, Sir Robert McLean, stipulated that a name beginning with 'S' would be appropriate for alliteration with Supermarine. Senior team members considered Shrew, Shrike and Scarab before Sir Robert insisted on Spitfire, reportedly because his daughter Annie was so nicknamed. On 10 June 1936 the Air Ministry confirmed that the name Spitfire would be adopted for the new fighter. Smith, history records, preferred the name Scarab.

After Mitchell's death, in 1937, Smith was not immediately made chief designer. Instead the role was given to Major Harold Payn, a former Royal Flying Corps pilot.

Smith had been hard at work on the general arrangement of the Type 300 from the very beginning and naturally started refining the aeroplane after its first flight in 1936. Much of his work was to ensure that the hand-built prototype could be converted into a design suitable for manufacture, a big problem because Supermarine suffered from a lack of production-engineering experience and key contract milestones were not being met. Smith pioneered the use of the local supply chain and used sub-contractors across England to develop sub-assemblies that came together for final assembly at flight test centres such as Eastleigh and Worthy Down, near Winchester.

Contractors for sub-assemblies included famous names from automotive, naval and aviation engineering and their work became important as Supermarine also needed to complete Air Ministry contracts for Walrus and Sea Otter amphibians. Fuselage production was concentrated at Supermarine at Woolston under Smith's direct care but other assemblies were contracted out to a host of small companies across England and into Scotland. He concentrated on the environs of Southampton and the engineering businesses in London and the East Midlands where the skills lay. Supermarine was just too small to cope with it all.

Air Ministry pressure on Vickers for Supermarine to release working drawings and locally made components caused some real problems that Smith needed to resolve. The Weybridge head office did not like the notion of sub-contracting because it reduced margins as well as bringing the risk of losing control of production, but the Air Ministry insisted that Vickers work in the national interest and even threatened to move Spitfire production away from Supermarine, to Bristol. It was only the lucid and compelling case made by Smith on

With the initial flying completed by 'Mutt' Summers in March 1936, the prototype Type 300 was given over to Jeffrey Quill to test fly. So from late spring, Joe Smith and Alf Faddy progressed the development with Ernie Mansbridge, the director of test flying at Supermarine. From late March, R.J. Mitchell seems to have had very little contact with the Spitfire's development other than a 'standing, silent presence at meetings', instead using his talents and remaining weeks on a high-speed flying boat and the Type 317/318 bomber project for the B12/36 requirement. Rex Features (Hugh Cowin)

the telephone to Air Marshal Sir Wilfrid Freeman, the Air Member for Development and Production, that saw this extraordinary threat withdrawn.

In 1939 it became clear that there were national security implications in Payn's appointment as Supermarine's design chief because his wife held dual nationality – British and German. This led to Smith taking over the role with the title of manager, design department, reporting to Rex Pierson at Weybridge. In fact it was not until 1941 that the Ministry of Aircraft Production approved the elevation of Smith to chief designer. A lesser man would have been peeved, but not Smith.

Smith was confident that the Spitfire could be improved and he would not hear of a follow-on design until the maximum capability had been drawn out of the Spitfire's design. He was prepared, said his subordinates, to listen to them and take good ideas forward with due credit to the originator.

The Seafire, the naval version of the Spitfire, was a project close to Smith's heart. Captain Eric Brown (then Lieutenant), recalls that Smith was very supportive of the test flying programmes, 'especially when he found that pink gin was tuppence a shot in the naval mess at Farnborough.' Through Smith's attention to detail, the Admiralty got the fighter it wanted to a standard demanded by the Fifth Sea Lord, Admiral Sir Denis Boyd.

Smith's genius certainly helped Supermarine to stay ahead of the game with piston-engined fighters, taking the Spitfire and Seafire through 40 main variants and into the Spiteful and Seafang. Where he came unstuck, though, was with the blank sheet of paper brought by the jet age. The Supermarine jet fighters – Attacker, Swift and Scimitar – never attained the stardom of the Spitfire and this must have disappointed Smith. Although the Scimitar was transonic and could carry nuclear weapons, it was considered dangerous by its crews and, according to Eric Brown, 'it woefully under-performed above 22,000 feet.'

Sadly Joe Smith, like Mitchell, succumbed to cancer and died early, aged 58, at his home in Chandler's Ford. His talent was to understand where he could make the greatest contribution, whether by supporting Mitchell in the early days of seaplanes and fighter development or eventually taking the lead after Mitchell's death in June 1937.

Alf Faddy

Born 1892
Died 30 November 1955
Supermarine design engineer, 1930–55

Alf Faddy – he never seems to have been called Alfred – was described in an obituary as a man of independent spirit and few words who exerted considerable influence on Supermarine and on the Spitfire, as well as many other aircraft types. He was a 'details man' in whose judgement and concepts both Joe Smith and R.J. Mitchell placed great faith.

There is no doubt that Alf Faddy was a key player in the Spitfire's story and, without him, and the people he was able to influence, the fighter would not have been such a success for Fighter Command and such a worldwide phenomenon. Alf drew the first drawings of the wing structure, for example, and suggested moving the wing tips forward from the original position and hence gave the Spitfire's elliptical wing its particular shape.

Faddy was born in the Borders and, like so many of his generation, won a place at grammar school, from where he went to an engineering apprenticeship at the great Newcastle-based firm of C.A. Parsons and Company. There he was involved in the development of steam turbines, an area in which Parsons had excelled since Victorian times. After completing his indentures and studying at night school, Faddy continued working in Newcastle upon Tyne for the company. In having this heavy engineering apprenticeship, he mirrored the career of Mitchell but, unlike his eventual boss, Faddy succeeded in joining up at the beginning of the First World War and elected for the Royal Naval Air Service.

He volunteered in 1914 and served in France initially before being posted to the flying-boat station at Felixstowe, where he perfected knowledge of amphibian design that must have reflected well when Faddy applied to join Supermarine in 1930, aged 38. His mentor at Felixstowe was Commander John Porte, the designer of ocean-going flying boats, who

Every year Supermarine brought together its design, development and works management for its Executive Christmas Lunch, a tradition that was upheld in wartime even if the fare, according to some participants, was not outstanding. This is the event in Southampton, probably at the Polygon Hotel, in 1942 or 1943. Prominent is a beaming Len Gooch, who became works engineer in 1941, and further to his right on the same table is Alf Faddy, seen turned to camera, his face immediately to the right of the tall figure in the foreground. Faddy is such an unsung hero of Spitfire design and development that this is the only known 'works' photo that shows him. Bill Fear and R.J. Fenner, two close associates of Faddy, are also thought to be present. Solent Sky

may well have introduced Faddy to the problems of longitudinal stability, an area that was not widely understood at the time but in which Porte and Faddy became specialists. This knowledge would have attracted Faddy to Supermarine, then the world's most important seaplane and flying-boat manufacturer.

After the end of the First World War, Faddy was employed by a small company that was licensed to build the Vickers Vimy bomber. In fact it seems that the aeroplanes were delivered to the Royal Air Force only to be broken up: a heart-breaking outcome but also a good grounding in both how the Air Ministry sometimes worked and how production was carried out. Faddy's role with this company included working in the capacity of flight test engineer as he flew on every delivery flight.

After the Vimy contract ceased, Faddy went to Parnall at Yate, near Bristol, to work on the company's experimental designs, including the Elf, an example of which has been restored by the Shuttleworth Collection at Old Warden.

Faddy started work at Supermarine, by now a Vickers company, on 7 July 1930 and his first task was to become involved in the company's design for Air Ministry Specification F7/30. This design, which Supermarine termed the Type 224, used a fixed undercarriage, a Rolls-Royce steam-cooled Goshawk engine and what was called a 'W wing', rather like the later Junkers Ju 87 Stuka or the Chance Vought Corsair. The design was rejected by the Air Ministry and the Vickers management was also less than impressed.

According to several sources at Solent Sky, the elliptical wing started to emerge at this time, and the first evidence of it is in Supermarine drawing no 30000. It seems that Faddy worked on Mitchell to adopt the elliptical wing, which had been proposed by Beverley Shenstone, but initially rejected as 'academic'. Faddy's argument was persuasive: the elliptical wing gave greater depth for retractable landing gear, which in itself would increase speed, and the weapons could be repositioned to best effect, with sufficient space for ammunition.

The new wing was designed by Shenstone, with Faddy providing the detail for the structure and 'productionisation' of the wing. It was a good joint effort and led to the development of the Type 300 with its elliptical planform shape that today everyone sees in the Spitfire. It was the pushing forward of the wing tip that allowed the single leading-edge spar to give both strength and flexibility.

Faddy was at Eastleigh for the first flight of the Type 300 prototype, K5054, on 5 March 1936. As the 'details man' on the structure, he was largely responsible for the engineering aspects of the maiden flight.

Later on, another area in which Faddy influenced the Spitfire was the development of the long-range photo-reconnaissance (PR) versions needed to fly high and with greater endurance than the regular fighter. Essentially this meant taking out the armament and instead putting fuel in the space that was liberated. Two early Spitfire Mk I airframes were converted in service, with Supermarine's help, and an initial sortie was flown over the naval bases at Emden and Wilhelmshaven on 10 February 1940.

The Air Ministry's Joint Directorate for Research and Development had a budget line for the development of the single-seat PR version of the Spitfire and this led, even at this early stage of the Second World War, to a redesign of the Spitfire and the development of a new engine by Rolls-Royce, the Griffon, based on the Schneider Trophy R-type engine. The Air Ministry requirement was for 470mph at 25,000ft and a cruising range of 1,050 miles at 330mph at 32,000ft.

Faddy's work led to the advancement of design in various significant areas, including airframe, pressurisation, flush undercarriage and bubble canopy (not introduced until the Mk XIV in 1944), as well as power plant. These areas of work also led to initial thoughts about a planned Spitfire successor as well as the long-range fighter that became the Mustang. Many members of the Supermarine design team, in fact, did not even consider the later marks to be Spitfires, instead regarding them as a new fighter design – and study of the comparative aircraft silhouettes would seem to support this thesis. Within Supermarine these iterations attracted the names Valiant and Victor, but such names were not adopted either by management or by customers.

The initial work on an advanced Spitfire started as early as March 1940 when a series of performance calculations was made by Faddy and sent to the Air Ministry. This resulted in a meeting with Wing Commander Sidney Cotton and Flight Lieutenant Maurice 'Shorty' Longbottom, both influential pioneers of photo-reconnaissance. Both saw the need for a single-seat, high-speed, high-altitude platform for the increasingly effective cameras that were being developed. As the Spitfire could generally out-perform its German equivalents, it appeared to be ideal for the photo-reconnaissance role if only its range could be extended and its service ceiling increased so that it could operate above the range of ground-based anti-aircraft artillery.

Development work for the photo-reconnaissance version took place at Hursley Park, the new base for Supermarine's design team after the company's relocation from Woolston in the wake of the bombing of September 1940. Efforts concentrated on accommodating fuel tanks within the leading edge of the wings – known colloquially as 'bowser wings' – in order to augment the rather small fuselage and wing tanks of the fighter version. Faddy used his experience from the Felixstowe flying boats and work by the National Physical Laboratory at Teddington to provide the necessary know-how concerning centre of gravity and the theory of balance. When design was finalised, the tanks were fabricated at Salisbury for fitting to a new series of limited-run Spitfire marks.

As a designer and draughtsman, Faddy was meticulous in the extreme, his maturity and experience playing an important part in the success of the Spitfire. The trust placed in him by Joe Smith, initially chief draughtsman and later chief designer, was vital in the early days of the design as it matured. One observer of the time said that Faddy 'drew with a soft pencil but designed with a rubber'. Gordon Mitchell, R.J. Mitchell's son, is among those who have confirmed that Faddy was an influence on the layout of the Spitfire, while Jeffrey Quill, the Supermarine chief test pilot, credited Faddy with an ability to bring the design team and test pilots together in such a way as to maximise improvements to the design of the aeroplane.

During the Battle of Britain, Faddy and his team were sent to front-line Fighter Command stations to show Royal Air Force engineers how to deal with fuselage repairs, whether caused by German cannon and machine gun bullets or just the result of heavy landings. The Spitfire was Fighter Command's first stressed-skin monoplane and the training that officers and mechanics had received in service had been based on canvas-covered aeroplanes. Propaganda at the time made much of the occasional practice that repairs, both in the front line and by the Civilian Repair Organisation, were sometimes contrived from flattened biscuit tins riveted into position. Faddy was able to explain just how unsafe this practice was and how the structural integrity of the Spitfire depended upon implementation of the safe repair procedure that he had devised.

When Alf Faddy died in Winchester in 1955, aged 63, he was still working, undertaking the detailed design of the Type 113 naval fighter, which became the Supermarine Scimitar, the first nuclear-equipped strike aircraft.

Faddy is most certainly an unsung hero of British aviation who made a major contribution to the Spitfire and later successes for British aircraft companies.

Beverley Shenstone

Born c1904
Died c1980
Aerodynamicist, Supermarine, 1932–38

It is clear from research at the Royal Aeronautical Society that R.J. Mitchell proposed an elliptical wing design for flying boats in the 1920s and that Ernst Heinkel in his sketches for high-speed mail planes in Germany followed similar thinking. It also seems that Canadian-born academic Beverley Shenstone was the first to appreciate the advantages of the design for a fighter aeroplane and start to translate them into hardware.

Beverley Shenstone is the man who persuaded Mitchell to adopt the elliptical wing – a modified ellipse that was unique in its shape and its combined use of two integrated aerofoil sections. By 1938 he had left Supermarine for the Air Ministry, later the Ministry of Aircraft Production, and eventually worked for British European Airways and became President of the Royal Aeronautical Society. Royal Aeronautical Society (National Aerospace Library)/Mary Evans Picture Library

After graduating from the University of Toronto with a Masters in Aeronautics in 1929, Shenstone went to work for Junkers in Germany. There he met Ludwig Prandtl, who worked closely with another great German aeronautical designer, Alexander Lippisch, on experimental wing shapes.

Shenstone arrived at Supermarine in 1932 as a young and enthusiastic academic, rather too eager for R.J. Mitchell, who thought his lack of an engineering apprenticeship and emphasis on academic study negated his claim to be an engineer. When Shenstone proposed the elliptical wing Mitchell at first rejected it, but Shenstone, who had met the great German designer Ernst Heinkel during the development of the He 70 record-breaking mail plane in the early 1930s, was able to persuade his boss of the potential for fighter aircraft. Working at Southampton, Shenstone's ideas were developed by Joe Smith (with the general arrangement drawings) and Alf Faddy (with work on the detailed structure) for the new monoplane fighter to meet Air Ministry requirement F37/35. That famous 'Mitchell Wing' design should be credited as much to Shenstone and Faddy as to Mitchell.

Spitfire wing forms, known to the engineering community as the NACA 2200 series, were very thin by comparison with conventional wisdom and may well have benefited from the thinking of Frederick Lanchester, who maintained in 1907 that it was better to spread the vortex flow along the wing instead of having it concentrated at the tip. Lanchester said that 'the wing plan of a bird has ordinates that approximate more or less closely to those of the ellipse.' Shenstone studied German analysis by Prandtl's doctoral student, Max Munk, that showed how 'induced drag is a minimum when the wing carries an elliptically distributed lift loading. The simplest means by which this loading can be achieved is by the use of an elliptic planform wing.' The theory was there and all Supermarine had to do was translate it into metal.

The rejection of Type 224 by the Air Ministry was a blessing for the Supermarine team as it allowed Shenstone to develop the lift distribution of the elliptical design across a larger speed range. His work allowed Mitchell to go to the Air Ministry on 5 December 1934 with a design that looked very much like the eventual Spitfire.

Shenstone and Faddy seem to have convinced Mitchell that a distorted elliptical wing with the main spar at right angles would work, although we shall never know this for sure because in those days meetings at Supermarine were frequent and never minuted. Mitchell then approved amendment of the design, with the wing tips taken forward to produce the best possible lift as well as to create that beautiful shape that many have tried to mimic.

Shenstone's influence on the wing design created the ideal means to reduce the twisting moment in the wings, a factor that is so important to the rigidity, stability and effectiveness of a fighter with its wing-mounted weapons. Without computer-aided design, the only way to judge the twisting moment was by the use of a model, and it was not until K5054 was built and had flown that the work of Shenstone and Faddy could be validated against a flexible airframe.

Shenstone should be regarded as major contributor to the Spitfire's success and deserves greater recognition.

CHAPTER 2
THE POLITICIANS

By the time Adolf Hitler, one-time *Gefreiter* in the Kaiser's army and Munich beer hall rabble-rouser, took power in Germany in 1933, Great Britain had won the Schneider Trophy outright and was starting to wake up to a new world order.

Europe was still reeling from the horrors of trench warfare and the financial crisis, had lost self-confidence, and had seen far-left and far-right governments establish themselves and threaten conventional democracy. This was not a good time to be a spokesman advocating rearmament or for forecasting yet another conflict between the Great Powers.

Lack of public and political sympathy for the blindingly obvious did not stop Winston Churchill, former First Lord of the Admiralty and former government minister but now in the political wilderness, from raising the need for preparedness, especially in the air, at every opportunity. Churchill had few friends at this time but those he had were aware of the needs, and many risked their political and service positions to provide him with the raw data of intelligence on what was happening in Germany at a time when others preferred to keep such information under wraps or simply did not want to believe it.

Britain's National Government was not alone in hiding its head in the sand. France had the largest forces on the ground and in the air; Britain boasted the largest naval forces (but most warships were not in home waters); the Scandinavians were desperate for neutrality and other smaller nations were trying to rebuild their economies. There was little space or appetite for bringing modern technology to the armed forces.

America was even worse off. The isolationist policies of successive administrations after 1918 also led to lack of investment in the armed forces, which were unwilling to embrace the modern technologies offered by private ventures in Britain or by their own country's developing aeronautical industry. America had also started to develop mass-production – Henry Ford started to pioneer this in Detroit before the First World War – and it had a number of small but very entrepreneurial aviation businesses such as Boeing, Lockheed and Douglas. In fact Lockheed and Douglas were busy with commercial airliner designs to link the east and west coasts of North America.

The financial situation and a complete lack of understanding of the potential implications of events in Germany meant that Britain was slow to rearm and there was little government support for such a policy. Despite warnings from a few quarters, uttered almost weekly from the sidelines by politicians like Churchill, the National Government of Ramsay MacDonald

Neville Chamberlain's arrival at Heston aerodrome with the signature of Adolf Hitler was a piece of skulduggery by the German leader that has forever blighted Chamberlain's reputation. He should also be remembered as the Chancellor of the Exchequer who forced the funding of the Spitfire through an otherwise hostile Cabinet. Rex Features (Universal Images)

was preoccupied with the difficulties arising from financial crisis, which even saw sailors in the Royal Navy mutiny over pay at Invergordon in September 1931. It took more than a year for the National Government to find room in the budget for a limited rearmament programme, and then only for air assets.

Rearmament was spurred on by the Air Member for Supply and Research, a certain Air Vice-Marshal Hugh Dowding, who had been appointed to the Air Council in September 1930. Unlike many of his contemporaries, Dowding – nicknamed 'Snuffy' – did not believe in the prevailing narrow interpretation of the Trenchard doctrine and its mantra that 'the bomber will always get through'. He was passionately devoted to the air defence of his country and saw the need to embrace modern technology. It was fitting, then, that he should become the first Air Officer Commanding the new Fighter Command in July 1936 and that the nation, through his foresight, would have the world's first integrated air defence organisation in time for the Battle of Britain.

Dowding worked with Group Captain (later Air Vice-Marshal) Sir Henry Cave-Browne-Cave to champion new thinking in aeroplane design as an 'operational requirement'. Cave-

Browne-Cave, a minor aristocrat who had been an engineering officer in the Royal Naval Air Service during the First World War, would also have a major part in the planning for what would become the Battle of Britain through his understanding of the merits of Mitchell's work and the need to modernise the Royal Air Force. He foresaw that air power would dominate much of any forthcoming war.

But the Spitfire's development was not straightforward. Although the Southampton-based Supermarine company had been bought by the industrial giant Vickers Armstrong in 1928, it was still fulfilling Air Ministry orders for biplane flying boats when, in 1931, Specification F7/30 for a new fighter-interceptor was issued to seven aircraft companies. Dowding and Cave-Browne-Cave wanted a machine capable of 250mph in level flight. By contrast, the Hawker Fury, the frontline fighter of the Metropolitan Air Force, as the predecessor of Fighter Command was called, had a service top speed of 207mph – and this compared with 407.5mph for the Supermarine S6B fitted with the Rolls-Royce R-type engine, showing perhaps that Air Ministry thinking was yet to catch up with the technology.

This should not have been an unrealistic target for Britain's aeroplane constructors, especially as the Specification was written in very general terms: highest possible rate of climb; highest possible speed at altitude; good visibility for the pilot; good manoeuvrability; ease of quantity production; ease of maintenance; provision for four rifle-calibre 0.303in machine guns and four 20lb general purpose bombs.

In the event the biplane Gloster SS37, now named Gladiator, was ordered into service as trials showed that it could out-climb monoplane rivals – including Supermarine's offering in the form of the Type 224 – and the conservative Air Ministry felt that the tried-and-tested biplane would perform better in service. Although the Gladiator could not reach the magic 250mph top speed required, it exceeded the maximum speed of the other six aeroplanes in the competition.

The Gladiator became the Royal Air Force's last biplane fighter – the Sea Gladiator was the last Fleet Air Arm biplane fighter too – and the first with an enclosed cockpit. The Gladiator would achieve fame defending Oslo from the Germans in April 1940 and the Sea Gladiator, flown by Royal Air Force pilots, defended Malta from the Italians later that same year. *Hope, Faith and Charity* might have been more than three actual airframes but they have gone down in the annals of aviation history for their spirited defence against overwhelming odds, a not unusual situation for British and Commonwealth flying units in the early years of the Second World War.

After the Air Ministry's rejection of the Type 224, things moved quickly at Supermarine, with Mitchell and his team creating their improved monoplane design, the Type 300, within six months. Despite the very obvious leap forward from fabric-covered biplanes, however, the new Supermarine design was also rejected by the Air Ministry, at least initially. Cave-Browne-Cave entered the Spitfire story again here: he is credited with having authorised, on 1 December 1934, the first £10,000 payment to Supermarine as a seed-corn investment for the assessment phase of an improved Type 300 monoplane fighter design – which would become the Spitfire. The prototype contract was designated F37/34 and stipulated eight machine

In the late 1930s the British government trod a difficult path between maintaining good relations with Hitler's Germany and rearmament against it. This atmospheric picture shows the Secretary of State for Air, Philip Cunliffe-Lister, bidding farewell to his German opposite number, General *Erhard Milch, State Secretary at the* Reichsluftfahrtministerium (ministry of aviation), *on the steps of the newly built Air Ministry on 18 October 1937. Looking on is* Generalmajor *Ernst Udet, head of the Luftwaffe's research and development department, the* Technisch-amt. Getty Images (Hulton Archive)

guns instead of four, because the Air Ministry had been convinced, mainly by Squadron Leader Ralph Sorley, that a modern enemy bomber would be fast and the punch packed by a fighter's armament would have to disable or destroy it with a burst of concentrated fire of no more than two seconds.

That funding kept the Type 300 project alive at a time when Supermarine's great rival, Hawker, had tested the Hurricane monoplane fighter at Teddington's National Physical Laboratory and set about answering Specification F37/34 calling for that eight-gun monoplane fighter. The Hurricane's maiden flight took place on 6 November 1935 with George Bulman at the controls. The Spitfire was running about six months behind its rival.

George Bulman was to play another important role in the story of Britain's rearmament two years later, when he was one of a small team invited to Germany to be shown the Luftwaffe's new equipment. His report to the Air Council caused a rapid increase in rearmament activity. It was scary stuff: large factories, funding through Hermann Göring's Nazi-backed industrial enterprises, aero-engine works to complement the airframe production, and a pilot training programme that had already been underway for a decade.

Another significant figure at this time was the long-time head of the Home Civil Service (a new position created after the First World War for better coordination of policy), Warren Fisher, who later became Permanent Secretary at the Treasury. Fisher was a friend and advisor to Neville Chamberlain when Chamberlain was Prime Minister and, having been in post since 1919, had myriad contacts that he used to good effect. Despite an academic background in Classics, which seemed to make him ideally suited to his first civil service appointment to the Inland Revenue, Fisher believed in new technology – luckily for the Spitfire – and in the need to invest in the production of new monoplane fighter aircraft.

Time was against Supermarine but the shadow of war was speeding up developments in the Air Ministry. New, clear thinkers were taking over and the government of the day finally got the message about the need to rearm even if a few still did not choose to believe that Germany was a serious threat.

Supermarine did not have to wait for a contract to back up that investment in the assessment phase. Early in 1935 the Air Ministry formalised Cave-Browne-Cave's work with a new Specification, F10/35, and a contract that used Mitchell's design drawings as its base. The new fighter design, still known at Supermarine as the F37/34 or Type 300, was soon to become the Spitfire.

Neville Chamberlain FRS PC

Born 18 March 1869
Died 9 November 1940
Member of Parliament, 1918–40
Chancellor of the Exchequer, 1931–37
Prime Minister, 1937–40

Neville Chamberlain is a misunderstood politician. His contribution to the development of the Spitfire has been overlooked by history and his reputation tarnished by his inability to understand the mind of Adolf Hitler. He was not alone in misreading tyrants: Franklin D. Roosevelt, the much-admired US President, misread Joseph Stalin yet history has not judged him so harshly.

Chamberlain was a former Mayor of Birmingham who entered national politics in 1918, his business skills and personality fitting the time. During the 1923 General Election he fought a close contest with the leader of the British Union of Fascists, Oswald Mosley, and won by a narrow majority, leading him to believe that right-wing extremism could be beaten through the ballot box rather than through any tougher measures.

Within four years Chamberlain was appointed chairman of the Conservative Party and joined the Cabinet in Stanley Baldwin's Government. Significantly for the Spitfire and other aviation developments, he became Chancellor of the Exchequer in the National Government of 1931. This role fitted Chamberlain's personal philosophies of thrift, hard work and personal achievement. He did not have sympathy for the 'scrounger mentality', which was prevalent in major conurbations even then.

By 1935 and the public emergence of German rearmament plans, *Aufrüstung*, especially with the emphasis on the Luftwaffe, Chamberlain took the view that enemy air power would be the greatest challenge of the next decade as it made Britain more vulnerable than ever before. The English Channel, despite the Royal Navy, would no longer be the bulwark of national defence that it had been since the Norman invasion 900 years before.

The writing had been on the wall since the revelations of a German whistle-blower and later Nobel laureate, Carl von Ossietzky, in 1931. Many of the European democracies had been slow on the uptake, not understanding that the Soviet Union was providing secret facilities for the development and production of aircraft and other armaments. Chamberlain did understand and after passing legislation protecting the unemployed, his top priority, he embarked on funding the rearmament of Britain's armed forces.

The Defence Requirements Sub-Committee of the Committee of Imperial Defence had followed the traditional British Government emphasis on Empire and 'East of Suez' by splitting funds between the Royal Navy for its capital ship projects and expeditionary funding for the British Army. It had brought forward the development of aircraft carriers and modernised battleships, but it still missed the latest technologies in the air and the capability gaps they created in Britain's traditional defence stance.

Chamberlain saw that the Royal Air Force vote of funding was insufficient to allow the service to modernise after the follies of the 'bomber will always get through' philosophy and the misplaced efforts at the Geneva Disarmament Conference to ban bombers, an aim that Baldwin held in such high regard. This conference faltered and died after Hitler came to power in 1933 and withdrew Germany from it as well as from the League of Nations. Peace, Chamberlain realised, would be hard to negotiate.

It took two years for Chamberlain to develop the funding lines for the development of the fighter force. By 1935 his annual budget reflected his thinking that the development of air power had to be supported by the Government. The Air Ministry was also rushing through development plans at the time with the Spitfire and the Hurricane being emphasised in debate and internal process. This process also saw the development of separate Royal Air Force commands, including the creation of Fighter Command, to which would come funding from the Exchequer in time for investment in radar, VHF (Very High Frequency) radio, new fuels and integrated communications, all of which would need Treasury approval and all of which Chamberlain oversaw and drove through.

The deputy leader of the Labour Party, Arthur Greenwood, attacked Chamberlain for spending money on rearmament. Labour's position was that rearmament was 'the merest scaremongering; disgraceful in a statesman of Mr Chamberlain's responsible position, to suggest that more millions of money needed to be spent on armaments.' Greenwood then

Neville Chamberlain's political skills were recognised by Winston Churchill in May 1940 when the new Prime Minister invited the man ousted just hours before to join the first War Cabinet. Chamberlain brought a talent for uniting the Conservative Party behind the National Government but sadly died in the immediate aftermath of the Battle of Britain, which his political courage in funding fighter production five years earlier had helped to win. Getty Images (Hulton Archive)

played a major part in the fall of Chamberlain in May 1940 when Labour refused to support him, as Prime Minister, when the *Blitzkrieg* was launched by Germany against France and the Low Countries.

Those who have branded Chamberlain a deluded appeaser often overlook his support for the Spitfire and other air-defence initiatives. Indeed, his policy of giving in to some of Hitler's demands can be judged now as having allowed time for development of the integrated air-defence system that in turn enabled Fighter Command, in 1940, to fight and win what otherwise might have been an unequal struggle.

Chamberlain's other great achievement, probably against his better judgement, was the appointment of Winston Churchill as First Lord of the Admiralty. After Chamberlain's fall, Churchill repaid this decision by the kindness he showed to his predecessor as Prime Minister in his dying days. Chamberlain died on 9 November 1940, ironically when his Government's original term of office was due to expire.

Sir Henry Tizard KCB FRS

Born 23 August 1885
Died 9 October 1959
Government Scientific Adviser, 1934–40

Henry Tizard is another great but relatively unknown figure in the development of air defence in which the Spitfire played a key part. A First World War fighter pilot and chemist who created the octane scale for fuel, Tizard was appointed chairman of the Aeronautical Research Committee in 1933 and, a year later, he chaired a government committee on air defence that became known as the Tizard Committee.

During the First World War and the inter-war period Tizard became immersed in aeronautics and the problems of air defence. His primary area was radar – radio ranging and detection, then known as radio direction finding – and its role in being able to guide fighter aircraft to the enemy instead of flying wasteful patrol lines, as had been his experience during the period 1916–18.

Tizard choose RAF Biggin Hill in Kent as his test station for radar-initiated interception using biplane fighters and leading to the creation of the Chain Home radar stations on the East and South Coasts of Britain. This development by the commercial company Cossor (now a subsidiary of Raytheon), teamed with Dowding's integrated air-defence plans pioneered at RAF Northolt, led to the successful system that allowed timely interception of Luftwaffe bombers by Spitfires and Hurricanes in 1940.

Realising that single-seat fighters could not on their own hope to intercept enemy night bombers, even with the help of ground-based radar direction, Tizard also pioneered airborne interception radar. This took longer to develop and was not operational until 1941, but it then played a major part in convincing the Germans that night bombing by larger formations would not be effective.

Henry Tizard was the sort of boffin that Britain seems to find in its darkest hours. During his six-year tenure as the Government's Scientific Advisor, he pioneered the development of radar, both ground-based for surveillance and airborne for fighter interception. His work generally helped the development of Fighter Command's new aeroplanes but he did not find favour with Churchill in 1940, and was replaced. Getty Images (Hulton Archive)

Tizard's other wartime duties included working for the US Government in joint defence developments, among them what the British called 'tube alloys' at the time and today we know as nuclear weapons. In 1945 he served as chairman of the Defence Research Policy Committee, led a study into UFOs, and was president of the British Association for the Advancement of Science.

Philip Cunliffe-Lister MC (Viscount Swinton)
Born 1 May 1884
Died 27 July 1972
Secretary of State for Air, 1935–38

Although perhaps not the most successful Secretary of State for Air, Philip Cunliffe-Lister is nevertheless important in the Spitfire story because he was the incumbent when the Spitfire first flew, when it was ordered and when it completed its pre-service trials. His hard work and ability to understand technology, as well as his championing of shadow factories, are redeeming features of his tenure.

First elected as an MP in 1918, Cunliffe-Lister was appointed Secretary of State for Air by Stanley Baldwin in 1935 as part of Baldwin's Cabinet reshuffle upon taking over from

Philip Cunliffe-Lister understood the need for modern technologies to counter the rise of Germany in the 1930s. Almost immediately after his appointment as Secretary of State for Air, he was ennobled as Lord Swinton and so lost touch with the House of Commons at a critical time in Britain's history. His backing for shadow factories for aeroplanes and aero-engines was right but he seems to have surrounded it in 'red tape' and been unable to cut through the log-jam at Supermarine that delayed initial production. Getty Images (Hulton Archive)

Ramsay MacDonald as Prime Minister. Soon after he was ennobled as Viscount Swinton and therefore did not contest that year's General Election, but he found that being in the House of Lords meant he could not answer for aircraft production and development in the Neville Chamberlain government.

Bizarrely, the Irish peer, Lord Winterton, did sit in the House of Commons and answered for the Air Ministry, but he was also completely out of touch. The result was a series of political embarrassments in the first part of 1938 that prompted Chamberlain to sack Swinton that May, but Chamberlain later came to regret that decision when he realised that continuity was as important as public image.

In so many areas Swinton was a key figure in the build-up to the Second World War, although serious historians of the Royal Air Force have never been able to understand his decision, without consultation, to appoint Sir Cyril Newall as Chief of the Air Staff over the head of Sir Hugh Dowding; Newall was far less able and experienced than Dowding. With hindsight, however, leaving Dowding at Bentley Priory, the headquarters of RAF Fighter Command, proved ideal as the Battle of Britain panned out – but it was happenstance rather than design. Newall did not excel as the Chief of the Air Staff and was replaced by Charles Portal in October 1940.

Swinton also deserves his place in the Spitfire story through his association with the creation of the shadow factories, especially the Spitfire facility at Castle Bromwich and the engine plants for Rolls-Royce. He understood that modern technology would be needed to defeat the Germans but that radar stations, Spitfire production and new airfields had to be in the right geographical locations. He also worked with Air Marshal Wilfrid Freeman in the Air Ministry to develop a process that would allow prototypes to be ordered once key performance indicators had been demonstrated.

Where Swinton failed was in his almost Edwardian beliefs that everybody else was as 'right-minded' as he was and that German private property was sacrosanct and therefore should not be bombed.

Sir Thomas Inskip CBE PC KC

Born 5 March 1876
Died 11 October 1947
Minister for the Coordination of Defence, 1936–39

Blessed with a sharp lawyer's mind, Thomas Inskip was a good but not brilliant administrator and a controversial political figure at a time when the United Kingdom needed the best minds. He was appointed in 1936 by Prime Minister Stanley Baldwin to bring together the strands of British rearmament. With Germany rearming faster than any other nation, many would have preferred Winston Churchill in the role but it is said that Baldwin thought Churchill would 'frighten the horses'.

Inskip, however, was close enough to Churchill in both philosophy and political thinking

Thomas Inskip was given the onerous task of coordinating the planned expansion of defence preparedness from 1936, including recommending which programmes and plans should be adopted. Luckily for Britain, he was persuaded that the bomber would not *always get through – contrary to the perceived wisdom of the day – and supported the funding of Spitfire and Hurricane development over spending on bombers.* Rex Features (Associated Newspapers)

to take forward the great man's vision, albeit slowly. He worked on rearmament but seems to have wanted a measured, legalistic approach, whereas others advocated radical and rapid rearmament. In fact, on appointment, Inskip was offered advice by Churchill. This advice was to coordinate strategy, settle inter-service debates and make sure that equipment ordered arrived on time, to the right standard and at the right cost. He took most of that advice, which has echoes in defence procurement up to the present day.

A year into his post Inskip chaired a Defence Review that was then published in 1938. Academics today say that his efforts to balance economic risks and rearmament were crucial if Britain was to navigate successfully the threatening international situation and maintain the country's own long-term economic stability. He seems to have been persuaded that a strategic bomber offensive alone would not destroy the enemy but that adequate fighter defences were also needed – hence his support for the Spitfire and the Hurricane.

Faced with tough choices and partisan briefings from the three Service chiefs, Inskip took a cautious approach. His championing of fighters, such as the Spitfire, goes some way to explaining why he received such negative press at a time when the case for bombers and more land forces had considerable media support.

He argued for the main effort to be directed at protecting Britain against air attack and preserving its trade routes, thus privileging the Royal Air Force and the Royal Navy, as well as the British Army's anti-aircraft units. This emphasis was vital in the Battle of Britain, of course, but the lack of priority for the British Army in the field quickly became overtaken by rapidly moving events on the Continent.

According to the Royal United Services Institute for defence studies, which in 2013 reviewed the 1938 White Paper, the Inskip Defence Review demonstrated the importance of balance and, crucially, of not closing off future options.

Sir Kingsley Wood

Born 19 August 1881
Died 21 September 1943
Secretary of State for Air, 1938–40

Sir Kingsley Wood became Secretary of State for Air in March 1938, six months before the Munich crisis enveloped Chamberlain's government. His Wesleyan upbringing endowed the steadfast determination he brought to the task of making more fighter aeroplanes.

Overturning some disastrous policies of his predecessor, Philip Cunliffe-Lister (later Lord Swinton), Wood expanded military aircraft production from a little over two a day at the time of his appointment to nearly 20 a day by the beginning of 1940. By that time the British aircraft industry was delivering combat aircraft to the front line at the same rate as the Germans were, but the Luftwaffe had had a head start of six years on the Royal Air Force.

The very great effort put into this exercise by Wood resulted in his physical and mental exhaustion. In early April 1940 he was removed to the less demanding role of Lord Privy Seal and replaced by Sir Archibald Sinclair. But Wood had brought the Spitfire to the front line and his actions played their part in the availability to Fighter Command of 19 squadrons when the Battle of Britain officially started in July.

If there is a debit side to Wood's work, it was his determination to bring Lord Nuffield into the Civilian Repair Organisation (CRO) as its director general, a role that seems to have taken Nuffield's eye off the completion of the Castle Bromwich factory, leading to its sequestration by Government and the handing over of its operations to Vickers. In the event the CRO's use of small and medium enterprises for military maintenance worked well and cleared the backlog from the Royal Air Force Maintenance Units, allowing the front line to have sufficient fighters for the Battle of Britain and later operations over Occupied Europe.

Wood was also instrumental in the creation of the Air Transport Auxiliary, which delivered over 308,000 aircraft from factories and CRO sites to Royal Air Force Maintenance Units and the front line in the period 1940–45. Wood provided the political muscle to turn various potentially uncooperative organisations into advocates – no mean achievement.

Kingsley Wood, the Secretary of State for Air, was a Spitfire supporter in the days when the programme needed its friends after its initial production problems. Wood clawed back some of the lead that Germany had over British aircraft production through the use of small and medium enterprises, mainly in the automotive industry. He is seen here with the Chief of the Air Staff, Air Chief Marshal Sir Cyril Newall, leaving No 10 Downing Street. They might be smiling for the camera but they frequently disagreed about fighter-versus-bomber production priorities. RAF Museum

CHAPTER 3
THE PIONEERS

Against a background of relative lack of government interest in aviation innovation as well as a financial crisis, Supermarine, a small aviation company on the South Coast, beat off French, Italian and American rivals to win the Schneider Trophy outright – the most prestigious aviation prize of its generation – thanks to victories in the three successive competitions of 1927, 1929 and 1931.

At this time many of the nations of Europe continued to believe that seaplanes and flying boats were the way forward as they still possessed overseas dominions and colonies that lacked the infrastructure for land plane operations but possessed plenty of water. The visionary aviator Sir Alan Cobham was a key figure in the inter-war seaplane and flying-boat revolution but even his exploits were ignored by the government of the day. Speed, too, was in the hands of seaplane designers like Mario Castoldi in Italy, Claudius Dornier in Germany and Gabriel Voisin in France.

French engineer Jacques Schneider also believed that seaplanes were the way forward for civil aviation. Using part of his family's fortune, derived from heavy industries including armaments, Schneider proposed to the Aéroclub de France an annual contest that he hoped would lead to development of better commercial aeroplanes. Participants needed to fly at least 150 miles (240 kilometres) and the winner would receive 25,000 Francs plus a trophy – the *Coupe d'Aviation Maritime Jacques Schneider* – that was worth the same as the monetary prize. If a nation was to win the cup three times within five years, the cup would belong to the winning team in perpetuity.

The first Schneider Trophy competition was held in 1913 off Monaco and another competition was held the following year. Competition was then suspended during the First World War, to be resumed in 1919. Nine more races were held until the competition was permanently suspended in 1931 when the British team won for the third time with the Supermarine S6b racing seaplane designed by R.J. Mitchell and powered by a Rolls-Royce engine. Sadly for Schneider, the races did not achieve his objective for the development of robust long-range aeroplanes, but they did show the way for designers to go faster and led to innovative British and Italian fighter designs, including the Spitfire, resulting from technical advances in fields such as aerodynamics and stressed-skin construction.

Britain's success in the Schneider Trophy competitions was thanks to the great designs of Supermarine chief designer Reginald Mitchell and a number of talented engineers at the

R.J. Mitchell engaged regularly with the pilots and engineers of the Royal Air Force High Speed Flight at RAF Calshot. In this 1931 picture he is chatting with (from left) Flight Lieutenants Freddy Long (second reserve), George Stainforth and E.J.L. Hope, in company with Lieutenant Jerry Brinton of the Fleet Air Arm. Solent Sky

Rolls-Royce company, whose tremendous contribution to the sports flying of the 1930s and the development of both the Spitfire and the Hurricane is often overlooked.

The young Mitchell joined Supermarine in 1917 with the intention of learning his chosen ambition to be a seaplane designer, having started in the railway locomotive business in Staffordshire. One of the notable things about Mitchell is that he trained as an apprentice through the drawing office and night school, as did so many of his contemporaries, following a path that is sadly lacking for similar talents today. Mitchell impressed, too, because he was not afraid of capturing the thoughts and ideas of others, developing them and creating an integrated, innovative solution.

His work with Supermarine led to the Schneider Trophy designs and more than 20 other aeroplane types, many of which reflected the times in being flying boats. When Vickers bought Supermarine from the powerboat enthusiast Hubert Scott-Paine in 1928, the deal included a five-year 'golden handcuff' for Mitchell. Bearing in mind the economic situation of the time, Mitchell must have jumped at the opportunity; his son Gordon, incidentally, told the author that the stability of the Vickers contract meant that Mitchell could afford to have him educated privately.

Mitchell and his contemporaries, such as Hawker's Sydney Camm, were working on the development of new monoplane airframes while George White and Henry Royce were developing revolutionary aero-engines.

As related in the introduction to Chapter 2, in 1931 the Air Ministry issued Specification F7/30 for a new fighter-interceptor and seven companies responded, one of them with two designs. The Bristol Type 123, Hawker PV3, Westland PV-4, Blackburn F7/30 and Gloster SS37 were all traditional biplanes. A more radical approach, never the best policy in a time of austerity in Britain, was also offered with three monoplanes, from Bristol with its Type 133 as well as from Supermarine with its Type 224 and Vickers with its Type 171 Jockey.

Supermarine's two monoplane rivals both looked like biplanes with the top wing removed. Bristol's Type 133, designed by Frank Barnwell and powered by the Bristol Mercury radial engine, looked very much like the earlier Bulldog, and incorporated a cranked wing but with retractable undercarriage. The Vickers Jockey, in which the famous designer Barnes Wallis had much input, was first mooted for a 1927 competition that led to the Hawker Fury. Although both companies learned much from these prototypes, especially in relation to stressed-skin and flight-control balance, they did not impress the Air Ministry. They lacked speed and agility as well as being fraught with potential production difficulties.

Mitchell's first effort was underwhelming – it was certainly not a Spitfire. The Type 224, although a monoplane design, featured an open cockpit, gull wings and a large, fixed, spatted undercarriage. It was powered by a liquid-cooled Rolls-Royce Goshawk engine, which, despite being the most powerful British aero engine of the time, only produced 660hp – the laws of physics did not allow a 660hp engine to endow a speed of more than 250mph. So it was that the Type 224, when it made its maiden flight in February 1934, disappointed not just the Air Ministry but the design team at Southampton as well. It certainly fulfilled the old adage: 'If it doesn't like right, it won't fly right.'

In fact the Type 224 suffered from a series of faults, including insufficient cooling for the engine and the tendency for liquid from the engine's wing-mounted condensers to stream off the wings in a climb. That cannot have been a comforting sight for the Royal Air Force test pilot assigned to the testing, Flight Lieutenant Hugh ('Willie') Wilson, who thought that the fighter would need to cruise for a spell at the top of its climb in order to cool off before the throttle was opened and it went into action. Wilson became the Royal Aircraft Establishment's chief enemy aircraft test pilot in 1941.

So it was back to the drawing board at Supermarine, where faith in the need for a monoplane fighter remained unshaken. In his lair next to the drawing office, overlooking the River Itchen in Southampton, Mitchell and his team created a new design, the Type 300, in less than six months. The Board of Vickers approved private-venture funding, perceiving that Mitchell was very much the right man to create a faster monoplane fighter, since he could draw from all of his experience of streamlining on the Supermarine S6b in the Schneider Trophy competition.

High-drag aspects of the Type 224 were addressed, especially the undercarriage, which was replaced by more compact, retractable gear with doors. The engine was also streamlined,

Supermarine's works and offices at Woolston on the River Itchen at Southampton show the graceful Art Deco *lines that blended function with aesthetic quality. Until the Spitfire came on line, the staple diet of the factory was the Walrus amphibian, an example of which can be seen at the top of the slipway prior to a test flight.* Solent Sky

helped by the work of Rolls-Royce on the PV-12, the forerunner of the Merlin. There would also be a major change to the wing shape.

Mitchell, Faddy, Bill Fear, R.J. Fenner and the team of apprenticed engineers were moving into a new era of flight. Much of the work now rested on academic study into aerodynamics, metallurgy and structural design. So it was that in the 1930s new faces appeared at Supermarine with university training and research backgrounds.

That famous and memorable elliptical wing, with reduced drag and increased lift, may have been difficult to mass-produce but it was key to the Spitfire's design. The elliptical wing may have had its roots in the early sketches for a mail plane by Ernst Heinkel and work by other German designers; Heinkel concentrated on a simple ellipse rather than the complex result of senior aerodynamicist Beverley Shenstone's work for Supermarine from 1932. Heinkel wanted to be as near as possible to aerodynamic perfection but an essential influence in the development of the wing design was Shenstone, who firmly believed that 'it must look nice' because he knew that usually meant 'it would fly nice'.

Part of Mitchell's genius as a designer was to take the initial thoughts of others and see their merits for Supermarine's own work. The Germans had been working on elliptical wings in the early 1930s as well and although they did not see service until the Messerschmitt Bf 109F flew a decade later, Mitchell and Shenstone were aware of Ernst Heinkel's practical

Prior to the Vickers take-over, Supermarine's works at Woolston was a simple combination of factory and aircraft hangars, with the drawing office and technical team based in the middle of the factory. To the right of the site is the Woolston floating bridge that connected Woolston to Southampton proper. Solent Sky

work on the record-breaking mail plane, the He 70, which first flew in December 1932; they saw the benefits and adapted the design process accordingly. In fact, Rolls-Royce in Britain took delivery in 1936 of a He 70 as a flying test bed, some weeks after the Spitfire had made its maiden flight, making the notion that Supermarine cribbed the Heinkel design for the Spitfire rather far-fetched.

With the engine, there was a need to reduce heat and yet still generate the figure of almost 1,000hp promised by Rolls-Royce. The Rolls-Royce team collaborated with the Royal Aircraft Establishment at Farnborough on the design of ducted radiators, using technological advances that included the Meredith-effect radiator. By means of careful design that was informed by the mathematics completed by F.W. Meredith in the early 1930s, this type of cooling radiator reduced the aerodynamic drag induced by a conventional under-wing radiator. Mitchell and Camm adopted the Meredith effect for the Spitfire and Hurricane respectively – and later Edgar Schmued of North American Aviation copied them for the P-51 Mustang's characteristic underbelly intake. Mitchell's team also worked on lightweight fuselage design as well as the weight and balance problems created by the heavier PV-12 engine. The gestation of the Merlin, in fact, proved to be as difficult as that of the Spitfire.

The prototype of the aeroplane that the Board of Vickers was soon to call the Spitfire,

This aerial view was taken immediately after the Luftwaffe inflicted considerable damage on the factory on 26 September 1940. Through the foresight of Supermarine officials, plans had been made as early as 1932 to disperse production and many small companies in locations far from the South Coast had been contracted. Solent Sky

K5054, first flew on 5 March 1936. The flight lasted eight minutes and it was documented in the First Flight Report, which is thought to have been compiled by Arthur Falcon and circulated to Messrs Mitchell, Westbrook, Payn, Clifton, Black and Faddy, in that order. The following day, 'Mutt' Summers took K5054 up again for 23 minutes, and further flights followed of 31 minutes on 10 March and 50 minutes on 14 March. By that time Summers was apparently satisfied with the modifications made, including a change of airscrew.

After one further flight on 15 March, K5054, now almost certainly known as the Supermarine Spitfire (or SS), was prepared to be ferried to the Aeroplane & Armament Experimental Establishment at Martlesham Heath for the first Royal Air Force trails in May. According to Arthur Falcon's notes, 21 different adjustments were suggested by Summers and agreed by Mitchell and the team.

For many pilots, the real issue with the beautiful and iconic Spitfire, and one that caused many accidents, was the narrow-track undercarriage. Considering the excellent relations between Mitchell and chief test pilot Jeffrey Quill, this is a surprise, but it is all about the design rather than the pilot's needs. The rival Hurricane had a wide track that allowed less experienced pilots to better control the aeroplane on the ground, especially on the landing run and particularly if the fighter was damaged or the pilot wounded.

The undercarriage design feature also caused some initial manufacturing headaches as the fuselage had to be supported on specially made or improvised trestles because the embryonic aeroplane could not stand on its legs. The Hurricane, which took about half the time to build, had a design that enabled the fuselage and the bottom of the mainplane to incorporate the main wheels and thus allow the aeroplane to be free-standing during production or when major repairs were made to the wings.

When, in late 1940 and early 1941, Spitfire production had to be dispersed as a wartime emergency measure, one method for the process engineering selected by Vickers was to separate the manufacture and fabrication of the wings, tail empennage and ancillaries. In the case of the dispersed sites in Salisbury, manufacture of these elements had to be in separate factories because of space constraints.

Where the Spitfire does appear to have succeeded in terms of manufacture was in the engine installation and cowling arrangement. Although many groundcrew men would complain about the arrangement of starter, engine and oil tank, it was possible to install the Merlin engine in the smallest of factories.

By December 1936 the Spitfire had been fitted with its weapons and an uprated Merlin engine, but much work on developing the aeroplane as a fighting machine and as an airframe capable of mass-production was needed before service entry in 1938. There were various small alterations to the design and work was needed to stop the Browning machine guns freezing up at altitude.

The close working relationship that Rolls-Royce established with Supermarine at this time, just months before Mitchell's death in June 1937, created one of the greatest combinations in aviation history, the Merlin-engined Spitfire, and all for less than £16,000.

By late 1937 the prototype Spitfire had returned to test flying after a forced landing at RAF Martlesham Heath following a hydraulic failure. It left the Supermarine works in a camouflage paint scheme of dark green and dark earth (brown) with what photographs appear to show a black/white underside, designed to aid recognition for anti-aircraft artillery spotters. It continued flying trials at the Royal Aircraft Establishment Farnborough until 4 September 1939, when it was written off, killing the Royal Air Force test pilot, Flight Lieutenant Gilbert White, also known as 'Spinner'. With little time to consider heritage after the outbreak of war, K5054 was broken up at Farnborough some time in October or November 1939.

Through the period of the Munich Crisis and the now infamous 'Peace in our time' speech by Prime Minister Neville Chamberlain in the House of Commons, three outstanding test pilots – Joseph 'Mutt' Summers, Jeffrey Quill and George Pickering – worked their magic on the Spitfire, helping to turn it from a prototype into a production aeroplane. Refinements included armament, hydraulics, radio fit and the reflector gun sight. The first two production Spitfires were retained at Supermarine for trials and development flying and a team of up to 25 pilots, led by legendary air racer Alex Henshaw (see page 115), was kept busy testing machines straight off the production lines at Castle Bromwich, Eastleigh and the various dispersed factories.

Noel Pemberton-Billing

Born 31 January 1881
Died 11 November 1948
Aviation entrepreneur, 1903–16

Noel Pemberton-Billing was one of those characters without whom the Spitfire would not have reached its birth, let alone its conception, but he had no direct part in its development. He tried several professions during his nearly life and at some he prospered, others not.

Perhaps the most significant factor in the Pemberton-Billing relationship with the Spitfire is the name 'Supermarine', which he used in 1913 to create an aviation business at an old coal wharf on the River Itchen's mouth at Southampton. It was an ideal telegraphic address at a time when the fastest means of communication was the Post Office telegram and the single name was enough to find an addressee anywhere in the world.

After serving in the Second Boer War in South Africa, Pemberton-Billing wanted to open an aerodrome in Essex, where aviation seemed to be focused in the late Edwardian era, and he tried to establish several flying fields in the county. He also started an aviation

Every inch the eccentric, Noel Pemberton-Billing had so many careers outside aviation that some might question his inclusion in this book. The answer is simple: he thought up the name 'Supermarine' and he began the industrialisation of Woolston.
Solent Sky

magazine, *Aerocraft*. Determined to rival the Wright brothers and the Blériot brothers, he sought private finance for an experimental aeroplane design and opened a factory in Essex. His experimental designs, however, were destined to fail and he had to sell up to pay back his debts.

Defeated by the move to concentrate aeroplane factories at Brooklands in Surrey, he decided to learn to fly and, in a typically extravagant gesture, he bet Frederick Handley Page, another aviation enthusiast and soon-to-be aviation industrialist, that he could earn his Royal Aero Club pilot's certificate within 24 hours. The bet was for £500 and Pemberton-Billing won, gaining licence number 683 at the Vickers School of Flying at Brooklands in one day during 1913. Vickers, of course, would play an important part in the Supermarine story 20 years later.

The money he won was invested in a steam yacht broking business, which he ran with Hubert Scott-Paine at Woolston, Southampton, on the estuary of the River Itchen. To this enterprise they added an aviation company that combined the knowledge both had of the air and the sea in the design and construction of a flying boat, the PB1 mono-hull biplane, in time for the Olympia Air Show in 1914. It was seen by HM King George V and, perhaps more importantly, by members of the Imperial German delegation, who ordered a production version, the PB7, there and then. The First World War prevented this aeroplane from being delivered.

War clouds meant that Pemberton-Billing, always a nationalist and imperialist, joined the armed forces again. This time, armed with his pilot's certificate, he applied to the Royal Naval Air Service as a probationary flight officer. Before joining up he had seen his company's PB9 fighter, a land plane, take to the skies above nearby Netley Common, flown by Victor Mahl, the Sopwith test pilot. It led to the PB23 'pusher' and the PB25 tractor-powered fighter, both early fighting machines.

By now Pemberton-Billing was becoming more interested in politics than aeroplanes and he applied for and was granted leave to design a fighter to combat the Zeppelin menace. Before departing from the RNAS he took part in the planning of the world's first long-range strategic bombing by aeroplanes, when the RNAS bombed the Zeppelin airship sheds on Lake Constance in November 1914. These German airships were to inflict sustained strategic bombing of an enemy capital when they attacked London in May 1915, having also struck King's Lynn in Norfolk – the first town ever to be attacked from the air – and Liège in Belgium earlier in the year. The air raids provoked an unusually immediate and decisive reaction from the War Office, which brought back aeroplanes from France and started setting up aerodromes on the East Coast and other approaches to London. The Cabinet also authorised retaliation.

In early 1916 Pemberton-Billing sold his shares in the Supermarine aviation company and contested a by-election for the parliamentary seat of Mile End. Although he lost there, he went on to win a by-election at Hertford and entered the House of Commons. He wrote a bestselling book, *Air War and How to Wage It*, but his health deteriorated and he left politics in 1921, moving into new technologies such as camera development and film.

Hubert Scott-Paine

Born 11 March 1891
Died 14 April 1954
Factory manager, Supermarine, 1913–16
Owner, Supermarine Aviation, 1916–23

Hubert Scott-Paine has been described as the Sir Richard Branson of his time, with his entrepreneurial flair for aeroplanes, airlines, fast boats, publicity and setting records. He should always be remembered as the man who employed R.J. Mitchell to design fast flying boats (aeroplanes that landed on their hulls in water) and racing seaplanes (which tended to use floats, or what the Americans call pontoons, for landing on water). Until his mid-20s he was plain Hubert Paine, but in 1917 he changed his name by deed-poll to combine his mother's and father's surnames.

By the time Supermarine was building fighter monoplanes, Scott-Paine was no longer directly involved in the company but he must have observed its activities from the sidelines across the water at Hythe while at the British Power Boat Company, where he built ever-faster speedboats. Some of these speedboats later became the 'light boats' of the Royal Naval Coastal Forces.

Scott-Paine began his 40-year career as a yacht broker for Noel Pemberton-Billing in 1913 and between them they created Pemberton-Billing Limited in June 1914 with another entrepreneur, Alfred de Broughton. Jacques Schneider's first trophy race at Monaco in 1913

Hubert Scott-Paine loved speed and innovation. He badly wanted his dream creation, Miss Britain III, *built almost a decade after he had sold Supermarine, to be powered by the S6b's R-type engine, but Rolls-Royce would not release one to him.* Getty Images

THE HIGH SPEED FLIGHT

Heroes were once daredevil adventurers who pushed the boundaries of known science. The High Speed Flight – or, to give it the Royal Air Force's preferred title, 'The High Speed Flight of the Marine Aircraft Experimental Establishment' – created such heroes in the late 1920s and early 1930s. They flew cutting-edge racing aeroplanes faster than people had thought possible just a decade before and their endeavours advanced the technology of high-speed flight.

These endeavours directly assisted Supermarine's R.J. Mitchell, the premier British racing seaplane designer, to think about transferring the technology of stressed-skin, monoplane construction with an advanced aero engine. This would lead to the Spitfire.

Following Britain's disastrous attempt on the 1925 Schneider Trophy air race and the country's absence from the 1926 contest, the Air Ministry was put under pressure to allow Royal Air Force pilots to participate, just as those from Italy and the US were doing. The result was the High Speed Flight, formed at Felixstowe in preparation for the 1927 Schneider Trophy race in Venice, where the British team flew two Supermarine S5s, a Gloster IV and the ill-fated Short Brothers' Crusader, which crashed in practice. The two S5s completed the course and came in first and second with speeds of 281.65mph and 272.91mph respectively.

Among the pilots flying for Britain in Venice was the highly decorated South African ace, **Flight Lieutenant Sam Kinkead** DSO, DSC*, DFC*, who flew the Gloster IV at more than 277mph to establish a new world record.

The sudden deterioration of the world's financial situation had a knock-on effect at the Air Ministry and it was forced to disband the High Speed Flight after the 1927 race, even though, ironically, the Treasury was prepared to fund the £200,000 needed for the 1928 race, also to be held at Cowes. In the end service pilots did participate in the racing but, during practice in March 1928, Kinkead died at the controls of an S5, prompting the Air Ministry to further review the risks of service pilots flying racing seaplanes.

Commanding The Flight, as it is often simply known, at this time was **Squadron Leader Augustus Orlebar** DFC*, a former Royal Flying Corps pilot, known to his friends as 'Harry', who would go on to command No 10 (Fighter) Group in 1941. Orlebar also claimed a world record in 1929 with a speed of 357.7mph in a Supermarine S6 seaplane powered by the supercharged Rolls-Royce R-type engine, which would be developed into the PV-12 and thus the Merlin within a matter of a few short years.

Flying Officer Dick Waghorn won the 1929 Schneider Trophy with an aggregated speed of 328.6mph in the same S6 (N247), which, incidentally, is now well cared for at the Solent Sky Museum at Southampton. A second S6 (N248) flown by **Flying Officer Richard Atcherley** was disqualified for cutting a corner in the race, but it mattered little as Britain had won.

Capturing the mood of seaplane flying for the past 100 years, this early-morning view of the second Supermarine S6b being recovered to the slipway at RAF Calshot was taken on 3 October 1931. The pilot is Squadron Leader Augustus Orlebar DFC*, captain of The Flight and world speed record holder. **Rex Features**

'Batchy' Atcherley maintained his association with Supermarine and the Spitfire during the Second World War in various command positions and through his connections with Winston Churchill, and in 1947 he commanded the Royal Pakistan Air Force after Partition. Waghorn continued test flying but was severely injured after the Hawker Horsley biplane bomber he was flying at Farnborough in 1931 went out of control in high winds and he died two days later.

Also flying in the 1929 race was **Flight Lieutenant George Hedley Stainforth** with the Napier Lion-powered Gloster VI, the company's first monoplane design. The experience of flying the monoplane racing seaplane was obviously beneficial even though it was withdrawn from the race itself. He achieved a world speed record in the Gloster and, two years later, in a Supermarine S6b.

A former soldier and fighter squadron pilot in the Royal Air Force, Stainforth is the epitome of the contemporary hero, depicted on cigarette cards and known to millions through his exploits with The Flight and the bid to bring the Schneider Trophy to Britain. Stainforth thus has a place in the annals of the Spitfire by being one of the select few who pioneered high-speed flight and thereby helped Mitchell's team develop the aeroplane. He also helped in the development of the Spitfire with flying trials at the Royal Aircraft Establishment, Farnborough in a mock combat that pitted a Messerschmitt Bf 109E-4 with Bob Stanford Tuck flying a Spitfire Mk IIa.

Despite the obvious British success in the 1929 race, and the presence there of both HRH The Prince of Wales and Prime Minister Ramsay MacDonald, the Government withdrew funding after a Cabinet-level decision. It was only thanks to the financial backing of Lady Houston that Britain achieved its third success in the 1931 race and kept the trophy in perpetuity. Her support embarrassed the Government into allowing the High Speed Flight to remain in being and enabled Supermarine to be awarded a contract for Mitchell to upgrade the existing S6 and develop it into the S6b – his greatest racing seaplane achievement.

In 1931 only the British team attended the trophy meeting, held again at Cowes. Contemporary reports state that a million people came out to watch in each of the two years when the races were run along The Solent, and at least half of them were women who, drawn by the cult-hero status of the pilots, wanted to see these dashing young men in their silver racing machines. Ferries to the Isle of Wight and trains to Portsmouth Harbour station were packed, stated the reports.

Flight Lieutenant John Boothman took one of the Supermarine S6bs (S1795) to 340.08mph to win the trophy in 1931 with a race-tuned 2,600hp Rolls-Royce R-type engine and then Stainforth, in the same machine, played an important part in the development of the Spitfire and its Merlin engine with his world record attempt that showed 400mph was possible. Ernest Hives at Rolls-Royce called that speed 'the mark that matters' and for the record attempt he created a sprint version of the R-type fuelled by a high-octane, highly explosive mixture. In achieving 407.5mph, Stainforth became the first man to exceed 400mph in an aeroplane – or anything else. He was the fastest man ever.

A close relationship was created between Mitchell, his early team at Supermarine and the High Speed Flight. Its new home at RAF Calshot, the military seaplane base, was only a short distance away from the Woolston works. Other important people in the Spitfire story with the High Speed Flight were **Flight Lieutenant E.J.L. Hope,** the engineering officer, **Lieutenant Jerry Brinton** Royal Navy (killed in a take-off incident on 18 August 1931), **Flight Lieutenant Freddy Long** (S6b pilot), **Flying Officer Leonard Snaith** (S6a pilot), who was to become a distinguished bomber squadron commander, and a second engineering officer, **Flight Lieutenant W.F. Dry.**

The High Speed Flight was disbanded in 1931 but reformed in 1946 for another world speed record attempt. It was commanded by former Spitfire pilot Group Captain Teddy Donaldson DSO AFC and included Spitfire aces **Flight Lieutenant Neville S. Duke** DSO DFC and **Wing Commander Roly Beamont** DSO. The Meteor, a Spitfire successor in RAF Fighter Command, achieved 616mph and a world record that year.

Leading from the front, Squadron Leader Augustus Orlebar briefs Lieutenant Jerry Brinton, the only naval flyer in the High Speed Flight, just four days before Brinton's death on 18 August 1931. In the background is Flight Lieutenant George Stainforth, who was every schoolboy's hero in the 1930s and the first man to exceed 400mph. Rex Features (Associated Newspapers)

focused the minds of the technologically savvy and attracted worldwide attention to fast seaplane designs. Pemberton-Billing was determined to become involved and Scott-Paine immediately saw the opportunities for their new company.

During this period Scott-Paine worked as the company's factory manager on the new site at Woolston on the River Itchen's estuary into Southampton Water. Besides flying boats and seaplanes, the company was designing and building landplanes, such as the PB9 Scout. When that aeroplane's designer, Carol Vasilesco, died, his replacement was Reginald Mitchell, a former engineering apprentice from the railway industry in Staffordshire who was also enamoured by the engineering of flight.

Although not ordered into production, the PB9 provided the company and its top team with valuable experience that led to work on fighters to engage the German Zeppelin scourge, including the quadruplane (four-wing) Nighthawk with its own searchlight, an innovation that required an auxiliary power unit. The old adage, 'If it doesn't look right, it won't fly right', was certainly proved by this design: the Nighthawk did fly, in 1917, but by this time the company had changed direction – and ownership – with Pemberton-Billing's adoption as a Member of Parliament.

In 1916 Scott-Paine bought out Pemberton-Billing's shares and created the Supermarine Aviation Company. It was mainly Scott-Paine's vision that inspired the company's two decades of leadership in flying-boat design, with the skill of his design team turning that vision into reality. Part of that reality was to establish an airline business in 1919, linking Southampton with France via the Channel Islands and taking part in the Schneider Trophy competitions, which had been restarted after the First World War. The first race was run in Bournemouth bay, just around the coast from Southampton, and the Italians won, although they were later disqualified and the race declared void. Italy hosted the event in Venice for the next two years and on both occasions the home nation won by default, in 1920 because there was no other contender and in 1921 because the French entry failed to start.

Italy was again the host in 1922 and this time Scott-Paine was determined to win, having secured private funding for the Supermarine Sea Lion II, a development of previous designs. Powered by the Napier Lion 450hp engine and flown by Supermarine's chief test pilot Henri Biard, the Sea Lion II won the race at an average speed of 145.7mph, starting the winning streak that allowed Britain to keep the trophy a decade later. Biard, incidentally, also flew the first cross-Channel aviation services and the first commercial service to the Channel Islands for Scott-Paine; he remained at Supermarine until 1933, when he was made redundant and replaced by Joseph 'Mutt' Summers from Vickers, the company's new owner.

By convention, the subsequent Schneider Trophy race was held in the previous winner's country, and Cowes, on the Isle of Wight, was the venue. The Sea Lion III was re-engined with a more powerful Napier Lion, developing 550hp, but only managed third place behind two Curtiss CR-3 seaplane racers. This failure to win in 1923 caused Scott-Paine to sell the Sea Lion III to the Air Ministry and then to sell his shares in Supermarine for £192,000 and invest the money in his airline, the British Marine Air Navigation Company, which merged a year later with Imperial Airways, the forerunner of British Airways.

Lucy, Lady Houston DBE

Born 8 April 1857
Died 29 December 1936
Schneider Trophy patron, 1931

Without Lady Houston's donation of £100,000 to the Government (and hence the Supermarine development contract) in 1931, it is doubtful that R.J. Mitchell would have been funded to develop the Supermarine S6b and that Rolls-Royce would have created the 2,300hp R-type engine that led to the Merlin.

Notorious for her personal relationships and political lobbying, Lucy Houston was highly effective at bringing public opinion behind renewal of Britain's participation in the Coupe d'Aviation Maritime Jacques Schneider and persuading the Air Council to support the Royal Air Force's High Speed Flight in its plan to win the trophy outright. Despite the win in 1929, the National Government of Ramsay MacDonald could see no benefit in developing high-speed aeroplanes for the nation in view of the world's financial crisis.

Without the generosity of the wealthy, Britain could not have achieved many aviation successes in the austerity of the 1930s. By donating £100,000, Lucy Houston shamed the government into supporting the High Speed Flight, which not only secured the Schneider Trophy for Britain but gave the nation a leg up in the development of war-winning technology. Lady Houston is pictured with Squadron Leader Augustus Orlebar at RAF Calshot in August 1931. TopFoto

Lady Houston declared that 'every true Briton would rather sell his last shirt than admit that England could not afford to defend herself' and she supported the Royal Aero Club's fundraising by, in effect, doubling it.

Besides supporting Supermarine's airframe development, Rolls-Royce also benefited and the company's managing director, Arthur Sidgreaves, told the media: 'It is not too much to say that research for the Schneider Trophy contest over the past two years is what our aero-engine department would otherwise have taken six to ten years to learn.'

A huge supporter of aviation in the early 1930s, Lady Houston also encouraged entrants in the MacRobertson London-to-Melbourne Air Race and funded the 1933 attempt – successful as it turned out – by Squadron Leader the Lord Clydesdale (later Air Commodore the Duke of Hamilton) in a Westland PV-3 to fly over Everest. It can be argued, persuasively, that lessons from this expedition included the need for specialist high-altitude flying gear, which arrived in Royal Air Force service just in time for the Second World War and high-flying Spitfire photo-reconnaissance aircraft.

Lord (Ernest) Hives CH MBE
Born 21 April 1886
Died 24 April 1965
Rolls-Royce, 1904–56

Ernest Hives worked for Rolls-Royce from its very beginnings, in 1904, and by 1916 he was head of the experimental department and therefore instrumental in the company's subsequent engine development, including the development of the PV-12 from the R-type racing engine. There is much justification, then, in calling Hives the 'father of the Merlin'.

Hives' design experience went back to the First World War and the development of the Rolls-Royce Eagle engine for the Vickers Vimy bomber, an example of which was converted to become the first aircraft to fly the Atlantic. He developed the Eagle into the Buzzard and this, in turn, led to the development of the R-type engine for the Schneider Trophy-winning Supermarine S6 series of racing seaplanes.

By 1936 Hives was general manager of the Aero Engine Division at Derby and he began work the following year to disperse the company's production capability to ensure security of supply if a European war erupted. Working with the Derby team, he set about moving production to other sites as well as dispersing the engineering facilities at Nottingham. Eventually there were factories at Crewe, Glasgow and Manchester, and additionally one in Detroit where the Packard company built Merlin engines under licence for the Canadian-produced Lancasters, Hurricanes and Mosquitos, and the North American P-51D Mustang. Not only did these actions protect production, which did not falter even after Luftwaffe attempts to destroy the Derby works, but they also hastened the use of new mass-production techniques, as pioneered by the Ford Motor Company, in aero-engine production.

Another major contribution by Hives to the progress of the Second World War was to

Rolls-Royce was Supermarine's most important industrial partner for three decades. Ernest Hives led much of the aero-engine development at Derby in that time and made a major contribution to the nation's industrial capacity to defeat the Axis powers in the Second World War. Solent Sky

create the shortest supply line of any engine manufacturer in the world. Not only did the Spitfire benefit from this ability to keep building and maintaining the Merlin, but also the other aircraft types that were fitted with this engine. This was the result of sound pre-war planning and the cooperation of various sub-contractors and associated companies such as Ford and Packard.

Hives increased the Rolls-Royce workforce from 7,000 in 1939 to over 55,000 by 1945, creating one of the world's greatest aero-engine businesses. Under Hives' leadership, Rolls-Royce Aero Engines also moved into the gas-turbine business – the jet engine.

Hives developed a good reputation for listening to the advice and comments of Rolls-Royce and service test pilots – even squadron pilots – who flew aeroplanes with Merlin engines. During the Second World War, the Fleet Air Arm and the Royal Air Force loaned pilots to the company to help with development and this cooperation paid dividends in feeding service experience into the development programme. With over 160,000 units produced, the Merlin became the most prolific piston engine in the world.

In 1950 Hives was elevated to the peerage and also became chairman of Rolls-Royce, a post he held until his retirement in 1956. He devoted virtually his entire working life – 52 years – to the company.

Sir Stanley Hooker FRS DPhil BSc FRAeS

Born 30 September 1907
Died 24 May 1984
Developer of the Merlin engine, 1938–45

Stanley Hooker trained as a mathematician rather than as an engineer, yet his contribution to one of the nation's greatest engineering companies is almost immeasurable. In January 1938 he started work at Rolls-Royce in Derby and brought his recent doctorate in aerodynamics to bear on the supercharger system of the Merlin engine.

After studying for a first degree at Imperial College, London and a DPhil at Brasenose College, Oxford, Hooker moved to the Admiralty but soon tired of the lack of interest there and applied to Rolls-Royce. At interview Ernest Hives famously told him that he was 'not much of an engineer' and Hooker chose that phrase as the title of his autobiography, published shortly before his death in 1984.

Hooker's supercharger work increased engine power for the Merlin 45 variant by 30 per cent at a time when the Royal Air Force badly needed more performance for the Spitfire to gain equality with the Luftwaffe's new Messerschmitt Bf 109F series of fighters over Normandy and Pas-de-Calais. This Spitfire was the Mk V, developed as an interim version based on the Mk I/II airframe fitted with the longer Merlin 45 engine, but it ended up being built in greater numbers than any other Spitfire, such was its robustness and flexibility, and it remained in service until at least 1950.

Hooker then turned his attention to developing two-stage supercharging for the Merlin 61 variant that powered the Mk IX. This Spitfire version turned out to be a real winner – although it was not produced in the same numbers as the Mk V – and was described by Captain Eric Brown as 'the most delightful Spitfire of all to fly'. Its performance certainly equalled that of the Focke-Wulf Fw 190, which it could now generally out-climb.

As the Merlin evolved, it became clear that, sound though the engine continued to be in its operational scope, it would need to be replaced in due course. That replacement was a gas-turbine engine and with it Hooker took Rolls-Royce into the jet age.

In 1940 Hooker met Frank Whittle, the pioneer of the jet engine. The following year the Air Ministry, seeking to put the first jet engines into production, contracted Rover for this task but the company proved incapable of delivering such a complex piece of engineering on the necessary timescale. So it was that Hooker took Sir Ernest Hives, the head of Rolls-Royce Aero Engines, to meet the Rover car company's Maurice Wilks in order to seek a mutually beneficial solution. The two captains of industry agreed to what was a basically a swap of factories, with Rolls-Royce taking over Rover's jet engine facilities at Barnoldswick in Lancashire (where a former cotton mill had been requisitioned in 1941) in return for Rover moving into Rolls-Royce's premises at Nottingham where the Meteor tank engine was produced.

After the end of the war Hooker and Hives fell out over the future development of Rolls-Royce engines, so Hooker left in 1949 to join Bristol – later Bristol Siddeley – and work on

Stanley Hooker was a key man in the development of the Merlin engine and therefore the success of the Spitfire. Using his mathematical and engineering knowledge, he worked on delivering more power from the engine through the use of superchargers in order to give Fighter Command an edge over the Luftwaffe. Solent Sky

jet engines that went on to power, among others, the Folland Gnat and the Avro Vulcan, and eventually the Harrier and Concorde. After Rolls-Royce overspent itself into bankruptcy with the RB211 engine in 1971, Hooker returned to the company as technical director, a job he had coveted before his departure but that Hives had denied him.

Hooker's greatest epitaph must be the comment made by Harrier test pilot Bill Bedford, who, when asked to name the greatest ever British engineer, stated 'it would not be Isambard Kingdom Brunel but Sir Stanley Hooker.'

Captain Joseph 'Mutt' Summers CBE

Born 10 March 1904
Died 16 March 1954
Chief test pilot, Vickers, 1929–39
First Spitfire pilot, 1936

Joseph 'Mutt' Summers has his place firmly carved in aviation history. As chief test pilot of Vickers Armstrong, the owners of Supermarine, he made the first flights in the Type 300 fighter, which became known as the Spitfire. Besides the Spitfire, Summers worked with Barnes Wallis on the 'bouncing bomb' for the Dambusters and took another 53 aircraft on their maiden flights, the last being the Cold War Vickers Valiant jet bomber.

Like many test pilots of his generation, his grounding in test flying was in the Royal Air Force as a fighter pilot and later he was posted to test flying on the Single Seat Fighter Flight at RAF Martlesham Heath at the tender age of 21, which must surely be testament to his abilities on the Gloster Grebes of the time. At RAF Martlesham Heath, the centre of Royal Air Force testing under the auspices of the Royal Aircraft Establishment, he cut his test-flying teeth on such types as the Bristol Bulldog, Gloster Gamecock and Hawker Hornbill – some of the fastest and most manoeuvrable aeroplanes of their day.

Because he was an officer on a Short Service Commission, he retired from Royal Air Force service in May 1929 but his talents were not wasted as he immediately joined the distinguished team at Vickers, which had only recently bought the Supermarine Aviation Company. With Vickers at Weybridge he first flew the Wellesley and Wellington bombers, which were in service with RAF Bomber Command in the early night-bombing operations of the Second World War.

It was in this period that Summers was promoted to chief test pilot for both the Weybridge and Southampton (Eastleigh) test facilities. This came at a time when there was real acrimony between Mitchell and the equally celebrated Barnes Wallis, who was sent down to Supermarine by the Vickers management because of their concerns about slow progress on the development of the F37/34 prototype, which became the Spitfire. Summers was able to smooth the ruffled feathers and suggested that Wallis should return to Weybridge and leave Mitchell's team to bring the Type 300 to its first flight.

Summers was selected to take the Type 300 for its maiden flight on 5 March 1936. It is for this flight, and perhaps also for flying the initial Dambuster 'bouncing bomb' trials, that he is best known. His day started at RAF Martlesham Heath, from where he flew the company Miles Falcon to Eastleigh aerodrome, the Supermarine test facility where K5054 was having final adjustments in the hangar. In several hours of ground-running during the previous days, the Rolls-Royce Merlin engine had performed flawlessly. Late in the afternoon Summers climbed into the cockpit. History does not record whether or not he had his trademark 'pee' against the rear skid, a habit that had occasioned his nickname 'Mutt' because, as one of his No 29 Squadron contemporaries is reported to have said some years earlier, he was like 'a dog cocking his leg'.

This historic picture taken on 5 March 1936 shows five men closely involved with the Spitfire's gestation. From left: Joseph 'Mutt' Summers, Vickers' chief test pilot, who is about to take the Supermarine fighter prototype into the air; Major Harold Payn, assistant chief designer; R.J. Mitchell (sitting on his car's running board); Stuart Scott Hall, Air Ministry resident technical officer; and Jeffrey Quill, Supermarine's chief test pilot. Solent Sky

That first flight lasted just eight minutes. Summers flew a series of initial tests to understand the stalling characteristics and tried some practice landings at altitude. He left the undercarriage down and concentrated on simple handling.

Much has been made over the years of the test pilot's comment to the ground crew of 'don't touch anything' but it is believed that Summers meant that he wanted the same configuration when the coarse-pitch propeller was fitted for the following day's longer test flight at cruise and maximum speed settings. Modifications were ordered by Summers after further test flying on 6 March, 10 March and 14 March, by which time the prototype had amassed 112 minutes in the air.

The aeroplane was painted in various shades of blue, which had been Supermarine's trademark colour since the early flying boats and was perpetuated through Mitchell's highly successful S-series racing seaplanes. The paint had an unusually smooth finish and was applied by experts loaned from Rolls-Royce. Later Rolls-Royce also helped with paint polishing and some performance-enhancing filling of panel joins as the engine manufacturer was still the doyen of the prestige motor car business. All this helped with initial handling and performance, so important for the reports to the Air Ministry from Stuart Scott Hall, the resident technical inspector.

Summers finished the Spitfire's factory test flying on 26 May with a cross-country flight to RAF Martlesham Heath and handed the aeroplane over to the Royal Aircraft Establishment for more test flying, this time in the hands of a variety of service pilots including Flight Lieutenant Humphrey Edwardes-Jones (the first service pilot to fly the Spitfire) and Flying Officer Sam McKenna (the first service pilot to force land a Spitfire, on 22 March 1937). The first service pilot killed in a Spitfire was RAE's Flight Lieutenant Gilbert 'Spinner' White, who crashed the prototype at RAE Farnborough on 4 September 1939.

At RAF Martlesham Heath all the love and attention by Supermarine and Rolls-Royce paid off as the Spitfire prototype reached 16,800ft and a speed of 349mph. Interestingly, the Spitfire was flown back to Eastleigh for Government-furnished equipment to be fitted, including its eight machine guns, but by now it was Jeffrey Quill in the cockpit as the acceptance trials continued through the summer.

Early in June 1936 Summers did fly the Spitfire prototype again, this time to Hatfield airfield where the Society of British Aircraft Constructors was holding a display and exhibition – an event that eventually became the Farnborough Air Show after the Second World War. The Spitfire was shown off there and attracted international attention and the promise of export sales.

Even if the mantle of test flying had passed on, Summers had not finished with the Spitfire. Under an enlightened scheme to get the most from the industrial experience and capabilities of production and flight test pilots, the Air Ministry ordered companies to send their pilots to support Fighter Command as non-combatant Home Guard officers. This seems to have been a rare moment of government – in the form of the Ministry of Aircraft Production and the Air Ministry – and industry thinking alike, exemplifying the crisis that the country felt in the summer of 1940 when the threat of German invasion was very real.

It was to No 11 Group that Vickers sent Summers in 1940. He flew both Spitfire and Hurricane to carry out post-inspection and post-overhaul test flying and, if any shortcomings were evident, the fighter had to be taken out of the line and replaced by a new build. In this way the limited resources of combat pilots would not be risked unnecessarily in fighters that were not fit to fight.

Summers had a narrow escape when a Hurricane he was evaluating for engine problems, reported by future fighter ace 'Ginger' Lacey, lost its propeller, forcing Summers to make a 'dead stick' landing with no power at RAF Middle Wallop – the incident amply justified the use of test pilots on the Fighter Command airfields.

By the end of the war, Summers had test-flown 310 different aircraft in 5,600 flying hours – longer in the air than any contemporary company test pilot.

Summers died in 1954, aged just 50, ironically of colon cancer, the condition that took the life of his friend R.J. Mitchell. His world record of maiden flights is never likely to be beaten and he is the only test pilot to have been granted the honour of a state funeral at Westminster Abbey.

Flight Lieutenant Humphrey Edwardes-Jones
Born 15 August 1905
Died 19 January 1987
First Spitfire service test pilot, 1936

Without this service test pilot's intervention, the Spitfire would not have entered service in time for the Second World War, let alone the Battle of Britain. His brief and very guarded telephone conversation with another visionary Royal Air Force officer, Air Marshal Freeman, resulted in a fast-track procurement order to Supermarine (Aviation) Ltd.

Humphrey Edwardes-Jones joined the Royal Air Force in 1925 and after training was posted to the Armstrong Whitworth Siskin-equipped No 1 (Fighter) Squadron at RAF Tangmere. No 1 was a Home Defence Fighter Squadron charged with protecting the approaches to London from France. Edwardes-Jones then went to RAF Duxford as a pilot on the Station Flight before being sent to No 2 Flying Training School in 1929. A posting to No 4 Flying Training School followed before he returned to a fighter pilot role as a flight commander with No 208 Squadron.

Humphrey Edwardes-Jones (centre) has a place in aviation history. He was the first service pilot to fly the Spitfire and without his moral courage to support the fighter at a critical moment, mainly through a single well-phrased telephone conversation, it would not have been ordered in time for the Second World War. This picture is one of very few that survive of him and was taken post-war. Jever Steam Laundry

SUPERMARINE'S MAIN MEN

Commander James Bird was general manager of the Supermarine works at Southampton and Eastleigh after the departure of H.B. Pratt (see below). He had been at Supermarine with Scott-Paine and ran the factory until Vickers bought the company in 1928. He remained at Southampton and it was his long experience with the company that allowed him to take production of the Spitfire from 14 a week to over 25 a week just a year after the Luftwaffe bombed the Supermarine works.

The structural engineer behind the Hooked Spitfire and the Seafire was **Alan Clifton**. He led the carrier team and whenever he could he went to all the trials, even those at sea. This gave the test pilots huge comfort. Described by Captain Eric Brown as being 'very easy and enthusiastic... particularly involved with the Seafire from the very beginning', he worked closely with Joe Smith, under whose careful supervision the Spitfire and Seafire were developed.

Charles Craven was the managing director of Vickers Supermarine until 'requisitioned' as special adviser by Lord Beaverbrook in his role as Minister of Aircraft Production. Craven took charge of dispersal planning prior to the devastating bombing of Woolston by German bombers in late September 1940, but he was back at Supermarine by late 1941, having found Beaverbrook impossible to work with. He was knighted in 1942 for services to the aeronautical industry.

The works manager at Supermarine during and after the Luftwaffe bombing of Southampton in September 1940 was **W.T. ('Wilf') Elliott**. During that period he moved his works management staff from Woolston to the Polygon Hotel: the team included production manager John Butler, assistant works manager Denis Le Penn Webb and works engineer Len Gooch. The chief planner of production was Johnny Bull aided by George Guard, who was chief estimator and head of the jig and tool offices. In the critical period up to 1942, Elliott set up a system that shortened the chain of command for important decisions, especially for sub-contractors.

Arthur Falcon was an apprentice in 1937 when it was the norm to serve five years indentured and to attend evening classes. In Falcon's case, these were held at University College, Southampton, where day-release courses were also undertaken. After working at Woolston on the Spitfire and Walrus, Falcon was sent to Eastleigh in June 1938 to work on fitting the wings, undercarriage and camera gun mountings, as well as installation of the engine. Apprentices also worked on preparing individual production aircraft for final inspection, including compass swinging and engine running.

By June 1939 Falcon was showing promise and was sent to the works engineer's department to learn the draughtsmen's craft with Len Gooch as the senior. It is through his endeavours that original documents have survived from the sale of Hursley Park and the subsequent 'clear-out' of filing cabinets and blueprint chests. Because of Falcon, we

Alan Clifton (above left) was an unsung hero of the Spitfire's design. He started on the original design when he was Mitchell's assistant and replaced Joe Smith as chief designer in 1946. Discussing the Spitfire with hatted 'Men from the Ministry' (above right) is W.T. 'Wilf' Elliott, the Supermarine works manager. At far right is Joe Smith, the man who took the Spitfire to production and developed its full potential. Solent Sky

now know the exact timings of the first and subsequent flights of the fighter that was to become the Spitfire.

Charlie Johns MBE was the chief inspector at Woolston and the Itchen Works. In the immediate aftermath of the bombing in September 1940, Johns was part of the management team that worked on the dispersal programme, which got Supermarine's production of Spitfires up and running again with remarkable efficiency.

Len Gooch OBE trained in the railway industry at Eastleigh where Southern Railways had its engineering depot. Mitchell would have approved his appointment in 1935, especially as he himself had been apprenticed in the same industry, albeit in Staffordshire. Gooch's first duties were in the project office for the new fighter. Aged only 28, he was promoted to works engineer in September 1940 (just before the bombing by the Luftwaffe) and was given responsibility for the dispersed factories. When he rose to the position of works manager in November 1941, he was responsible for the production process from Southampton to Trowbridge and Reading. Post-war Gooch rose to become chairman of Vickers Automated Systems Ltd.

Major Harold Payn AFC was the Vickers nominee at Supermarine in 1928 after the recall

This remarkable photo was taken on 1 April 1944 when Sir Stafford Cripps, Minister of Aircraft Production (1942–45), visited Supermarine's experimental department at Hursley Park. Those present represent the senior and middle management of Supermarine. Seated, from left: W.T. Elliott, an unknown senior naval officer, Hew Kilner (managing director of Vickers), Sir Stafford Cripps, James Bird, Mrs Perkins and Group Captain Perkins (liaison officer). Standing: E.L. Cooper, Arthur Black, Joe Smith, two officials, Len Gooch, Frank Perry (resident technical officer), unknown, Ernie Mansbridge, unknown, Alan Clifton and Arthur Shirval. Solent Sky

of Barnes Wallis following his dispute with R.J. Mitchell over desk space and governance. Payn became Mitchell's assistant because he was not only a decorated Royal Flying Corps veteran but also had a good grasp of aeronautical engineering. He was appointed head of design on Mitchell's death and was closely involved in getting the Spitfire into production.

In September 1939, after routine security checks, Payn's career hit the buffers when it was discovered that his wife had been born in Germany. He was immediately replaced by Joe Smith in an acting capacity as manager of the design department, although not yet as chief designer. Payn was one of the few in Mitchell's team who witnessed the first flight of K5054 on 5 March 1936.

In 1937 **H.B. Pratt** was appointed general manager of Supermarine and stayed in that position until June 1941. His responsibilities were the two factories by the River Itchen and he worked hard to support the team under him. With Charles Craven, Pratt was a major architect of the original dispersal plan that Beaverbrook crassly ignored. He also fell foul of Beaverbrook's team in other ways, leading to his sacking by Ministerial directive.

As his last duty, Pratt signed the 30 June 1941 report to the Vickers' directors, left the Supermarine offices and shortly afterwards shot himself. The impact was felt in London as Beaverbrook was transferred to the Ministry of Supply and Craven, on the direct orders of the Prime Minister, was sent to the Ministry of Aircraft Production to ameliorate some of the aftershock.

Denis Le Penn Webb started work at Supermarine as an apprentice, completing his training in 1931. He rose through hard work, from inspection to the design and technical offices, to the top of the aviation manufacturing game as assistant to **Trevor Westbrook**, the works manager and one of those to witness the first flight of K5054. From there, Le Penn (the name by which he was generally known) became assistant works manager at Southampton in 1941 and then moved to High Post to take up the role of assistant experimental manager, which he retained until the end of the war.

After the High Post operation moved to the former RAF station at Chilbolton, Le Penn moved again to the British Aircraft Corporation as a project manager on the ill-fated TSR-2 strike aircraft project, which was cancelled at the behest of the White House by Harold Wilson's Labour government just after it started to prove itself in trials.

In the mid-1990s Le Penn wrote a series of personal *aides-mémoire* that are lodged with the Solent Sky Museum and have been consulted for this book. He was a great critic of Lord Beaverbrook's handling of the dispersal operations and, in a private note, reckoned that these hasty actions may have cost Fighter Command some 150 Spitfires in the 1940–41 period.

Denis Le Penn Webb had a long and deep relationship with the Spitfire, so his memories and notes shed useful light on areas that have received little study until now. He advocated a reappraisal of Joe Smith's role in the original design of the Spitfire, from a position of one who was there.
Solent Sky

This experience in fighters and training led to a test pilot's post at the Aeroplane & Armament Experimental Establishment at RAF Martlesham Heath. It was to this station that 'Mutt' Summers delivered K5054, the Supermarine Type 300 monoplane fighter prototype that became known as the Spitfire shortly afterwards.

His first flight in the prototype convinced Edwardes-Jones that it was a winner. When he called the Air Ministry, given the need for security, his enthusiasm was nevertheless sufficient to convince Air Marshal Freeman to spend taxpayers' money and order the fighter straight away.

Edwardes-Jones did, however, come close to force-landing the fighter prototype after he forgot to lower the undercarriage until the last moment. As all contemporary Royal Air Force fighters and training types had a fixed undercarriage, he advised that an undercarriage warning klaxon should be fitted and this was duly done. The Royal Air Force did not adopt a two-seat trainer for its piston-engined single-seat fighters and so any pilot's first Spitfire flights tended to be fraught.

Later in 1936 Edwardes-Jones was posted to command No 213 Squadron, equipped with the Gloster Gauntlet Mk II biplane fighter, but he continued to advise the Air Ministry on future fighter development and tactics. No 213 went on to be a squadron in the Mediterranean theatre, first with Hurricanes and then Spitfires.

On 27 May 1940 he transferred his Squadron Leader's pennant to No 17 Squadron, another Hurricane unit, and took the unit to Brittany after covering the Dunkirk operations. After France capitulated, he was posted to RAF Exeter to command the Exeter Sector in No 10 Group. He kept his relationship with the Spitfire throughout the rest of his service career with postings to Algiers with No 210 Group in 1943 after Operation Torch and then to the staff of HQ Mediterranean Allied Air Forces at the end of the Second World War.

Air Marshal Sir Humphrey Edwardes-Jones retired from the Royal Air Force as Commander-in-Chief of the Second Tactical Air Force in 1961.

Jeffrey Quill OBE AFC FRAeS
Born 1 February 1913
Died 20 February 1996
Supermarine chief test pilot from 1938

Described by Captain Eric Brown as 'the master of the Spitfire', Jeffrey Quill will be forever linked with the great fighter aeroplane. He flew every mark and almost every variant, and perhaps the only cloud over his glittering career was the fact that he was not the first man to fly the prototype.

Quill's contribution to the development of the Spitfire as a fighting aeroplane was immense. It was the careful and deliberate testing of the flight envelope in 1936–37 and then the development of the production versions through the early part of 1939 where Quill added most value.

As a man, he was open and honest; as a test pilot, thorough and exacting. His appointment to the position of Supermarine's chief test pilot before he was 25 years old and his working relationships first with Mitchell, then with Smith, were key to developing the Spitfire as he translated the service views into corporate speak.

Quill's flying career started in 1931 with his appointment as an Acting Pilot Officer in the Royal Air Force Volunteer Reserve (RAFVR), a route followed by many air-minded boys in the early 1930s. He showed his worth as a natural pilot by going solo at No 3 Flying Training School (Grantham) within six hours and was assessed as exceptional. His first training aeroplane was the Avro Tutor, after which he moved to an advanced course on the Armstrong Whitworth Siskin Mk IIIa. In 1932 he was posted to No 17 Squadron, on the Bristol Bulldog, and he soon became a participant in the Hendon displays, which he had watched as a teenager on exeat from Lancing College.

Believing that a pilot must be fully familiar with his aeroplane, Quill was a devotee of aerobatics and the need, as he put it, to 'practise assiduously'. He reckoned to have performed aerobatics almost every time he flew until well into the 1980s. His skill at flying in bad weather, through cloud and without the full panel of instruments, led to his posting to the Meteorological Flight at RAF Duxford, where his award of the Air Force Cross was merited by the fact that the Flight always achieved its twice-daily weather reporting up to 25,000ft, with the benefit of an occasionally functioning heated flying suit in the open cockpit of the the Siskin Mk IIIa.

In the small aviation community of the mid-1930s, Quill's capabilities came to the attention of Vickers, the owners of Supermarine, and more particularly to the attention of 'Mutt' Summers, the chief test pilot. At that time aviation companies and the Air Ministry relied on a very high degree of mutual trust and cooperation and it was not long before Quill was offered employment at Weybridge as Summers' assistant, leaving the Royal Air Force in 1936. Although Quill was to make his name with the Spitfire, his first tasks were related to the ungainly Vickers Wellesley, the single-engine medium bomber that almost cost Quill his life when he was forced to bail out in unsuccessful spin-recovery tests.

Before the Type 300, the Spitfire prototype, K5054, was due to be delivered to RAF Martlesham Heath for service flying evaluation and trials, Quill worked on the modifications required after Summers' initial evaluation in March 1936. Quill's logbook records 26 March as his first flight.

Working with the Aeroplane & Armament Experimental Establishment, Quill took the Spitfire prototype through a series of tests before the new fighter was given its release to service. These modifications to flying characteristics and handling at slow speed were as much to blame for the delay in service entry as the production issues being confronted by Supermarine at Southampton. With the death of R.J. Mitchell, Supermarine's management made some changes and confirmed Quill as the company's chief test pilot. Although Joe Smith was yet to be confirmed as the chief designer, he was in charge of the Spitfire project and worked closely with Quill on the development of the first production aircraft and then on the subsequent changes.

In 1940, several test pilots with previous Royal Air Force fighter experience were released from their civilian jobs and seconded to front-line fighter squadrons to gain first-hand experience that they could feed back to their employers. Quill's RAFVR commission was reactivated and he joined No 65 Squadron at RAF Hornchurch on 5 August 1940, now with the rank of Acting Flying Officer. In 18 days of operational flying, Quill accounted for a Messerschmitt Bf 109E and a shared kill on a Heinkel He 111, as well as learning much about the need to arm the Spitfire with cannon able to punch through the armour of German bombers. Other improvements suggested by his short service interlude were better cockpit ergonomics, stiffer ailerons (to assist with the high wing loading in combat turns) and a better rear-view mirror. It is highly likely that these changes saved the lives of numerous fighter pilots over the next five years.

Back at Southampton (or more specifically at the Eastleigh aerodrome) Smith had been working on the replacement for the Spitfire Mk I/II, in the shape of the Mk III. This was a redesign with clipped wings and the capability to exceed 400mph in level flight. Its first flight was made on 16 March 1940 but its development called for the skills of Quill, who returned to carry out the flying needed.

The Spitfire Mk III was an attempt to build on the lessons learned in performance and productionisation, as well as to capture the developments at Rolls-Royce to uprate the Merlin to 1,390hp with the Merlin XX. Other improvements were a strengthened undercarriage, retractable tail wheel, bullet-proof windscreen and optically flat cockpit hood panels. The Mk III did not see production but was used to develop the thinking for the Griffon-powered Spitfires that followed, including the Mk IX for which the first Mk III acted as prototype.

The 1942 British propaganda film *First of the Few* has a very young David Niven playing the part of 'Geoffrey Crisp', who is portrayed as an amalgam of Stainforth, Atcherley, Waghorn and Quill. In the flying scenes shot at RAF Northolt in November 1941, a Spitfire Mk II was mocked up to resemble K5054.

Quill continued development flying at Eastleigh and even trained at the Royal Aircraft Establishment Farnborough to understand German cockpit instruments after a plan was hatched to steal a new Focke-Wulf Fw 190A from a French airfield. Luckily for Quill, who was supposed to perform the deed, one of the German fighters landed in Britain in error and was recovered intact. Lieutenant Eric Brown was the German-language and procedures instructor during preparation for this adventure and he and Quill became close friends.

Quill and Brown worked together on the Hooked Spitfire and the Seafire programmes. For these development flights, Quill was commissioned into the Royal Naval Volunteer Reserve as a Lieutenant Commander (A) and flew with front-line, carrier-embarked squadrons, making 75 deck landings without incident. Again the trained test pilot's mind resolved many of the problems faced by young Seafire pilots whose loss rate to deck accidents was greater than that in the face of the enemy. Brown called Quill 'an inspired choice' for the job. Quill validated the curved approach and landing technique that Brown had developed for the early Seafires, and helped the US Navy to understand the difficulties faced by big-engined fighters on small decks.

No man equals Jeffrey Quill in his relationship with the Spitfire. Many at the factory were surprised when Vickers did not select the talented young test pilot to fly K5054 on its maiden flight. In the years that followed Quill earned the respect and affection of all those with whom he worked. Solent Sky

Quill went on to help Joe Smith to develop the Spiteful and Seafang, as well as the naval jets, taking the Attacker into the air for its first flight on 27 July 1946. By now exhausted from continuous test flying, Quill retired from that role but remained engaged in the industry, taking an active role in the development of the TSR-2 and Tornado strike aircraft. He also displayed Spitfire AB910 post-war. One of his last overseas trips was to Munich in 1994 for the 20th anniversary of the Tornado's first flight when he delighted a select audience with tales of flying.

Group Captain J.F.X. 'Sam' McKenna AFC FRAeS

Born 20 December 1907
Died 19 January 1945
Supermarine test pilot, 1938–45

Not only did Sam McKenna undertake early flying trials with the prototype Spitfire but he also went on to have an illustrious wartime career at the Aeroplane & Armament Experimental Establishment (A&AEE), which was moved from Martlesham Heath to Boscombe Down after war broke out in order to make it less vulnerable to attack. So highly thought of is McKenna, especially during his tenure as the Commandant, that every year's best-performing graduate of the Empire Test Pilots' School (ETPS) is awarded the McKenna Trophy at the McKenna Dinner.

As well as being a pilot, McKenna was an engineer, aerobatic pilot and one of those rare breed who displayed at RAF Hendon before the Second World War. His knowledge of aerodynamics and thermodynamics meant that he was a natural fit for the A&AEE but first there was a posting to the Farnborough-based Royal Aircraft Establishment as a test pilot specialising in aerodynamics in the period 1932–34.

McKenna then went back to the front line in Aden until 1937, when he joined A&AEE, at Martlesham Heath, at exactly the right time to be closely involved in the development of the Spitfire. Getting back into test flying, McKenna impressed his seniors with his skill, which led them to believe he would have considerable promise as a test pilot. This was an exciting time for British military aviation with the delivery of the Bristol Blenheim light bomber, the Hawker Hurricane and the prototype Spitfire. McKenna would become a professional service test pilot familiar with all these types, particularly the Spitfire.

McKenna continued to rise through the A&AEE, first as a Flight Commander on promotion and then becoming the chief test pilot and the first Commandant of the ETPS.

After Edwardes-Jones' first experience with the Spitfire, McKenna took over the project. He claimed a place in history as the first pilot to 'belly-land' the Spitfire, making him also the first person to belly-land a new-generation, high-speed monoplane fighter. This experience was an important lesson for the Operational Training Units as pilots made the transition from fixed-wing undercarriage trainers, many of them open-cockpit biplanes, to the sleek new generation of fighter aircraft.

Every inch a service test pilot, Sam McKenna (right) had many firsts to his name, including the first ETPS Commandant and the first Spitfire forced landing! He spent a wartime career testing and improving fighters, but perished at the controls of a Mustang near Old Sarum in the final months of the war. He is seen with Group Captain H.A. 'Bruin' Purvis, who was in charge of the Engine Development Flight at Farnborough. RAF Museum

For this successful saving of the prototype Spitfire – it was flying again within weeks – McKenna was awarded the Air Force Cross and sent to America to join the British Air Commission's Washington-based Flight Test Branch. This small team carried out what would today be termed initial release to service flying of US equipment, and the flying prototypes of new designs, passing on his experience to his US counterparts.

In 1944, McKenna returned to the A&AEE and set up the ETPS. He sadly died at the controls of a North American Mustang IV that he was testing near RAF Old Sarum, north of Salisbury, on 19 January 1945. Apparently, the Mustang lost an ammunition hatch cover, causing oscillation and the eventual separation of the wing from the fuselage, all at high speed. Recently, the Boscombe Down Aviation Collection has been coordinating efforts to salvage the remains of the Mustang, much of which has remained buried at the crash site.

Squadron Leader (Air Marshal Sir) Ralph Sorley OBE DSC DFC

Born 9 January 1898
Died 17 November 1974
SO2 Operational Requirements, Air Ministry, 1933
OC4 Armament Training Station, 1937
Aeroplane & Armament Experimental Establishment, 1940
Founder, Empire Test Pilots' School, 1943
AOC Technical Training Command, 1946

Ralph Sorley played a major part in the gestation, development and service life of the Spitfire. He was one of the finest technical officers of the Royal Air Force in its first 50 years and deserves much greater prominence in the Spitfire story.

Because of this former Royal Naval Air Service fighter pilot's understanding of air-to-air combat, the Hurricane and Spitfire were specified to carry eight machine guns rather than the usual four such weapons. This went against the orthodoxy of the time that preferred machines to be spaced rather than grouped, negating the impact of concentrated rounds on a target. Sorley fought against this doctrine and won.

There is evidence to suggest that Sorley was involved in the initial ideas for the Supermarine Type 327 twin-engine 'Spitfire' with six 20mm Hispano cannon grouped in threes in the wing root of each elliptical wing. In a specification issued by Supermarine in August 1938, this aeroplane was to be powered by two Merlin engines and would have been the long-range Spitfire successor.

Even if the Browning 0.303in rifle-calibre weapon was shown to be inadequate after 1940, it set the standard for armaments that would develop, in no small part due to Sorley, into the mix of 0.50in machines and cannon in the Spitfire's ultimate E-wing.

Sorley was appointed Commandant of the Aeroplane & Armament Experimental Establishment in 1940, soon after its move from Martlesham Heath to Boscombe Down, and then to the Air Council as Assistant Chief of the Air Staff before being moved in 1943 to the Ministry of Aircraft Production as Controller of Research & Development. While at the MAP he created the Test Pilots' Training Flight, which became the Empire Test Pilots' School – still the world's leading such establishment. Patrick Shea-Simonds, a naval reserve pilot who was one of the test pilots for the Spitfire's planned successor, the Spiteful, would go on to command the Empire Test Pilots' School.

After the Second World War, Sorley championed the air-to-air missile for air defence and joined De Havilland to see this happen in the form of the Firestreak missile.

Ralph Sorley (right) was a fighter pilot with a deep understanding of armament. He championed guns of heavier calibre for the fighter force, especially the Spitfire. He is seen here, probably at A&AEE Boscombe Down, with Prince George, Duke of Kent, who died in a Sunderland crash in August 1942 – the first member of the Royal Family to die on active service for 400 years. RAF Museum

George Pickering AFC

Born 21 October 1906
Died 2 June 1943
Spitfire test pilot, 1937–43

George Pickering was the classic central-casting image of a test pilot: tall, handsome, respectful, cool and utterly professional. Like his contemporaries, Pickering was bitten by flying at an early age and by 1924 he was commissioned into the Royal Air Force.

After graduating from No 2 Flying Training School at RAF Digby, where he had soloed in an Avro 504K, Pickering was posted to test flying boats at the Marine Aircraft Experimental Establishment in Felixstowe and then posted for operational flying to Malta. Here he was awarded the Air Force Cross for a noteworthy rescue of the Bishop of Malta in rough seas by flying boat in 1927.

During his Royal Air Force service, Pickering tested various biplane fighters on floats, including the naval Hawker Nimrod and then the Supermarine Stranraer, Scapa and Southampton flying boat prototypes. With his flying boat and seaplane background, Pickering was a natural for Supermarine when his short service commission ended in 1934. By the time he had retired, Supermarine had been a Vickers company for six years and had a full order book. Pickering was given the flight test of the Walrus and is reported to have looped the biplane amphibian over The Solent.

At Woolston, Pickering flew all the flying boats coming off the line and worked closely with Mitchell, who became a close family friend. By the time the Spitfire prototype was ready for testing, he was effectively No 3 in the Supermarine test pilot hierarchy after Joseph 'Mutt' Summers and Jeffrey Quill.

Pickering first flew the Spitfire prototype on 25 March 1936 on test flight No 6 and logged 33 minutes in what he called the 'SS fighter', standing for Supermarine Spitfire. With Quill, he continued test flying the prototype for the 33 pre-delivery flights before it went to the Royal Aircraft Establishment.

Along with Jeffrey Quill, then chief test pilot, Pickering was part of the company's export sales drive to interest the French in the Spitfire, flying aerobatics for the French Air Force staff at Eastleigh in May 1939. In the event, a single demonstration Spitfire was delivered to France in 1940 and it fell into the hands of the Luftwaffe that June when France capitulated.

Besides the Spitfire, Pickering also flew the company 'hacks' including the Miles Falcon, which was present at the Spitfire's first flight, and a Miles Magister. His communications trips embraced the airfields associated with the dispersed sites, including Chattis Hill, Worthy Down, Henley and Aldermaston.

Back at Eastleigh, Pickering continued sharing the development flying with Quill until, in 1941, he was involved in a serious incident when a production Spitfire Mk Vb broke up in flight and was pushed into a 500mph dive. As the fighter broke up, Pickering was thrown out and had to take to his parachute. He landed badly and was off flying duties for several months while he recovered.

Test pilots were the superstars of the age. Two key players in the Spitfire story were Jeffrey Quill (left) and George Pickering, seen here talking to King George VI, with Vickers' managing director Alex Dunbar (right). Pickering's career was halted when he bailed out of a Spitfire at high speed, but he did recover, only to be killed in a freak accident in a Universal Carrier armoured vehicle. Courtesy of Jennie Sherborne

Some time in 1940 or 1941, Pickering is reputed to have flown a Spitfire Mk II under a bridge that spanned the A33 trunk road from Basingstoke to Southampton on what is now the M3 but was then the newly constructed Winchester by-pass. Until it was demolished to take the new motorway, this landmark was known as Spitfire Bridge, and a side road called Spitfire Way now marks the location.

Following convalescence, Pickering was fit to return to flight status on 1 June 1943. Apparently keen to celebrate, he went to his sister's public house at Ivinghoe in Bedfordshire. In an act of characteristic bravado, he met some soldiers and talked himself into a drive of the Universal Carrier open-top light armoured vehicle at the Chilterns training area. The following morning he took control of the vehicle and it overturned, killing him. He was only 38 years old.

CHAPTER 4

THE PRODUCERS

With the Spitfire prototype, K5054, having impressed the Air Ministry enough for contracts to be placed, the hand-built prototype had to be translated into a mass-produced aeroplane.

With its complex curves and panels, this was never going to be easy. The carefully conceived shape of the Spitfire's fuselage, hand-crafted for the prototype at great expense in terms of both time and money, needed to be manufactured rapidly and cheaply by machinery. Additionally there was the challenge for Supermarine of finding the necessary skilled workforce, as the growing demands of rearmament meant that many suitably skilled workers in the Southampton area were already involved in shipbuilding and the manufacture of other military equipment. Supermarine was also still committed to Air Ministry contracts for flying boats and seaplanes, with orders extant for the Walrus amphibian and the Stranraer long-range patrol flying boat.

The Air Ministry's first Spitfire production contract, dated 3 June 1936, was for 310 airframes to be manufactured and assembled by Supermarine at Woolston, with flight testing to be carried out at Eastleigh. Other parts of the operation went to a number of tested contractors with whom the Ministry and Vickers already had good working relationships.

Wing integration was in the hands of General Aircraft (Feltham) and Pobjoy Airmotors (Rochester), with the tips coming from General Electric (Preston) and the ribs and other strengtheners from both G. Beaton & Son (Willesden) and Westland Aircraft (Yeovil). The last part of the wing jigsaw was the D-shaped leading edge, for which Pressed Steel (Coventry) was responsible.

J. Samuel White (Isle of Wight) was contracted to fabricate the fuselage frames, while the horizontal control surfaces – fabric-covered at this stage in the Spitfire's life – were to be created by Aero Engines Ltd (Bristol). The tail empennage was the work of Folland (Hamble), which went on to create most of the empennage jigs and tooling, if not the tails themselves, for almost every Spitfire and Seafire ever produced. Engine mountings came from Singer (Coventry), the specialist machinists.

Coincidental with the order for the first 310 Spitfires – and an order for 600 Hurricane airframes made at the same time – came the realisation within government that factories at Rochester (Short Brothers), Kingston upon Thames (Hawker) and Southampton (Vickers Supermarine) were vulnerable to air attack as they were situated so close to the Channel

Shadow factories optimised the new industrial revolution of the 1930s: clean, light, open spaces in which production lines could be built. This is the Castle Bromwich Aircraft Factory in late 1941 or early 1942 with a batch of Spitfire Mk Vb fighters nearing completion. Detail visible includes the open wireless compartment aft of the cockpit into which a radio would be fitted at the Maintenance Unit to which the Spitfire would be delivered. Solent Sky

coast. This concern focused the mind of the Secretary of State for Air, Lord Swinton (formerly Philip Cunliffe-Lister), who could see that the use of shadow factories would provide at least a partial solution. He became a champion of them.

With the prevailing air doctrine – 'the bomber will always get through' – remaining the guiding factor behind policy, money was allocated to the Shadow Factory Scheme in the government's 'Statement Relating to Defence' in March 1936. The plan was for the Air Ministry to be given control of a series of capital projects to construct factories that would be run by the non-aviation sector of industry, especially the motor industry.

The plan anticipated that the first shadow factory would be completed by May 1937, that the first components from the dispersed sub-contractors would be available by September, and that the first new aero engines from factories at Crewe and Glasgow would be ready by November. A highly mobile support service, the Emergency Services Organisation, was also set up to repair bomb-damaged factories.

The main shadow factory was built at Castle Bromwich, Birmingham, between Fort Dunlop and a military aerodrome – useful for test flying – that had been used by the Royal Flying Corps during the First World War. Sir Kingsley Wood, who succeeded Lord Swinton

The sheer number of Spitfire Mk F 21 fuselages under final erection shows the capabilities of a shadow factory. This one is South Marston near Swindon in 1944. This facility also produced Miles Master trainers at this time and Short Stirling bombers had been built here in previous years. Spitfires were also repaired here under the Civilian Repair scheme. Solent Sky

as Secretary of State for Air in May 1938, entrusted the Castle Bromwich works to William Morris, maker of Morris cars, who had been ennobled recently as Lord Nuffield.

Construction work at Castle Bromwich began in July 1938 and the plans were both lavish and ambitious. The aeroplane factory was to be the largest industrial plant in Britain, covering 345 acres and employing 12,000 skilled workers from the surrounding area, many of them with experience in the automotive industry. The entire site was to be completely self-contained, with its own power generation and facilities for all aspects of Spitfire manufacture except aero-engine production and some elements that needed specialist manufacture, such as tyres and rubber piping. Staff facilities included canteens and doctors' surgeries.

Building fighter aeroplanes was certainly found to be more complex than Morris Motors had initially thought and Lord Nuffield's organisation was found wanting. By the time the Ministry of Aircraft Production came into being in May 1940, with Lord Beaverbrook at its helm, still no Spitfires had been produced at Castle Bromwich. It did not help that the plant was also initially plagued with labour troubles, including strikes and working to rule. The whole matter was of critical national importance and the Ministry of Aircraft Production existed to provide direction. As a result of a telephone conversation between their Lordships, Vickers-Armstrong took over the Castle Bromwich production facilities and by the end of the war over 11,900 Spitfires, 50 Seafires and 200 Avro Lancasters had been built there.

Remarkably, the Castle Bromwich factory only twice received the attention of Luftwaffe bombers, in 1940 (before it entered full production) and in 1943. Today there is little left to show for its wartime life: much of the site has been taken over by Jaguar Land Rover and the rest is a housing estate along the Chester Road over which Spitfires (and Lancasters) would once have trundled from factory to aerodrome for test flying by such legends as Alex Henshaw and Peter Ayerst.

Another shadow factory, also conceived in 1938, was built at South Marston, near Swindon, and kept in public ownership until bought by Vickers after the Second World War. Originally conceived as a 'shadow' to the Phillips & Powis Aircraft factory at Woodley, near Reading, it was in production by 1940 making the Miles Master, an advanced trainer that many a Spitfire and Hurricane squadron received as a 'hack' and continuity trainer because it used a Merlin engine and had similar approach and landing characteristics. Records of South Marston production show that 121 Spitfire Mk 21s were assembled there and in addition 50 Spitfires were modified as Seafires for the Royal Navy. Some Mk IXs were also built there, including one of most famous heritage Spitfires, MH434 of the Old Flying Machine Company at Duxford. South Marston also carried out service upgrades, especially to fuel systems and hydraulics.

Back at Supermarine, meanwhile, the problems that arose during the build-up to manufacture were so considerable that nearly two years had elapsed since the Spitfire's maiden flight when, on 14 May 1938, the first production Spitfire became airborne at Eastleigh. At one stage during 1938 dismay about the delays led the Air Ministry to consider denying subsequent Spitfire contracts to Supermarine and transferring them elsewhere, leaving Supermarine to finish making flying boats and start building the new twin-engined Bristol Beaufighter. During the Second World War, in fact, it became commonplace for companies that designed aeroplanes to see the production contracts go elsewhere, usually to peacetime rivals, as first the Air Ministry and then the Ministry of Aircraft Production masterminded production.

But by working double shifts, coordinating the myriad sub-contractors (not just in the local area but across the length and breadth of the country) and working closely with Rolls-Royce, Supermarine's management got on top of the problems, such that by August 1939, on the brink of war, the company had managed to deliver 240 of the now much-vaunted Spitfire Mk I versions out of that first order for 310, as itemised in the table on the next page, compiled from Supermarine's quarterly reports to the Vickers' directors. It helped that the last Stranraer twin-engine flying boats were completed by March 1939 so that the Spitfire really could become the focus of attention.

In order to increase manufacturing capacity, in 1939 Supermarine used reclaimed land on the banks of the River Itchen to build the 'Itchen Works', primarily for the production of its amphibians (Walrus and Sea Otter) but later for Spitfire fuselages as well. Some Walrus production was also transferred to J. Samuel White on the Isle of Wight and, for a while in December 1939, Supermarine transferred some of its Spitfire workers to its Walrus line when Spitfire components were in short supply.

After Supermarine had been awarded the contract, the first task in moving towards manufacture was for assistant chief designer Joe Smith and his team to create standard drawings. Smith had been the chief draughtsman in Mitchell's time and when the great man died, in 1937, he was the natural successor. Smith also oversaw the creation of machine tools and jigs as well as the qualification process for the sub-contractors. The Air Ministry supported this search for the right sub-contractors, realising that Supermarine could not do everything required for the Spitfire as well as keep Walrus and Stranraer production going. Denis Le Penn Webb (see page 81), whose role later involved the supervision of several hundred sub-contractors, reckoned that only 25 per cent of a Spitfire could be produced at Supermarine, and many small items, such as rudder pedals and some rib pressings, had to be contracted out.

The placing of orders was the responsibility of production manager John Butler and works manager Wilf Elliott. As production ramped up, Victor Jackson took over the sub-contractors' office and he and a small staff were responsible for progressing the work and meeting the schedules.

Air Ministry figures for the first production contract for Southampton show that the price of a Spitfire from Supermarine was £8,783, without engine or radio (fitted as government-furnished equipment at Eastleigh) and also without weapons (fitted by Maintenance Units at places such as Brize Norton). The contract document declares that the cost of material was £4,998 per airframe, with additions for labour (£1,317), tools (£561) and works' overheads (£1,599). That left a profit for Supermarine of £308 per Spitfire.

By April 1940 Supermarine had delivered 604 production-standard Spitfires to the Air Ministry, yet service training and enemy action during Operation Dynamo over Dunkirk meant that only 280 remained in the front line when Air Chief Marshal Dowding reported

SPITFIRE PRODUCTION AT SUPERMARINE

Quarter ending	Number produced	Notes
30 September 1938	8	–
31 December 1938	49	–
31 March 1939	65	–
30 June 1939	118	–
30 September 1939	102	Shortage of Merlin engines and government-furnished equipment
31 December 1939	138	First contract for 310 completed
31 March 1940	124	Still suffering from component delays
30 June 1940	231	–
30 September 1940	360	Bombing of Southampton on 26 September; dispersal begins

Part of Supermarine's expansion programme with the Spitfire order was the construction of the Itchen Works, upstream from the Woolston headquarters. These Spitfire Mk I fighters from the first production contract appear to be awaiting delivery of Merlin engines from Rolls-Royce. Pre-war production at Supermarine was hampered by the lack of process that Wilf Elliott and his team needed to put into gear. Solent Sky

to the War Cabinet on 3 June 1940. By the end of the Battle of Britain, Supermarine had delivered more than 1,000 Spitfires.

Plans for the dispersal of Spitfire production in the event of war were discussed as early as 1937, when H.B. Pratt, Supermarine's newly appointed general manager, and Charles Craven, Vickers' managing director (and later industrial advisor to Lord Beaverbrook at the Ministry of Aircraft Production), looked at available production space. The actual details, however, were not worked out until August 1940, when several overflights by Luftwaffe reconnaissance aircraft prompted Vickers' management to think hard about what they would have to do if the Germans destroyed the Supermarine works.

In the quarterly report of 30 September 1940, Vickers' directors were told of contingency plans to continue production, especially of fuselages, at new locations. The key to this dispersal programme was to map out locations and floor space but nothing was to be done that might risk production, a vitally important consideration that was not helped by the fact that the Castle Bromwich line for the Spitfire Mk II had still not come on stream.

As a taste of things to come, Junkers Ju 87 Stuka dive-bombers attacked the Eastleigh flight sheds on 11 September and then there was a raid on Woolston on 15 September.

Following this, there was a telephone conversation between Craven (in London) and Pratt in which some dispersal preparation was discussed. By the time the Luftwaffe returned on 26 September some completed fuselages had been transferred to Hendy's Garage, although nothing substantial in terms of equipment seems to have been moved.

The bombing of Southampton on 26 September killed 92 people and the damage at Supermarine was so extensive that production came to a halt. The official report on the raids stated that the works 'were seriously damaged by enemy action on 26 September' and went on to add that 'damage was confined to buildings and work in progress, and damage to plant, machines and tools was remarkably little.' Lord Beaverbrook visited Woolston that night and took personal charge of the dispersal of the Supermarine effort in the Southampton area, quite probably treading all over the carefully laid plans hatched in the preceding months by Pratt and Craven, who visited the works the day after the raid.

All Spitfire production at Supermarine was dispersed to Wiltshire and Berkshire as well as some assembly and test flying in the north of Hampshire. An early move by the team from the Ministry of Aircraft Production was to have the fuselage jigs sent to Salisbury. This looked good on paper but the disadvantage was that the cathedral city had no suitably skilled workforce, so the workers initially had to be brought in by bus from the Southampton area – about an hour each way.

Building on the planning already carried out by Supermarine staff, Ministry officials examined the use of other facilities in and around Southampton, including small workshops and even a steam laundry in the suburbs. Most of Supermarine's office staff moved to Hursley Park, south of Winchester: there the design team occupied the stately home, the experimental facilities were housed in large new buildings concealed from the air within clumps of trees in the park's grounds, and Sleepy Hollow Barn was used to store the accounting records that were so important to support Supermarine's invoices to the Ministry of Aircraft Production. Hursley Park had only recently been requisitioned following the death of its owner, Sir George Cooper, and post-war it remained in Vickers' ownership until sold to IBM in 1963, by which time it had been responsible not just for Spitfire development but also for successor designs like the Spiteful and a new age of jet fighters. Versions of the Spitfire designed at Hursley, and occasionally fabricated in the facilities there, were test-flown at Worthy Down (the naval air station where the Royal Navy trained its telegraphists and air gunners), Chattis Hill or Eastleigh, depending on workload.

Production facilities were more difficult to find. This is where British ingenuity came to the fore, through the simple expediency of a map, pencil and ruler. Every significant town within about 60 miles of Southampton was assessed, each team equipped with an experienced Vickers manager such as Charlie Johns (the chief inspector) or George Guard (the chief estimator), plus a police constable in case the owners of premises needed to be reminded of the Emergency Powers Act. They were tasked to look for suitable buildings and note their measurements, then report back to works manager Wilf Elliott.

A key to the success of the Dispersal Factories Plan was the selection of the right premises into which Supermarine could move its experienced workforce and where, eventually, some

SUPERMARINE'S DISPERSED SITES
Locations of sub-contractors

1 Musselburgh
2 Glasgow (2 firms)
3 Prestwick
4 Darlington
5 Liverpool
6 Manchester
7 Stalybridge
8 Huddersfield
9 Leeds (2 firms)
10 Wakefield
11 Brough
12 Barnsley
13 Sheffield
14 Rotherham
15 Doncaster
16 Nottingham
17 Shrewsbury
18 Wolverhampton
19 Dudley
20 Birmingham (25 firms)
21 Norwich
22 Bromsgrove
23 Coventry (9 firms)
24 Northampton
25 Warwick
26 Rugby
27 Bedford
28 Oxford (2 firms)
29 Swindon (2 firms)
30 Bristol (5 firms)
31 Trowbridge

32 Newbury (2 firms)
33 Reading (3 firms)
34 Slough (4 firms)
35 London (105 firms)
36 Tiverton
37 Taunton
38 Salisbury
39 Farnham
40 Exeter
41 Yeovil (3 firms)
42 Romsey (2 firms)
43 Winchester
44 Horsham
45 Crawley
46 Bournemouth, Poole and Parkstone (13 firms)
47 Southampton, Eastleigh and Hythe (19 firms)

48 Portsmouth (2 firms)
49 Brighton and Hove (3 firms)
50 Isle of Wight (3 firms)

training could take place. But initially Beaverbrook's idea of 'total dispersal' caused problems, sometimes with possibly unnecessary loss of production through ministerial meddling.

Few of the companies involved in dispersal production complained about the prospect of playing a part in Spitfire production. Many of them, such as motor agents and garages, were suffering through lack of business and were more than happy to accommodate the plans of the Ministry of Aircraft Production. However, it is said that the Bishop of Salisbury remonstrated with Lord Beaverbrook about the risk that Salisbury, with its fine medieval cathedral, would become a target for the Germans. The Beaver's reply was apparently succinct: 'No Spitfires, no cathedral.' The Bishop got the point but it did not stop a local factory owner from contacting the Mayor, who took up his case against the requisition of his small works. Supermarine's man on the spot, 28-year-old works engineer Len Gooch, who managed much of the dispersal operations, simply reminded the Mayor that he was the chairman of the newly established Spitfire Fund and it would look rather hypocritical if Salisbury did not do its best to help Spitfire production.

Eventually Salisbury boasted eight sites, including accommodation and catering in the former W.H. Smith bookshop. Two purpose-built premises were constructed on Castle Road, which leads north from the city centre directly to the aerodrome at High Post, where final assembly and test flying took place. When High Post became too busy in 1941–44, Spitfires were taken along the A30 to Chattis Hill, a former First World War aerodrome. Among the accolades that Salisbury can claim is the manufacture of all Spitfire Mk XII fighters and completion of the first two-seat Spitfire, a converted Mk VIII, as a private venture for Vickers in the Castle Road No 2 factory. Wessex Garages built fuselages from jigs moved from Woolston, while Anna Valley Motors made specialist fuel tanks in the leading edges of the wings – known as 'bowser' wings – for photo-reconnaissance Spitfires.

In July 1944 High Post was the scene of one of the most extraordinary developments of the Spitfire. Troops on the Normandy coast beachhead claimed to be missing English beer and word got back to Supermarine. A small team worked in the evenings to calculate the stress of carrying beer barrels on the wing attachments for 500lb bombs, having ruled out filling the Spitfire's wing tanks with beer. The local brewer, Strongs of Romsey, provided new barrels that were inspected, fitted and then filled with best bitter. In order to prevent a meddling official from stopping the project, the task was given a job number and the paperwork looked completely official. The High Post tests were completely successful.

Besides Salisbury, there were three other main dispersal sites, in Trowbridge, Reading and Newbury. The dispersal to these four main sites outside Southampton inevitably caused some disruption but Spitfire production never ceased. A statement in one of the quarterly reports to Vickers' directors provides some insight: 'The introduction of cannons [sic] into the armament was required to be put into immediate production. These changes were particularly unfortunate as they occurred at a time when production was recovering from the dispersal of all components into at least four different centres.'

The Vickers' Board Report for 30 December 1940 stated that in the previous quarter – the first since the bombing of Woolston – the number of Spitfires delivered was 177, the

After D-Day, Spitfires were unofficially employed to take beer to the troops in Normandy after development work at High Post with the 'Type XXX depth charge'. This photo at forward aerodrome B57 Lille-Nord is probably staged as the beer transport went from England to the Continent, not vice versa. The pilot is Captain Nils Magne Jørgensen (Norway) with his No 332 Squadron Mk IX fighter. Solent Sky

figure for the previous quarter having been 360. Some Supermarine men, however, believed that it was Beaverbrook's 'bull in a china shop' dispersal plans, rather than the Luftwaffe's actions, that caused this dip in Spitfire production. The policy of duplicated and even triplicated sub-contracts helped the cause and worked well, even if it imposed strains on the fleet of Queen Mary transporters, lorries and vans that ferried components and assemblies to their destinations. The effectiveness of Supermarine's transport pool was enhanced by the addition of vehicles belonging to the garages requisitioned for the dispersed sites.

It took until April/May 1941 for Spitfire production at the dispersal sites to regain the production figures required for the Royal Air Force, showing that the impact of the September 1940 bombing on Southampton was probably greater than the Luftwaffe could have imagined. Supermarine's Spitfire production grew from about 14 a week in December 1940 to 25 a week by September 1941. This goes part of the way to explain why Mk I fighters were still being delivered in 1941 when the front squadrons had already started to be equipped with the Mk II from Castle Bromwich in late 1940.

By late 1941 the workforce employed at Southampton and the four dispersed centres totalled 9,600, with 3,000 at Southampton, 1,600 each in Reading, Salisbury and Trowbridge, and

PERSONNEL IN SUPERMARINE'S DISPERSED FACTORIES

Immediately after the Luftwaffe bombed the Itchen and Woolston works on 26 September 1940, the dispersed factories and contractors were grouped into five main areas, each with its own manager.

Contractors in the Southampton area were managed by **Alfred Nelson**, probably working first from the Polygon Hotel, the top floor of which had been requisitioned in 1940 for the management team, and later at Hursley Park. Under Nelson's control were 23 locations where the means of production had been established, including final assembly and experimental facilities. Besides actual manufacture, there were locations with training facilities and a tool-room for making production equipment (such as jigs), and there were numerous stores. Although dispersed in case of further air raids, these sites were still in the Southampton area so that workforce continuity could be maintained as much as possible. The following list gives the main sub-contractors

- Detail and sub-assembly – Sunlight Laundry
- Finishing shop – Marwell Hall (now a world-renowned animal centre)
- Fuselage assembly – Hendy's Garage (Pound Tree Road, Southampton)
- Fuselage and jig production – Seward's Garage
- Machine shops – Short's Garage
- Pre-production finishing – Hendy's Garage
- Sheet metal and press shop – Chiswell's Garage
- Stores – Holly Brook Stores, Hursley Road, Leigh Road and Park Place (Southampton), Bishop's Waltham, Botley and Sholing
- Tank covering – Austin House Garage (where training was also carried out)
- Tank and pipe manufacture – Weston Rolling Mills and Hendy's Garage
- Tool-room – Lowther's Garage
- Transport repairs – Garratt's Garage
- Wing assembly – Hants & Dorset Bus Company, Southampton depot
- Woodworking – Newtown Works

The use of garages taken over from motor traders was a 'win-win' result: mechanics would have been available, such premises were generally large, and during the war there was little need for maintenance of cars.

Ladies from the Women's Voluntary Service (WVS) supported the dispersed workforce. The WVS was established in 1938 as a corps to support the air raid precautions regime, including provision of clothing of those bombed out in the Blitz, and by 1941 it was a million strong. Several dozen WVS personnel were employed to support the Spitfire

Part of the great success of keeping Spitfire production going after the air raids in September 1940 was the dispersal of production capacity first to Southampton itself and then to towns within 60 miles of the Supermarine works. The initial plan was masterminded by H.B. Pratt in 1937 and taken up by the Ministry of Aircraft Production in 1940. This is the top floor of Seward's Garage in Southampton where fuselages were crafted and jigs manufactured. Solent Sky

production effort by becoming rivet sorters at the Park Place store in Southampton – vital but repetitive work.

After Southampton, the next largest facilities were created around the Wiltshire county town of Trowbridge, where **Victor Hall** was installed as the local manager. His domain stretched across to the final assembly and flight test sheds at RAF Keevil where the Spitfires produced in the Trowbridge 'cluster' of factories were flown and where the Air Transport Auxiliary would have arrived to collect finished fighters for delivery to Maintenance Units (such as Brize Norton, Colerne and Hullavington) for the military equipment to be fitted.

Wessex Garages in Salisbury provided the floor space for the second stage of fuselage production for Spitfires, which would then go up to High Post aerodrome for final assembly and test flying. The Salisbury cluster employed workers from Southampton until a local workforce could be trained in the necessary skills, which included the new and challenging 'art' of welding aluminium. Solent Sky

The facility built in Trowbridge (where a Tesco superstore now stands) manufactured Mk VIII, Mk IX and Mk XIV Spitfires for the rest of the war.

Again, garages came to the fore in Trowbridge, including Forestreet Garage (details and fittings), Rutland Garage (pipes and coppersmiths) and Curries Garage (where the premises were large enough to store completed fuselages), and there were two transport centres at Eyken's Garage and Moore's Garage. There was also a purpose-built site at Bradley Road where wings, sub-assemblies and moulds were made, and where a tool-room was sited. 'Goods inwards' and fuselage stores used the Haverton cloth mills. Another factory was created at Hilperton Road were sub-assembly and details work was carried out.

Within the Trowbridge cluster were further workshops at Devizes (Southwick for leading edges) and Westbury (where Spitfires were assembled in the Bolton glove factory).

The Salisbury cluster was managed by **William Heaver**. The cathedral city proved a rich source of garages and semi-skilled labour, including a large number of educated women, who formed more than 60 per cent of the Salisbury workforce by 1943 and continued to work at Supermarine after the end of the Second World War when jets were being tested at High Post and later Chilbolton.

Two factories were built on Castle Road in Salisbury. These were positioned to take advantage of the former Roman road that continues north and past the High Post aerodrome, where the Wiltshire Flying Club and Royal Artillery Flying Club facilities had been taken over for the 'duration'. Some 1,935 Spitfires were built at Salisbury and flown from High Post, Chattis Hill and later Chilbolton. Chattis Hill not only used the racehorse gallops for a landing strip (just as had been done in the First World War) but the facilities were also large enough to accommodate overhaul facilities for Merlin engines.

Fuselages were made at Castle Road Factory No 1 and at Wessex Garages, which also made leading edges and tail units. Wings were made at Wilts & Dorset Bus garage and Castle Road Factory No 2, where leading edges were made too. Anna Valley Motors produced tail units.

As with other sites, the need to move materials – whether components from stores or large assemblies like fuselages and wings – necessitated the development of a transport network that was maintained by Castle Road Garage. The use of diesel-powered Petter tugs became commonplace and they were employed to tow the Spitfires, and their wing assemblies, up to High Post for final assembly and flight test.

Berkshire offered two sites for dispersed Spitfire production from late 1940. **Ken Scales** looked after the Reading cluster until late 1941, when **Ron Gould** replaced him. Vincent's Garage, near the main railway station, became a centre for fuselage production, wings were made at the Great Western Garage, and new factory space at Caversham was used for engine installation and the fabrication of fuselage formers. Aldermaston, now the home of the Atomic Weapons Establishment, was the main test airfield for Reading-built Spitfires, and a strip at Henley was also used.

The Newbury cluster, managed by **Tom Barby**, was small and concentrated mainly on detailed fittings and assemblies apart from at Elliott's, the furniture maker, where major assemblies were fabricated. Elliott's also became an experimental and trials facility that used skilled craftsmen to improve production engineering and develop new processes. The other six locations were mainly garages (Nias, Pass's and Stradling's), the Venture Bus Garage was taken over for stores, and there was a machine shop at Hungerford, eight miles west of Newbury.

1,800 in Newbury, where there were also repair operations. The Beaverbrook entourage – the 'Beaverboys' as they were known – had departed the Supermarine works and production had increased, perhaps by coincidence.

Widening the perspective beyond Supermarine's dispersed operations, the total number of people involved in building the Spitfire numbered over 20,000 at its peak. Many remember their times at the factories with a fondness derived from achievement and being part of the greater whole. Today the survivors among these Spitfire People still have a deep affection for the fighter 'which saved Britain'. With male conscription to the armed forces, many of the recruits in the factories were women, and they showed a cool determination to contribute despite long hours, often harsh conditions and the occasional air raid.

Spitfire manufacture, of course, was just a part of the aviation industry as a whole: in 1935 the industry employed 35,000 semi-skilled, skilled and professional people but, according to Ministry of Aircraft Production statistics, the figure grew to 335,000 by the declaration of war against Germany in September 1939. This huge surge in the workforce made aeronautics the country's biggest employer until the arrival of the National Health Service in 1948.

The Supermarine Spitfire Memorial Book records as many names as possible of those who, between 1932 and 1945, designed, developed and manufactured the Spitfire. This mighty tome was instigated at the behest of former Supermarine chief test pilot Jeffrey Quill at the Southampton Hall of Aviation – today's Solent Sky Museum. Despite a huge effort, it is destined to remain incomplete, for the passage of time makes the task ever more difficult.

Lord Beaverbrook (Max Aitken)

Born 25 May 1879
Died 9 June 1964
Minister of Aircraft Production, 1940–41
Minister of Supply, 1941–42
Minister of War Production, 1942

The business flair and energy of Canadian-born Max Aitken made him a millionaire by the age of 30 and it was around this time that he moved to England, becoming an MP in the general election of 1910. After the death that same year of Charles Rolls, of Rolls-Royce, Aitken bought Rolls' shares and gradually increased his holding in the company, although his attempt to acquire a controlling interest was thwarted. Aitken's first investment in the *Daily Express* in 1911, however, did lead to him taking control of the newspaper by 1916, and he is remembered today as much for being a press baron as for his ministerial successes during the Second World War.

During the First World War Aitken was a huge supporter of his native Canada's contribution to the war effort and, post-war, he raised hundreds of Canadian war memorials to remind successive generations of the sacrifice made by his country. It was during the war, in 1917,

In May 1940, one of Churchill's first acts had a profound impact on the Spitfire. He appointed Max Aitken, a trusted friend, to the Cabinet position of Minister for Aircraft Production. As Lord Beaverbrook, he had revolutionised the newspaper industry and was set to do the same to the production of fighters – his main priority. Not only did his roughshod methods work but his media persona was always cheerful, as here in Downing Street in June. Getty Images (Topical Press Agency)

Lord Beaverbrook might have been a maverick but his great skill was getting things done to the satisfaction of Churchill and he traded on his close relationship with the Prime Minister. He was not an effective administrator and needed to have a team follow him around to pick up the pieces. This photo of the pair was taken aboard HMS Prince of Wales *en route to Newfoundland for Churchill's vital first meeting with US President Roosevelt.* Getty Images (Keystone)

that he was elevated to the peerage and took the title Beaverbrook from a place name of his Canadian childhood.

It was two decades later that Beaverbrook came into his own and had a major influence on the Spitfire – sometimes good, sometimes not so good. It is ironic that he has become known as the champion of war production yet until September 1938 his newspapers, including the *Daily Express*, consistently took an appeasement stance, suggesting that there would be no European war and that Germany would not fight Britain.

On 10 May 1940 Winston Churchill became Prime Minister and one of his first acts was to create a Ministry of Aircraft Production (MAP). He chose his old ally, friend and confidant Lord Beaverbrook to run this war-critical department of state, which became effective from 14 May. Building aircraft to defend the nation and to take the war to the Germans was the prime concern of the National Government in 1940. It was the Spitfire and the Hurricane that would keep the Luftwaffe from gaining air supremacy and it would be a revitalised Bomber Command that would attack the German war effort.

Much about Beaverbrook's style of ministerial management was unorthodox, antagonistic and interventionist. He used his own home for the head office; he recruited key figures – the 'Beaverboys' – from industry to make up for his own deficiencies in understanding the means of production and the means of delivery; he 'railroaded' companies, people and government to achieve his aims.

Perhaps Beaverbrook's finest achievement was persuading Churchill to allow key people and departments to be transferred from the Air Ministry to the MAP, while his greatest disservice was the dip in Spitfire production that occurred in late 1940, caused, Supermarine believed, by his fundamental lack of understanding of the means of production rather than, as Beaverbrook asserted, the pre-war methods that Supermarine had in place.

The MAP took over and gave new direction to the Royal Air Force Aircraft Storage Units (ASUs) and Maintenance Units (MUs) that received aeroplanes, particularly Spitfires and Hurricanes, from the aircraft factories at this critical time. They were highly inefficient: 'stores is for storing – if they were for issuing, they would be called issuants' was a common refrain of the time. When the MAP was established, in May 1940, the MUs had received over 1,000 newly produced aircraft for fitting with government-furnished equipment but had only delivered about 650 into service because of the grossly inefficient pre-war processes involved. Beaverbrook crashed straight through that by taking over the MUs and sending in the Beaverboys.

The effect of the MAP on aircraft production was almost immediate. The total number of aircraft produced from January to April 1940 was 2,729, including 638 Spitfires, Hurricanes and Defiants. By the time the Battle of Britain was in full swing, total production delivered to the Royal Navy and Royal Air Force in the next four-month period, from May to August, had increased to 4,578, of which 1,875 were fighters. This was twice the volume achieved by the German aircraft industry, which had so many different models to produce and suffered from political interference and an inefficient system for sending them to front-line units.

Beaverbrook encouraged his subordinates to adopt a management style that relied little on form-filling and memoranda (so different from the Air Ministry and the Ministry of Supply) and instead to use the telephone and personal visits to make things happen. As a result due process was ignored, records were not kept, and time was wasted later in trying to formalise decisions, including contracts.

Beaverbrook broadcast a rousing speech on the BBC Home Service on 24 July, with the Battle of Britain officially still in its 'Channel Phase'. He called on the nation to keep up the good work in supplying materials, money and time for the vital production and repair of fighter aircraft. He thanked everyone for their efforts, from the manufacturing company that sent four and a half tons of surplus metal to the housewife who donated a saucepan. Such innovative approaches, including the Spitfire Funds and other money-raising efforts, were highly effective in raising morale, if less so in real manufacturing terms.

A major achievement by Beaverbrook in the quest to increase Spitfire production was to wrest the Castle Bromwich factory from Lord Nuffield and use the Emergency Powers Act to disperse the production of Spitfires from the devastated Supermarine works at Woolston

The Warminster Spitfire Fund raised £5,000 to buy a Spitfire for the nation in 1941 and a cheque was duly sent to Lord Beaverbrook. In fact, the Spitfire Mk Vb serial number BM359 allocated went on to fight in Russia as well. Author's collection

to numerous small factories in southern England. In doing so, he galvanised small businesses and brought the best out of many skilled craftsmen in many towns and cities.

But he also liked to be the centre of attention and make dramatic moves, and in doing so trod on many well-laid plans and clever people. Some did not survive contact with 'The Beaver'. At Supermarine, for example, he cut through the existing management and caused the loss of experienced, dedicated staff; the fact that his industrial advisor, Sir Charles Craven, asked to return to Vickers after less than 12 months speaks volumes.

In a private memoir published in 2001, *Never A Dull Moment*, Supermarine manager Denis Le Penn Webb (see page 81) wrote of the practical and sensible schemes already in place for dispersal that would have seen the maintenance of Spitfire fuselage production and would have meant only a slight delay in wing production. Other components were already widely dispersed with at least two if not three alternative sources of supply. Webb also questioned the wisdom of four centres, as directed by Beaverbrook, rather than one with three out-stations, and wrote: 'I reckon that this unnecessary and unthought [sic] through move cost the Royal Air Force some 150 Spitfires in lost production.' He added that the damage caused at Supermarine by the bombing of 26 September 1940 was not as bad as was made out and that Beaverbrook made theatre out of it.

Away from the airframe side, Rolls-Royce's own engine shadow factories at Glasgow and Crewe were made to function as part of the whole fighter aircraft production enterprise by Beaverbrook's rapid action.

Beaverbrook's sudden changes of tack and quick-fire action plans caused real problems in the well-ordered ranks of the Ministry and in industry. While some criticism can be laid at the door of those who did not fully understand the urgency of the situation, Beaverbrook ignored the expertise in the factories and experience of the managers who knew both product and workforce.

After a particularly vicious row in Cabinet, Beaverbrook offered his resignation in May 1941 and a reluctant Churchill accepted it. Because Beaverbrook's style of management and leadership ran directly opposite to that of the civil service and contemporary norms, there were few in the MAP who mourned his departure. Beaverbrook's immediate successors, John Moore-Brabazon (1941–42) and John Llewellin (1942), built on his efforts but toned down the rhetoric. From November 1942 the Minister was the dull but efficient Labour politician, Sir Stafford Cripps, the arch-appeaser of 1936, who took the department through the final years of conflict until a Labour Government was elected. The last Minister was Ernest Brown, who saw the MAP absorbed into the Ministry of Supply from July 1945. Power had, by that time, passed into the hands of the Director-General and the Minister had become more of a figurehead.

'I needed his vital and vibrant energy,' Churchill wrote of Beaverbrook in his memoirs after the Second World War. The Prime Minister seemed to be content with Beaverbrook's brash approach, probably because he recognised the slowness of decision-making inherent in the British civil service.

After leaving the MAP, Beaverbrook was appointed, in turn, Minister of Supply, Minister of War Production and Lord Privy Seal. He remained close to Churchill throughout the war, influencing policy, often to the annoyance of other Cabinet Ministers and the Chiefs of Staff. He even travelled to Washington DC and Moscow with the Prime Minister for meetings with Roosevelt and Stalin.

The current Lord Beaverbrook, also christened Max, is an Honorary Air Vice-Marshal of the Royal Auxiliary Air Force.

Lord Austin (Herbert Austin)

Born 8 November 1866
Died 23 May 1941
Car manufacturer

Herbert Austin and William Morris dominated the first six decades of the British car industry. During the Second World War they also helped oil the wheels of aircraft production, especially of Spitfires at a time when Supermarine was geared only for the craft production of flying boats.

The son of a farmer, Austin went to Australia when he was 18 and learned his trade in sheep-shearing machinery in New South Wales, where he joined another future car baron, Frederick Wolseley, in the Wolseley Sheep Shearing Machine Company before both men returned to England in 1893, bringing their business interests back with them. Since the sales of sheep-shearing equipment were seasonal, Austin looked for other avenues, first bicycles and then early motor cars, to occupy the company during slack periods. Vickers, which

Car baron Herbert Austin was quick to grasp the potential of the internal combustion engine and what it would do for motor transport. His Austin Motor Company pioneered cheap motor cars in the 1920s and 1930s, but his skill as an organiser led to his appointment to ensure that the shadow factories and sub-contractors were properly organised and delivered on time. Rex Features (Associated Newspapers)

would later buy the Supermarine business at Southampton, bought Wolseley's car business in 1901 and Austin transferred with it, but soon he struck out on his own and founded the Austin Motor Company at Longbridge, Birmingham.

With the outbreak of the First World War, Austin went into the military hardware manufacturing business and it won him both a fortune and a knighthood. He was elected the Conservative MP for Birmingham King's Norton in 1918 and later became close to both Lord Swinton and Neville Chamberlain.

With the development of shadow factories, initially under Swinton and then Sir Kingsley Wood, the expertise for building both airframes and engines in large numbers came predominantly from the car industry, which had embraced mass production for two decades. Austin, now a peer, was a natural choice to supervise the implementation of industrial aspects of developing new facilities and extending existing ones. Government grants and soft loans helped bring the production facilities into being and Austin's knowledge of the local politics in Birmingham undoubtedly helped with the Castle Bromwich facility.

Lord Nuffield (William Morris)

Born 10 October 1877
Died 22 August 1963
Car baron

It was William Morris rather than Herbert Austin, his great rival in the pre-war motor industry, who was put in charge of shadow-factory development.

At Cowley near Oxford, Morris, a former bicycle apprentice mechanic, started his own business making motor cycles in 1901 and then motor cars from 1912, when the famous 'Bullnose' Morris was introduced. In 1927, a year before the launch of the first Morris Minor, Morris beat Austin to the acquisition of assets of the failed Wolseley Motors, which

A clever man, Lord Nuffield was a car maker, not a street fighter like Beaverbrook. Nor was he, it seems, a good industrial organiser, for he lost control of the Castle Bromwich Aircraft Factory in May 1940. He did, however, develop the Civilian Repair Organisation into a vital cog in the machinery of keeping the front-line squadrons supplied with fighters, especially Spitfires. Rex Features (Associated Newspapers)

had been founded by Vickers in conjunction with Austin 26 years earlier.

With rearmament plans underway in the mid-1930s, the Air Ministry needed expertise to turn around the first production order of 310 Spitfires because it was clear that Supermarine's management were unable to handle manufacture on this scale, owing to the sheer size of the requirement and the company's lack of workers with the right skills for mass production. Morris, by now Lord Nuffield, was placed in charge of the Castle Bromwich shadow factory and he claimed that 50 Spitfires a week would roll off its production lines.

When Lord Beaverbrook took over as the first Minister of Aircraft Production in May 1940, he was alarmed to find that Nuffield's team had yet to produce a single Spitfire at Castle Bromwich. In a telephone conversation Beaverbrook out-manoeuvred Nuffield into giving up the factory, after Nuffield said words to the effect, 'If you think you can do any better why don't you do it.' Nuffield never knew what hit him and returned to Cowley to develop the Civilian Repair Organisation, which mended damaged aircraft, including Spitfires, at that critical time in the Battle of Britain.

Despite his falling out with Beaverbrook, Nuffield made a major personal and collective contribution to the motor industries' Spitfire Fund, which raised £105,026 to fund the acquisition of Presentation Spitfires. With Nuffield's own contribution of £5,000 in March 1941, announced by four-time ace and Dunkirk veteran Flight Lieutenant Harbourne Stephen DSO DFC RAFVR of No 74 Squadron at a press conference in London, a Spitfire Mk Vb was allocated and delivered, marked 'NUFFIELD', to the Royal Air Force on 14 March 1942. It served at RAF Hornchurch with No 154 (Motor Industries) Squadron, a unit that also benefited from the fund. The Squadron was named in recognition of the motor industry donors as part of a publicity campaign that saw many units linked to fund-raising organisations within the industry as well as overseas territories.

There was a set scale of contribution to Spitfire Funds for individuals and works' groups. The tariff included the following: Rolls-Royce Merlin, £2,000; fuselage, £2,500; wings, £1,800; undercarriage, £800; airscrew, £350; tail empennage, £500; cockpit canopy, £15; VHF radio, £50; compass, £5; individual rivet, 6d. These figures were completely arbitrary but they gave individuals a sense of ownership and patriotism. The whole concept of 'buying a Spitfire' appealed to many in Britain and the Empire, keen to find a way to contribute and harnessed by the media-savvy Beaverbrook in his big speech of 24 July 1940.

Not to be outdone, the Rootes Group – manufacturer of Hillman, Humber, Singer and Sunbeam cars as well as Commer trucks – also benefited from the publicity when the Ministry of Aircraft Production enlisted the help of Pilot Officer Wilfred Duncan Smith to present a £15,000 cheque to the Ministry for three Spitfires for No 154 Squadron.

Nuffield's support for the war effort and raising money for Spitfires continued despite Beaverbrook removing the Castle Bromwich facilities from his control and handing them over to Vickers Armstrong. Within weeks of this transfer, production got underway and the first Mk II Spitfires were coming off the line, the rate eventually reaching 300 a week. These would be followed by the bulk of Mk IX production and many of the Mk XVI, culminating in 11,964 Spitfires in six variants delivered from the site when production ceased in 1946.

Alex Henshaw

Born 7 November 1912
Died 24 February 2007
Chief test pilot, Castle Bromwich Aircraft Factory

Alex Henshaw deserves the epitaph of 'Mr Spitfire' more than anyone. He personally tested more than 10,000 Spitfires built at the Castle Bromwich facility. He flew relatively few marks and variants of the classic fighter because he was a production test pilot, so it was the same few versions in very large numbers that passed his careful scrutiny. Henshaw's civilian status meant that his contribution to the war effort and the story of the Spitfire was perhaps all the greater, although test flying was no less risky than active service.

Henshaw was a household name before the Second World War. An accomplished aviator and engineer, he was probably Britain's best-known pilot in the 1930s with an incredible list of accomplishments to his credit.

He learned to fly at the Skegness & East Lincolnshire Aero Club and was fortunate enough to be given a De Havilland Gipsy Moth by his father in which he took his pilot's

Alex Henshaw was every inch a pilot. In 1939 he wanted to do something for the war effort and found the perfect niche as the company production test pilot at Castle Bromwich. This factory mass-produced Spitfires (and later Lancasters) off the blueprint and Henshaw's team test-flew every machine that came off the line. Rex Features (Associated Newspapers)

licence in June 1932, aged 19. A year later he competed against the best pilots in Britain for the King's Cup in a Comper Swift and was awarded the Siddeley Challenge Trophy. He had to bail out of an Arrow Active and then started flying the aeroplane that made his name a legend – the Percival Mew Gull. This was the aeroplane in which he achieved his ambitions to fly long distances and set records: the Mew Gull had 'real legs'.

The Mew Gull entered the Spitfire story on 5 March 1936 when it was present at Eastleigh for the maiden flight of the Type 300 prototype, K5054, and is represented in Michael Turner's classic painting of a scene from that day. When Turner was doing his research for the painting, Henshaw was the only known eyewitness to the event and helped him position the groups of people and the aeroplanes.

On 3 February 1939 Henshaw flew the Mew Gull from Gravesend, Kent to Oran in French Algeria, stopping just long enough to refuel. Then he crossed the Sahara desert, pushing on through the equator to the Belgian Congo. From there he flew to Portuguese Angola and then to Cape Town's Wingfield aerodrome, flying the 6,377 miles in 40 hours – an average ground speed of 159.5mph. The outward leg set a new record.

Staying little more than a day in Cape Town, he climbed aboard the quickly serviced Mew Gull – Henshaw was a trained mechanic too – and retraced his course, landing back at Gravesend on 9 February after a total of 12,754 miles. The return leg was also a record, as was the solo round trip – which was not bettered until May 2009.

Henshaw's remarkable achievement, which won him the Royal Aero Club's Britannia Medal, shows the mettle of the man who would later survive some horrendous crashes while testing Spitfires.

When Germany invaded Poland on 1 September 1939, Henshaw immediately considered how best to serve his country. He thought about enlisting in the Royal Air Force but found that the inflexible training machine would mean that he would have to go back to flying school and start all over again. At the invitation of Jeffrey Quill, the chief test pilot at Supermarine, he joined Vickers Armstrong as a test pilot and was assigned to the Castle Bromwich factory. Here he worked with the redoubtable Bernard Cook, works manager, and later a Vickers director. The whole rationale for production test flying was to ensure that the Spitfires delivered to the front line were as near perfect as possible.

In June 1940 Henshaw became the chief test pilot and led a team of 25 service pilots including Flight Lieutenant Peter Ayerst and the Czech ace Flight Lieutenant Venda Jicha. Two of the pilots seconded to Vickers' testing team were killed in Spitfires in the course of their test work and the essential statistics for Castle Bromwich are the more impressive for that: 12,767 Spitfires and Lancasters tested in 37,023 test flights totalling 9,116.2 flying hours with only 130 forced landings.

Although Henshaw remained a civilian throughout the Second World War, he was given the rank of Sergeant Pilot in the Royal Air Force Volunteer Reserve in order to legally fly an armed Spitfire in defence of the Castle Bromwich works.

In his later years Henshaw described the days at the Castle Bromwich Aircraft Factory as routine – 20 new Spitfires or Seafires to test in a day – punctuated by the sheer terror of a

Weak from his two-way flight across Africa in his Mew Gull in February 1939, a young Alex Henshaw is carried through the crowds who came to greet him at Gravesend airfield. The airfield became a vital fighter base in the Battle of Britain and Henshaw an indispensible production test pilot at Castle Bromwich. Rex Features (Associated Newspapers)

production fault every once in a while. One occurred on 18 July 1942, when he put Mk Vb EP615 down between houses in Willenhall, near Wednesfield, after engine failure on a flight from RAF Cosford. The engine's skew gear meshed with one or more magnetos, causing the engine to stop when he was over a built-up area with no handy fields in which to land. That flight could easily have been his last.

Despite an outstanding war record of test flying Spitfires and Lancasters, Henshaw only received an MBE (Member of the Order of the British Empire) from the Attlee government in 1945 and many thought that he should have been honoured more highly – but Henshaw always said that he was only doing a job that needed to be done.

Among his more agreeable tasks was the occasion in 1941 when the Prime Minister and Mrs Churchill visited Castle Bromwich, described in Henshaw's autobiographical account of flying the Spitfire called, picturesquely, *Sigh for a Merlin*. Henshaw provided Mr Churchill with a full aerobatic display in a Spitfire Mk Va, including his signature inverted pass. The official photographer's camera also caught the PM with Henshaw talking about the Spitfire, a moment that features on the front cover of this book.

After the end of the war Henshaw did not experience a Spitfire again until 5 March 2006, 70 years after the first flight of K5054, when the Aircraft Restoration Company, Britain's premier Spitfire rebuilding facility, invited him to fly in a two-seat Spitfire. This was his last flight, for he died at home in Newmarket the following year, aged 95. His logbooks and records are held by the RAF Museum.

CHAPTER 5
THE COMMANDERS

Spitfire Mk I K9789, the third production aircraft from the Supermarine line at Southampton, was flown to RAF Duxford from the Eastleigh aerodrome on 4 August 1938. This marked the first delivery to the Royal Air Force and started a 20-year front-line relationship that continues to this day with the Battle of Britain Memorial Flight.

The entry into service of any new type was, and is, challenging and demanding, especially when the threat of a new European conflict was rapidly emerging. In an historical context, the entry into service of the Spitfire must be seen against the chilling events unfolding on the Continent of Europe and, perhaps to a lesser degree, in Westminster, and the continuing conflict in China that involved two Chinese factions, the Soviet Union and Imperial Japan.

In Europe, the Spanish Civil War had entered its third and final year. The Condor Legion of more than 7,000 German 'volunteers' served on the Nationalist side in the conflict from July 1936 until March 1939, when they were withdrawn for training prior to the invasion of Poland. The first production Messerschmitt Bf 109 and the prototype Heinkel He 112 were sent to Spain, creating a 'trial by combat' of the competing designs. Although this conflict presented a clear opportunity for technical intelligence gathering, it seems that very little of what may have been gleaned was passed to Supermarine, Hawker or other companies in the British aviation industry.

In March 1938, Austria and Germany created the political union that came to be known as *Anschluß*, which, despite being contrary to the various treaties that defined the peace after the end of the First World War, did not result in any armed action, but it certainly heightened tension and confirmed warnings from Churchill and his followers. Hitler, emboldened by his success in Austria, turned his attention to the Sudetenland in Czechoslovakia, causing even more political tension and creating a real sense of urgency in British rearmament.

As the first Spitfires were being moved from the Itchen-side factories to Eastleigh aerodrome for flight testing, the German armed forces, including the Luftwaffe, began experimenting with battle plans for Operation Green, the invasion of Czechoslovakia.

European tension seems to have galvanised the Vickers group and the pace of production increased as the Westminster politicians in London, and their French colleagues at the Quai d'Orsay, struggled to find a peaceful solution to Hitler's obvious drive to create the Greater German Reich.

When it came to accepting the first production Spitfire into service, before the advent of operational development, conversion or training units, it had to be decided which squadron and air station would receive it. In a classic out-flanking move, the highly talented and newly promoted Squadron Leader Henry Cozens, Officer Commanding No 19 Squadron at RAF Duxford, convinced a friend at the Air Ministry that Duxford was a superior air station to the planned Catterick deployment, not least because it was closer to London and easier for boffins, officials and senior officers to see the game-changing fighter.

Fighter Command, and especially No 19, was still equipped with obsolete – or at least obsolescent – biplane fighters that represented little more capability than had been available at the end of the First World War 20 years earlier. The Spitfire was 170mph faster in level flight, carried more hitting power, had a longer range and better communications, and the pilot sat in an enclosed cockpit. The Spitfire also had the double-edged sword of a retractable undercarriage: this was good for speed but early on there were instances of pilots landing inadvertently with wheels up owing to all their previous flying experience having been with fixed undercarriages.

Production Spitfires were not, however, delivered with pilots' notes, a detailed conversion course nor a company instructor. It would have been pretty daunting stuff to fly a new single-seat, high-performance fighter without the benefit of a dual-seat conversion trainer or, as in today's Royal Air Force, a flight simulator. But in 1938 that was the norm.

Cozens and his fellow squadron commander at No 66 Squadron, Squadron Leader Laurence Fuller-Good, were tasked with flying intensive trials to complete 400 hours as soon as possible and report back to the Air Ministry. From London, the report was circulated to Supermarine and Rolls-Royce in industry and to HQ Fighter Command at Bentley Priory, Stanmore for service consideration.

No 66 had been reformed as part of the Fighter Command expansion in 1936 from No 19's C flight. The rivalry and camaraderie were ideal for the accelerated service introduction of a new type and the intensive trials were completed after only 200 hours. These included some of the first firing trials with the new Browning rifle-calibre machine guns over ranges such as the RAF Sutton Bridge Practice Camp on the edge of The Wash.

By October 1938 the Air Ministry was confident enough to show the Spitfire to the public for the first time. The venue chosen was the opening of Cambridge Airport on 8 October, when Sir Arthur Marshall, chairman of Marshall of Cambridge, welcomed Sir Kingsley Wood, the Secretary of State for Air, to see the new facilities, including a training school. During the next few years Marshall's company trained over 10,000 pilots for the Royal Navy and the Royal Air Force as one of the main civilian flying schools, equipped with the De Havilland Tiger Moth. The company also undertook overhaul and repair as part of the Civilian Repair Organisation throughout the Second World War.

Although nobody was killed in the intensive flying trials, the first production Spitfire to be written off was the eighth example, which lost its port wheel assembly on touching down at RAF Duxford on 3 November 1938. The pilot, Pilot Officer Gordon Sinclair, was unhurt, which was just as well for he went on to become a double ace in the Battle of Britain.

Key recommendations included a bulged cockpit canopy, a faster starter motor, improved

Previously unpublished, this photo shows a section from No 19 Squadron at RAF Duxford at the opening of Cambridge Airport in October 1938. This was the first time operational Spitfires appeared in public and the squadron number is clearly visible on the fin. The Spitfire in the middle was flown that day by Squadron Leader Henry Cozens, the officer commanding No 19. **The Marshall Group of Companies**

engine oil seals and a hydraulic undercarriage system to prevent the pilot exfoliating his knuckles every time he needed to lower or retract the wheels. All the recommendations were accepted and actioned within 12 weeks, which is a credit to the lack of red tape and the slick staff work in Fighter Command.

These improvements even included the technically innovative propeller changes required to improve performance and handling at critical flight stages, including during take-off and landing. Work had been set in train in 1937 to create Rotol – a joint venture between Rolls-Royce and Bristol – to improve every area of airscrew technology for both Spitfires and Hurricanes, and it was Rotol that conceived the world's first five-blade propeller configuration for late-model Spitfires.

As 1939 dawned, the Air Ministry saw the importance of promoting the Spitfire and began to bring the new fighter capability to the attention of the general public. On 20 May 1939 a massed gathering of Spitfires and Hurricanes departed from RAF Digby to fly around the Midlands and the northern England for Empire Air Day; it was to be the last such event as war was just four months away. Then these fighters would be sorely tried and tested – and they would meet the expectations of the nation.

By 3 September 1939, when Germany failed to respond to the British government's ultimatum requiring German forces to be withdrawn from Poland, the Royal Air Force had

187 Spitfires in front-line service with, perhaps surprisingly, 36 Spitfires already written off in flying accidents.

Although initial trials showed that the Spitfire was faster and more manoeuvrable than the Hurricane, it was the Hurricane that was now in service in far greater numbers than its Supermarine rival. The Hurricane, however, carried more ammunition and was therefore destined, with its slower rate of climb, to be used to engage bombers, while the Spitfire was supposed to 'take care' of the fighter cover.

In the summer of 1939 forward squadrons in south-east England practised formation flying that might have impressed at the Hendon Air Pageants but were about to be shown as dangerous and tactically inept.

Spitfires were not deployed to France with the Advanced Air Striking Force (mobilised on 24 August 1939 in a rare bit of pre-planning) nor as part of the air component of the British Expeditionary Force. In great secrecy, photo-reconnaissance Spitfires were sent to France, operating from places like Lille-Seclin, very close to the Belgian border, using as a cover the Camouflage Unit – which was also known as Sidney Cotton's air force.

At home there was little to do for the Spitfire squadrons other than to fly in formation, except for some moments of excitement for auxiliary squadrons in Scotland protecting the Rosyth naval base. The first scrambles at Rosyth resulted in Spitfire victories against Junkers Ju 88 and Heinkel He 111 on 16 October 1939. Those Spitfires from auxiliary air force squadrons No 602 and No 603 also brought down the first German military aircraft to fall on British soil since the First World War when a Heinkel was defeated over East Lothian on 29 November.

Many squadrons were engaged in painting and repainting camouflage and squadron codes on their Spitfires. The first iteration was the Temperate Land Scheme of dark 'earth'/dark green upper surfaces that had been devised in 1936. The Royal Air Force national roundel of red/white/blue was also modified and, perhaps most importantly, recognition markings were applied to the under surfaces – black (night) and white on the port and starboard wings respectively. After trials in 1937, the Air Ministry agreed that these markings would give clear recognition for anti-aircraft batteries and the Observer Corps, and it was also said that they would help with quick identification in dogfights, of which there had, so far, been none. These new markings had been painted on the first Spitfires and Hurricanes by the time of the Munich Crisis in September 1938.

The complexity of the problems that faced the Air Ministry in bringing the Spitfire into service is characterised by some facts in Dr Alfred Price's outstanding *Spitfire: Pilots' Stories*. He lists 83 Spitfires that had been delivered by Supermarine but were not yet at the front line, some simply stored awaiting a delivery pilot. An incredible 71 were at Maintenance Units awaiting government-furnished equipment such as armament (weapons from Royal Ordnance were contracted for separately and delivered to the Maintenance Units for fitting) and radio equipment, including the new VHF voice system.

When Lord Beaverbrook created the Ministry of Aircraft Production in May 1940, he railed against the delay in bringing the Supermarine fighter to the front line. He rang the

*This is every commander's dream: a line-up of well-turned-out fighter aircraft and
equally well-trained pilots. These Spitfire Mk Vc fighters have been posed for publicity
at RAF Hawkinge in May 1942. Setting this up would have taken considerable coordination
between the command functions on a squadron – Squadron Leader Robert Oxspring
(the OC), his engineering and ops staff, and of course the groundcrew of No 91 (Nigeria)
Squadron.* Rex Features (Everett Collection)

changes quickly and not without banging together a few heads. The Spitfire was established
in production at Southampton but Castle Bromwich's delays caused some serious problems
at the time of greatest need in mid-1940, when fighters were destroyed in combat, on the
ground or lost through technical problems over France and the English Channel.

Castle Bromwich started building the Mk II in June 1940 at a monthly production rate
of 10, which increased to 23 in July, 37 in August and 56 in September. Eventually, 921 Mk
II standard Spitfires would be built in the Midlands out of 5,665 in total, the remainder
coming from Southampton and the Wiltshire factories. Production at Castle Bromwich grew
to 320 Spitfires a month in 1942 and by 1945 the bulk of the Mk Vs and all Mk IXs were
coming out of this factory.

Training of aircrew remained a considerable problem. During the Battle of Britain, the
lack of trained pilots caused Fighter Command to 'trawl' for pilots from Army Cooperation
and Coastal Commands – bomber pilots were too valuable in case the Germans invaded.
Eventually even Fleet Air Arm pilots were brought into the mix. The numbers were building
up even if the pilot training programme was suffering from the old pre-war stereotyping,
prejudices and inefficiencies.

Production and training gelled just in time for the Battle of Britain proper – the Spitfire's finest hour – to begin in August. Although the Hurricane made the greatest contribution in terms of numbers, the Spitfire has symbolised this crucial phase of the war both nowadays and, as local newspaper reports reveal, at the time as well – although the term 'Battle of Britain' was not recognised until after the end of the Second World War.

A new school of enlightened historical research looks upon the date for the starting of the battle as arbitrary and based on a convenient British date rather than an examination of the operational picture following the German invasion of the Low Countries and France on 10 May. Royal Air Force Fighter Command came under increasing pressure in the skies over France and Belgium in May 1940 with Hurricanes based in northern France and Spitfires operating at range from predominantly No 11 Group air stations in Kent and Sussex. Spitfire loss rates at this time were around five per cent of those scrambled as against Hurricane losses at seven per cent.

Air Marshal Sir Wilfrid Freeman GCB, DSO, MC

Born 18 July 1888
Died 15 May 1953
Air Member for Research & Development, 1936–40
Vice Chief of the Air Staff, 1940–42
Chief Executive, Ministry of Air Production, 1942–45

Wilfrid Freeman is a key figure in the Spitfire story. It was his drive and determination that galvanised the Air Ministry into ordering the Spitfire in time for the outbreak of war. Although a relatively unknown figure in the wider world, Freeman was one of the most important and influential people in rearmament during the period immediately before the Second World War.

After a distinguished career as a fighter pilot and as an air-power commander, Freeman took membership of the Air Council with alacrity and plunged in with characteristic relish. His remit as Air Member for Research & Development was simple: choose the aircraft with which to rearm the Royal Air Force. The Spitfire seems to have been top of his list.

Following an official visit to Germany by air force and industry leaders, newly appointed Air Chief Marshal Sir Cyril Newall worked with Freeman and the Minister for the Coordination of Defence, Sir Thomas Inskip, to increase funding for fighter production – Hurricanes and Spitfires – by means of a programme known as Scheme J. This would see the Metropolitan Air Force, which was charged with Home Defence, increased in size and later, after Germany's union with Austria, the Supply Committee of the Air Council was able to order equipment without recourse to HM Treasury – an excellent move to cut red tape but one that was almost too late.

Freeman's R&D remit was extended in 1938 to include aircraft production as it was clear that the areas of R&D and production should be linked in these formative years. This

BATTLE OF BRITAIN TIMELINE

12 May

As the *Blitzkrieg* developed, the first skirmishes between the Spitfire and its German opponent, the *Jagdwaffe*, the Bf 109E, were fought over Amsterdam on 12 May 1940 (some sources state 13 May), and the Netherlands sued for peace on 14 May.

16 May

Churchill, under pressure from the French government to send more fighters to France, firmly pushed back with Fighter Command, under the leadership of Air Chief Marshal Sir Hugh Dowding, who was convinced that every fighter, especially Spitfires, would be needed to defend British skies – how right he was proved to be.

23 May

Spitfires of No 54 Squadron shot down Bf 109s over Calais-Marck airfield; among the victorious pilots were Flying Officers Al Deere and Johnny Allen.

24 May

This day was a snapshot of the hectic air battles over northern France. It saw the last operational flight of P9374, flown by Flying Officer Peter Casenove of No 92 Squadron. Shot down near Calais, the Spitfire lay buried in the beach sand only to be exhumed and become the earliest flying example in the world. No 92 Squadron, led by Bob Stanford Tuck, was in constant action during this time along with other units from No 12 Group air stations, forward based in Kent and Essex.

29 May

This was a day of intense air operations over the beaches of Dunkirk and the ports of Calais and Boulogne as the British Expeditionary Force was withdrawn from the Franco-Belgian front with Hurricanes still operating from French airfields to the south and west of Paris.

4 June

The evacuation of Dunkirk (Operation Dynamo) was completed, with 338,226 Allied soldiers and some civilians saved – but Fighter Command lost 67 Spitfires in protecting the shipping. Over 100,000 British troops and airmen remained in France south of the River Somme and were even reinforced.

14 June

The surrender of Paris.

18 June

Churchill made the famous speech to the House of Commons in which he used the term 'Battle of Britain'. The Prime Minister said that the Battle of France was over – 'I expect that the Battle of Britain is about to begin'. That night, Flight Lieutenant 'Sailor' Malan of No 74 Squadron destroyed two Heinkel He 111 night bombers as he began his progress to becoming a Spitfire ace.

30 June

This is regarded by German sources as the first day of the Battle of Britain as this was date on which *Reichsmarschall* Hermann Göring ordered his forces to engage the fighters of the Royal Air Force and draw them into battle. In his directive he ordered that bomber strikes were to be focused on attacking British coastal convoys, South Coast radar stations, aircraft factories and the airfields of Fighter Command. The reputation of the Spitfire was such that many Luftwaffe *Kampfpiloten* (fighter pilots) claimed to have been shot down by one.

10 July

Traditionally the first day of Phase One, known to the Luftwaffe as *Kanalkampf*. Attacks on convoys continued until 12 August.

16 July

Hitler released Directive No 16 for the invasion of Britain under the operational code words *Unternehmen Seelöwe* (Operation Sealion).

12 August

The intended start date for Phase Two, with Luftwaffe action against radar stations and forward fighter airfields across Britain, codenamed *Adlerangriff* or 'Eagle Attack'. In the event, it was delayed until the next day.

A close shave for Pilot Officer Andrew Mamedoff after combat over the Isle of Wight on 24 August. He returned with such damage that the tail end collapsed on landing. Museum of Army Flying

13 August

The delayed *Adlertag*, 'Eagle Day', took place. No 609 Squadron's Spitfire destroyed 13 enemy aircraft that were attacking Portland, Dorset.

15 August

Variously known as 'The Greatest Day' or 'Black Thursday', this date saw Fighter Command fly 974 sorties against 1,786 individual Luftwaffe raids, with losses of 30 against 75.

18 August

'The Hardest Day': the day of the greatest losses on both sides.

20 August

Churchill's famous speech to the House of Commons citing 'The Few' for the first time.

23/24 August

Phase Three: the first bombs fall on London.

7 September

Phase Four: massed raids on London.

15 September

Every single aircraft of No 11 Group was in action on this date, which is now commemorated as Battle of Britain Day. Eight squadrons of Spitfires engaged German formations attacking London.

17 September

The German land invasion was called off.

26 September

The Spitfire factory at Woolston, Southampton was bombed.

29 October

The last substantial raids against English targets.

31 October

This is regarded as 'The Last Day'. Summing up the Battle of Britain for the Spitfire, more than 215 were lost in combat or through bombing, and about 45 in flying accidents

*Eloquent and brimming with moral courage, Air Chief Marshal Sir Wilfrid Freeman (centre)
saw to it that the Spitfire was ordered, funded and developed. His tenures on the
Air Council and later as the Chief Executive of the Ministry of Aircraft Production were
critical to the Spitfire. Here he is listening to Air Marshal Alec Coryton, Controller of
Research & Development.* RAF Museum

enabled the emphasis to be shared between airframes and aero engines as well, with the
latter including the construction for Rolls-Royce of the Crewe site, which was functioning
within a year of the start of building work.

But it is the Spitfire for which Freeman can take most credit. His vital telephone conversation,
on 26 May 1936, to Flight Lieutenant Humphrey Edwardes-Jones at RAF Martlesham
Heath has gone down in the history of the Spitfire as a pivotal moment. Edwardes-Jones was
the first service test pilot to fly the Spitfire and his somewhat guarded comments on an open
line to Freeman resulted in an immediate decision to order 310 Spitfires from Vickers. It is
said that Freeman consulted no one but used his authority as a member of the Air Council
and put his job on the line for something in which he believed – and he was proved right.

Freeman struggled against some misguided judgements by the political leadership in
1939, overwhelmed as they were by the prospect of war. The issues over the control and
effectiveness of the Civilian Repair Organisation (CRO), run by Lord Nuffield, became
critical. It was the chaos of the CRO and lack of drive in aircraft production that led in May
1940 to the creation of the Ministry of Air Production (MAP), which proved to be as vital a
step as any other administrative decision in the ramping up of Spitfire production. Freeman's
relationship with Lord Beaverbrook, who was appointed Minister for Aircraft Production,

was strained and by November 1940 this resulted in Freeman being moved, under protest, to become Vice-Chief of the Air Staff, a new post created for him but not wanted by him.

In December 1941, when Churchill departed to Washington DC, taking the Chief of the Air Staff, Air Chief Marshal Lord Portal, with him, Freeman became acting Chief of the Air Staff. This allowed him to see clearly the problems that Beaverbrook had created in the MAP by dispensing with process and planning. Freeman's talents had been missed and after Beaverbrook had departed the Ministry, in April 1941, it was clear that, for better control, the job required a champion of air power who understood the complexities of the Royal Air Force. With the support of Portal, Sir Charles Craven, chairman of Vickers Armstrong and Chief Executive of the MAP, and a man of some influence, approached Churchill to have Freeman brought back into the MAP as his successor to run what was in effect the largest industry in Britain.

On 19 October 1942 Portal and Craven got their way. Freeman was appointed Chief Executive of the MAP, with full executive powers. It did mean moving to the retired list but Freeman accepted this move as he could immediately set to work on a series of highly important developments, including the Merlin-engined Mustang and the development of the Hawker Tempest.

When Freeman returned to the MAP there were over 1.6 million workers under its control, and by 1944 the figure rose to two million, of whom 800,000 were women – about 40 per cent of the workforce compared with a proportion of around 10 per cent for the rest of British industry.

Among Freeman's achievements in the role was to promote the improvements to the Spitfire necessary to bring it up to scratch compared with German fighters. His first priority, however, had to be the heavy bomber force, especially the Halifax and Lancaster. It can be argued that the Spitfire did not need his attention at this stage of its development, and the fighter was well supported at Vickers, Supermarine and the MAP.

In the wider re-equipment of the Royal Air Force, Freeman can also take credit for the development of the Hurricane and the Mosquito. He has been called the 'Czar of Procurement' and certainly he set the standards needed for the future shape and size of the British aircraft industry. Sadly his successors did not equal his calibre.

Air Chief Marshal Sir Cyril Newall AM KCMG

Born 15 February 1886
Died 30 November 1963
Chief of the Air Staff, 1938–40

Despite a strong 'bomber' pedigree, Cyril Newall was a late and perhaps not totally convinced convert to the 'fighter' school of thinking. Nevertheless, as Chief of the Air Staff before and during the Battle of Britain, he lent the weight of the Royal Air Force behind Spitfire production and repair.

Air Chief Marshal Sir Cyril Newall may not have been the brightest bulb in the Royal Air Force chandelier but he eventually turned from the 'bomber will get through' philosophy to supporting fighters. His appreciation of Whitehall politics was not keen and he fell foul of the 'big beasts', particularly Lord Beaverbrook. He is seen here (left) in Cairo in happier times as AOC Middle East Command 1931–35, with Lieutenant General Sir John Burnett-Stuart, GOC British Troops in Egypt 1931–34. RAF Museum

Newall was an early aviator, having learned to fly in 1911 at Larkhill, the world's first dedicated military aerodrome. During the First World War he was awarded the Albert Medal for his courage in walking into a burning bomb store and controlling the fire. By the end of the war he was deputy to the founding father of the Royal Air Force, Lord Trenchard, in the Independent Bombing Force. After war service he remained in the Royal Air Force and worked through the ranks, commanding at each one.

His experience with the Independent Bombing Force and his adherence to the Trenchard doctrine of strategic bombing made him believe that the 'bomber will get through', an oft-quoted political mantra of the time. In the rearmament debates of the 1930s Newall supported the bomber faction against the fighter faction, which was championed by Dowding, Churchill and other crystal-clear thinkers.

Newall's appointment as Chief of the Air Staff, the most senior position in the Royal Air Force, on 1 September 1937 was an unexpected move by Lord Swinton, the Secretary of State for Air, and it shocked the Royal Air Force establishment, confirming that the bomber faction was in the ascendency. By convention, the outgoing Chief would recommend his successor and the Secretary of State would ratify it before the proposed appointment went to No 10 Downing Street for agreement and finally to the Monarch for the seal of approval. The outgoing Chief, Air Chief Marshal Sir Edward Ellington, had recommended that his successor should be Hugh Dowding, who was more senior than Newall, and everyone had expected that to happen.

Newall's main area of deficit was failing to understand the way in which politicians think and work. Although he did come to support the production of increased numbers of Spitfires and Hurricanes, he was, perhaps, a little slow to recognise that the bomber would not always get through and in fact wrote a memo to Lord Swinton to that effect in 1938, in somewhat guarded terms. He was, however, won over to the fighter faction later that year following the report by the Minister for Defence Coordination, Sir Thomas Inskip, calling for more Spitfires and Hurricanes. Newall understood enough to support the radical changes needed in the aircraft industry, including the creation of shadow factories, double-shift working and the bringing in of new talent to manage the industrial output.

His lack of understanding of how politics worked applied both at Westminster and within the Royal Air Force. At the beginning of the war Newall was criticised by Lord Trenchard for not launching a strategic bomber offensive. In the autumn of 1940 Sir John Salmond, a former Chief of the Air Staff and Director of Armament Production at the Ministry of Aircraft Production, held Newall responsible – along with Hugh Dowding – for the lack of night fighter protection for British cities. Finally his political shortcomings led to his dismissal at the request of Winston Churchill in October 1940.

Not realising that the relationship between Lord Beaverbrook and Churchill was significant, Newall picked a fight with Beaverbrook about control of aircraft production at a time when the latter was riding high with the Prime Minister's support at the Ministry of Aircraft Production. Newall was retired from the Royal Air Force and sent to New Zealand as Governor-General, a post he held for the rest of the war.

Squadron Leader Henry Cozens AFC

Born 13 March 1904
Died 21 June 1995
OC No 19 Squadron, 1937–40

Spitfire development certainly benefited from the skill of its development and production test pilots, but its entry into service and subsequent initial operational success can be attributed to Henry Cozens.

Leading 'A' Flight of No 19 Squadron up from RAF Duxford in May 1939 is Squadron Leader Henry Cozens, closest to the camera. The formation in echelon starboard has been arranged for the press, who were flying in a Blenheim. Bright and competent, Cozens was well connected in the Air Ministry and managed to get command of the first Spitfire squadron. His initial work on development of the Spitfire for operational service was invaluable and allowed Dowding to have 11 operational squadrons at readiness on 3 September 1939. Imperial War Museum

Cozens commanded No 19 Squadron at RAF Duxford in 1938, then flying the Gloster Gauntlet open-cockpit, biplane fighter before it became the first unit to receive Supermarine's new monoplane fighter that August. By his own account, Cozens used his influence in the Air Ministry to have the Spitfire's service debut at RAF Duxford, near Cambridge, rather further north, at RAF Catterick, 'which would be too far for distinguished visitors to reach from London.'

Air Ministry orders were that the Spitfire should be flown extensively and it was! Both No 19 and No 66 Squadrons received early production Spitfires in August 1938 and commenced intensive flying trials programme. In fact they found themselves able to report back to the Air Ministry after just 200 hours with a series of recommendations that would benefit the fighter in service and be applied to all, or almost all, of the 310 Spitfires in Supermarine's first production batch. As production slowly got underway, those early Spitfires were received on squadrons at the rate of about one a week, apparently without any armament, so it was well into 1939 before No 19 received all 16 of its Spitfires, allowing it to be deemed 'operational' and finally able to dispense with its Gloster Gauntlets.

One of the key innovations proposed by Cozens to Supermarine senior test pilot Jeffrey Quill was the constant-speed propeller, which gave the airscrew the right pitch settings for every speed. In other words, the propeller had automatic gearing for a fine pitch for take-off with a coarser pitch for climb/cruise and combat power. An hydraulic undercarriage retraction system was also fitted quickly when it became clear, mainly through Cozens' bandaged knuckles being displayed to management at Supermarine, that the manual pump-action system was unsatisfactory. Cozens can also take credit for the bulged cockpit canopy, improved oil seals and starter motors for the Merlin engines.

Cozens received the Air Force Cross for his daring work, including the first night firing of armament (which by all accounts caused disquiet among early Spitfire pilots because of the recoil effect) and the successful introduction to service of a new type without losing a pilot. He survived the Second World War and retired in 1947 as an Air Commodore.

Air Chief Marshal Sir Hugh Dowding GCVO KCB

Born 24 April 1882
Died 15 February 1970
Air Officer Commanding Fighter Command, 1936–40

Sadly never totally recognised in his lifetime for his genius, Hugh Dowding is one of the great names in both the Spitfire story and the defeat of Hitler's plans for the conquest of the United Kingdom.

Dowding created Fighter Command and his amazing ability to recognise and harness modern technology, from the eight-gun fighter to radio direction finding (as radar was called in the beginning), enabled him to create the world's first integrated air-defence system that brought together the best of the Royal Air Force with the power of the civilian Observer

Hugh Dowding was the hero of the Battle of Britain: without his leadership Fighter Command would not have been ready for combat let alone survived the Luftwaffe's onslaught. A fighter pilot by training, he understood his people but he was not comfortable with the 'political' demands of his role, such as entertaining King George VI at RAF Bentley Priory on 6 September 1939. Rex Features (Rota)

Dowding did not always see eye to eye with Douglas Bader, but here, five years after the Battle of Britain, the two seem to have much to discuss. Political history in the immediate aftermath of the war almost wrote out Dowding's achievements and in more recent years it has been fashionable to question Bader's leadership. To the serious historian, both have their honoured place in the Spitfire story. RAF Museum

Corps and the air-defence guns of the Royal Regiment of Artillery, which Dowding had joined as a young man in 1900.

After flying in the Royal Flying Corps and commanding No 16 Squadron, he took up a series of command and staff appointments, including in the Middle East and the Air Ministry, where he began to understand both what new technology had to offer and the risks of adopting it too quickly. Regarding the latter, he had signed off the ill-fated R101 airship without a proper risk assessment and held himself to blame for allowing it to fly untested with the resultant loss of life when it crashed on its maiden overseas voyage. He took that failure to heart and ensured that the air defence of Britain would benefit from tried-and-tested technology and operating procedures.

Working closely with the then Air Commodore Park, Dowding created a trials unit at RAF Northolt, a fighter station charged with the air defence of metropolitan London. This fundamental work formed the foundation for the system that helped Fighter Command win the Battle of Britain.

In the 1930s the concept of ground-directed air defence was unknown. The fragile biplane fighters of the era were short on 'legs' (range) because they had been designed with small fuel tanks and their engines were less efficient than those in use only five years later. The fighters also lacked firepower and, very often, radios.

Although new technologies such as radio detection and ranging (radar), VHF (Very High Frequency) radio for voice communications, and radio transponders (IFF or Identification, Friend or Foe) were at the experimental stage of development, Dowding, by then close to the normal age of retirement, embraced the these innovations because he believed that they could be an effective counter to massed bomber formations.

In July 1936 Royal Air Force Fighter Command was established with Hugh Dowding as it first Air Officer Commanding. He moved his headquarters to Bentley Priory at Stanmore, north London, where an operations room – the 'bunker' – was set up deep underground.

The United Kingdom was divided into Group areas, each with its own headquarters that controlled a number of sectors and the squadrons within those sectors. The system that Park and Dowding constructed became known, naturally enough, as the Dowding system, and it allowed information to be passed, filtered and acted upon with speed and agility.

The first line of defence was formed by the Chain Home radar stations that Dowding had erected from the River Humber to Cornwall to detect raiding aircraft coming from the Continent. A two-tier approach of high-level and low-level detection was added in 1940 by harnessing the IFF radio pulses from a friendly fighter, known to fighter pilots as 'Pipsqueak'. Dowding was also insistent on ground-to-air communications, with ground-based direction from an experienced fighter controller sitting in a station operations room with a vast plan/position map stretched out in front of him.

All this procedure came from trials of the Dowding system in a hut at RAF Northolt and became known as ground-controlled interception. Germany had nothing like it until the strategic bombing of the Reich in 1943 and even then the Nazi command failed to understand the merits of dispersed and redundant capabilities that allowed one sector to take over from another in the event of it being rendered unserviceable.

At the height of the Battle of Britain, when the Luftwaffe turned its attention to attacking the air stations of Fighter Command, particularly in Park's No 11 Group (Kent and Sussex) and Air Vice-Marshal Quintin Brand's No 10 Group (Hampshire to Cornwall), operations rooms were bombed and some put out of action. The period of black-out was limited by a pre-planned deployment of the Ops room to other locations close by, including shops and village halls. The unsung heroes of these enforced moves were the General Post Office telephone engineers who could restring telephone lines, a key part of the communications set-up, in a matter of hours.

Dowding fought hard to keep the Spitfire squadrons under his command engaged in British-based operations in 1940, despite the increasingly desperate calls from the French government, relayed by Churchill, for more fighters to be sent to France after the German *Blitzkrieg*. In theory, the French Air Force was larger than the Royal Air Force but its fighters were less effective, and command and control were poor, with fighters maintaining wasteful standing patrols rather than being directed from the ground to known raids or reconnaissance sorties by the Germans. The French did not want to coordinate with the deployed British Hurricane squadrons, except to 'require' that they were painted in the same style of markings. The French Air Force, like much of the French military and some British army seniors, was stuck in the notion of fighting the last war and having plenty of time to do everything – even, in the French case, to the extent of ordering fighters from America after the Germans invaded Poland.

Although a few camera-equipped Spitfires of No 2 Camouflage Unit, the cover name for the in-theatre photo-reconnaissance capability, were operating from Lille-Seclin airfield covering targets in western Germany from Aachen to the Ruhr industrial areas, Dowding did not let his precious Spitfires deploy except in exceptional circumstances. In May and June 1940, Spitfires from No 92 and No 609 Squadrons respectively escorted Winston Churchill to Paris and Orléans for meetings, but none were used in an offensive role.

Over Dunkirk, Dowding pushed the Spitfires into mounting fighting patrols over, and inland of, the beaches, but they were forward deployed to Manston and Rochford rather than to French airfields south of the Somme.

He took some important steps in releasing to operations foreign fighter pilots under training, including Canadians, Poles and Czechs. He was always concerned that the lack of good spoken English among continental aircrew from Belgium, France, Czechoslovakia and Poland would hamper the finely balanced radio communications system he had set up, but any such concerns were marginal when compared with the fighting dedication of the pilots and their groundcrew.

Another of his wise policies was to circulate squadrons from the front line in No 11 Group to less demanding areas, such as No 13 Group in the north. By this means tired pilots, particularly his talented flight and squadron commanders, were able to rest, which saved them from burning out in the air and causing Fighter Command to lose more top pilots. They could also pass on their experience to younger pilots, some of whom had just 10 hours on Spitfires before coming to the front line.

Dowding's genius of preparing for the Battle of Britain four years before and his steady leadership, getting the best out of his subordinate commanders, and the equipment at his disposal, should give him a place in the gallery of British military heroes. He won the Battle of Britain because he husbanded the available Spitfires, inspired his subordinates, and was well prepared for the country's first major air battle in history. Despite his nickname, he was not 'Stuffy' but instead just a tad 'old school'.

By October, the Battle was won. The Luftwaffe could not keep up with the attrition of the fighting – but, to be honest, Fighter Command was also experiencing problems as Spitfire production faltered after the Supermarine factory at Southampton was destroyed on 26 September. Production would pick up in early 1941, but it was nevertheless a trying time.

Thereafter the problem for Dowding was that the daylight defence of Britain had been successful but he had no real solution to the night-time blitz on London and the Midlands. Spitfires were particularly tricky to operate at night, especially with their narrow-track undercarriage – and the wider gait of the Hurricane was not much better.

In the end Dowding's nemesis was Air Chief Marshal Sir John Salmond and his report on the shortcomings of night fighting. The report was critical of Dowding, who did not fully endorse its recommendations. Dowding wanted airborne radar to be developed and was prepared to wait for it. His rival, Air Chief Marshal Sholto Douglas, an officer of limited ability but one with a staunch mentor in Sir Archibald Sinclair, the Secretary of State for Air, saw the way the politics were moving and lost no time in supporting Salmond, and in due course, in November 1940, Douglas replaced Dowding. The role that followed for Dowding was to identify areas of over-manning in the Royal Air Force, a task that was bound to cause friction – and indeed it did. Dowding had made a life-long enemy of the new Chief of the Air Staff, Lord Portal, by the time he retired in 1942.

Sholto Douglas oversaw the winter 1940–41 offensive operations over Occupied Europe in which more pilots and aircraft were lost than in the Battle of Britain. Douglas was finally able to practise his 'Big Wing' theories and they were found wanting in combat, because the time required for aircraft to form up inevitably reduced the time available in the combat area. Dowding's disciple, Keith Park, was also replaced by Air Vice-Marshal Trafford Leigh-Mallory, whose divisive failure to support No 11 Group in the Battle of Britain was a result of rivalry over the 'Big Wing' fantasies.

Air Vice-Marshal (Sir) Keith Park GCB CB MC* DFC
Born 15 June 1892
Died 6 February 1975
AOC No 11 Group Fighter Command, 1939–40
AOC Malta, 1942–44
AOC Middle East, 1944–45
AOC Allied Air Command, South-East Asia, 1945

Standing in Waterloo Place, abutting the venerable Athenaeum, the London Club, is a statue of a reserved New Zealand pilot and leader who, more than anyone except possibly Sir Hugh Dowding, prevented a British defeat in the Battle of Britain. It took 70 years to be erected but the statue of Air Marshal Sir Keith Park is well deserved and appreciated.

The juxtaposition is ironic as the Athenaeum is best considered conservative and traditional, whereas Park was anything but, having a skill for bold leadership and a flair for being unconventional. Park excelled not only during the Battle of Britain but also in Malta, where he took the fight back to Sicily and North Africa.

Park was born in New Zealand to a middle-class Scottish family and was educated there. He joined the Territorial Army in the New Zealand Field Artillery and later went to sea in the Merchant Navy. He was called up to the Reserve in 1914 and joined his regiment as a non-commissioned officer, travelling to Europe in time to take part in the Gallipoli landings of April 1915.

He was given a field commission for his courageous leadership in the trenches of the

Keith Park was a tactical leader of the highest calibre. He carried the absolute trust of his boss, Air Chief Marshal Sir Hugh Dowding, and that was a major factor in the Fighter Command success story. The two great exponents of air supremacy had worked together before the Second World War and there was no better team when it came to defending Britain in 1940. RAF Museum

Dardanelles and later commanded a battery at Suvla Bay, before joining the Royal Horse Artillery on transfer to the British Army, leaving the Turkish campaign in January 1916.

Historians point to his admiration for General Sir William Birdwood, the Australia & New Zealand Army Corps commander, as important in forming Park's views on command. Birdwood's creative leadership style was to figure in Park's style of command in the Second World War both in Britain and in overseas theatres.

Another formative experience for Park during the First World War was the Battle of the Somme, where superior German aerial reconnaissance allowed the German artillery to target their British counterparts with devastating counter-battery fire. He took advantage of an offer from the Royal Flying Corps to inspect gun positions from the air and noted, in contrast to more conventional soldiers of the period, the value of the 'third dimension'.

After being wounded and unable to ride, Park left the Royal Horse Artillery and joined the Royal Flying Corps in December 1916. For the next 30 years, he made the air domain his own through commands from squadron to group.

On qualifying to fly, Park joined No 48 (Fighter) Squadron, which was one of the first to fly the Bristol Fighter, a two-man biplane that remained in Royal Air Force service into the 1920s. In the Bristol Fighter, Park and his gunner, Sgt Arthur Noss, achieved several distinguished combats and Park was awarded the Military Cross in August 1917 during some of the toughest air battles of the First World War. The aggressive use of fighter aircraft and the concept of operations must have begun to mature in Park's mind at this time. During his spell with the Royal Flying Corps, Park became a quadruple ace with at least 20 victories. Being based forward near Dunkirk, his operations were aggressive and effective which, less than 25 years later, would be the hallmark of No 11 Group and particularly the employment of Spitfires from Malta.

Park was commissioned into the new Royal Air Force and went to the new Staff College at RAF Andover in 1922. This establishment was the crucible for new talent and new thinking – and for bringing together an officer corps that would have to fight the Second World War in the air.

Fighters were always in Park's blood. He was posted to HQ Royal Air Force Middle East as Air Staff Officer Operations and then back to Air Defence of Great Britain, the forerunner of Fighter Command, before commanding No 111 Squadron. Within six months he was posted to RAF Hornchurch as station commander and then back to HQ Fighting Area before being appointed to command RAF Northolt in January 1931.

His remarkable career also included being Air Attaché, Buenos Aires and attending the Imperial Defence College before another fighter station command at RAF Tangmere, a place synonymous with the Battle of Britain and air operations to take the fight to the enemy in Occupied France.

As an Air Commodore, Park was appointed Senior Air Staff Officer to Sir Hugh Dowding in 1938 and it was this two-year partnership that created and implemented the great success of the Battle of Britain, operationally and tactically respectively, with limited means and not always the best of co-operation from other commanders.

In April 1940 Park was promoted to Air Vice-Marshal and left HQ Fighter Command at Stanmore for RAF Uxbridge and No 11 Group a matter of six miles away. This was the time of great German expansion with the invasions of Denmark and Norway on 9 April, and the planning, as yet unrevealed, for the invasion of Belgium, the Netherlands and France. In France, the Royal Air Force had deployed Hurricane fighters with the Air Component of the British Expeditionary Force and with them the Advanced Air Striking Force; both were commanded separately from Fighter Command, which was charged with the air defence of Great Britain (at that time not at range but very much domestically on the mainland).

Dowding and Park, working together to husband pilots and machines for the onslaught to come, resisted all attempts to send precious Spitfires to France but did operate a system that allowed Spitfire squadrons to deploy flights forward to French airfields in the morning, as long as they returned to British bases in the evening.

Dunkirk was the first test of both Park, as a tactical commander, and of the Dowding system to control the stream of fighter aircraft over the beaches and the wider Pas-de-Calais region. At the same time, Park needed to train his operators and practise contingency plans, as well as ensure that aerodromes were protected with anti-aircraft artillery.

When Hitler moved against the Low Countries and France on 10 May, there was an almost overwhelming urge to support the three victims of German aggression but Dowding ordered Park to hold firm and not deploy forward, other than on a daily basis. No 12 Group did send fighters on aggressive patrols to Amsterdam, for example, but No 11 Group concentrated on covering the daily transport flight. The British air forces deployed in France had a logistics trail that relied upon transport aircraft rather than ferries and trucks, and it was found lacking in the ability to provide sheer volume.

By July, what should have been a concerted national effort to support the hardest-pressed area, No 11 Group, had become acrimonious with the self-serving Air Vice-Marshal Trafford Leigh-Mallory in No 12 Group allowing his fighters to roam into No 11 Group's area in search of 'prey'. This compares badly with a lesser-known but more effective commander in No 10 Group, Air Vice-Marshal Quintin Brand, who provided unquestioning support for No 11 Group from his airfields such as Middle Wallop and Boscombe Down.

To see his squadrons in action, Park used a personal Hurricane, kept at his former command, RAF Northolt, just down the A40 from Uxbridge. In this machine he flew the Group Area and dropped in unannounced on his squadron commanders. He used a Hurricane rather than a Spitfire for two reasons: first, there were more Hurricanes and Spitfires were more precious; second, the Hurricane's wide-track undercarriage meant that the fighter was easier to land and Park required fewer hours to remain competent for flying.

Park's great legacy to the nation, the Commonwealth and possibly the world was his willingness to listen, his confidence in his pilots and their leaders, and his preparedness to ignore dogma. He allowed his commanders to exercise their judgement in tactical employment of limited fighters against seemingly overwhelming odds.

This creative marshalling of forces, particularly the Spitfire squadrons, the bulk of which were allocated to No 11 Group, was a key battle-winning factor. As the Germans stepped up

Falling victim to Whitehall intrigue in Fighter Command, Park was posted to the Mediterranean, first to defend Malta and then as AOC Middle East Command taking the fight to the enemy. Here he is briefing Lord Moyne DSO* PC, British Minister for the Middle East, at the Royal Air Force HQ in Heliopolis. Previously instrumental in attracting Jamaican recruits to the Royal Air Force, Moyne was murdered by Jewish terrorists in Cairo on 6 November 1944. RAF Museum

the momentum by attacking airfields and aircraft production facilities, losses on the ground mounted and there were real concerns about the ability of the Civilian Repair Organisation to mend and return aircraft, especially Spitfires, to service at the required rate, as well as for new airframes to be delivered in a timely manner from the Maintenance Units where government-furnished equipment was fitted.

As the tempo of the Battle of Britain developed, Park was unable to spend as much time out at Squadron locations, using his personal charm and charisma to support his pilots and the groundcrew. He subsequently spent more time in the No 11 Group bunker at RAF Uxbridge, a facility closer to London that was bound to mean more dealings with all sorts of distinguished visitors.

There was the famous occasion on 15 September 1940 – today commemorated as Battle of Britain Day – when Winston Churchill arrived unannounced at a time when every available fighter was committed and there were no reserves. On 6 September 1940 HM King George VI and Queen Elizabeth were at Brooklands shortly after the Luftwaffe had attacked aircraft factories there, including the Hawker works. Park had that morning assembled 17 squadrons, predominantly Spitfires, to protect Brooklands and Weybridge, and the Royal couple missed that great air action. After noon, a further 19 squadrons were scrambled against 100-plus German raiders and for the first time No 12 Group put up five squadrons in a Big Wing in support of No 11 Group. On that occasion it worked but the time taken to put the squadrons into the air meant the No 12 Group fighters often hit the bombers on their return flights after the damage had been done.

Park's tactical genius now came to fore. With the Chain Home radar stations only giving 20 minutes' warning of German formations building up over France, the squadrons had to get Spitfires and Hurricanes off the ground in less than five minutes, and in just 15 minutes get to 20,000ft for Hurricanes or 25,000ft for Spitfires.

Park and his principal controller, Group Captain Gilbert Harcourt Smith, created comprehensive books of instructions with appendices and directives covering every aspect of the deployment of fighters. This included the integration with other Groups as well as Park's authorised opposite strategy to the Big Wing that involved bringing up single squadrons or pairs of squadrons from the same airfield and allowing them, sometimes only two flights strong, to ripple through the engagement as required rather than being all up and all down, as the Big Wing would dictate. The two men were to work together again in May 1943 when Park's Senior Air Staff Officer was Harcourt Smith, who was eventually promoted to Air Vice-Marshal.

Park was dismissed as AOC No 11 Group in November 1940. In a calculated move to insult Park, Air Chief Marshal Sholto Douglas, who had replaced Dowding, made Leigh-Mallory the new Air Operating Commanding in his place. Park is said to have been bitter about his treatment for the rest of his life.

Park was able to vindicate his theories in another theatre, when he replaced Air Vice-Marshal Hugh Lloyd in Malta and brought with him Wing Commander John Thompson, an ace from No 11 Group during the Battle of Britain, where he had pioneered aggressive head-on attacks against massed bomber formations. This was a combat indicator that Park wanted to go on to the offensive.

Thompson, in command of the Ta'qali, then Hal Far and finally Luqa Wings (the only man to lead all three Malta Spitfire wings), would play a key part in the Fighter Interception Plan that called for Malta's Spitfires to be deployed north of Malta and Gozo. These operations, which involved use of the newly arrived Spitfire Mk Vb at altitude, saw 142 enemy aircraft destroyed in July 1942 for the loss of only 38 Spitfires.

Malta still suffered daily and nearly starved more than once during Park's tenure. He not only defended the islands but also went on the offensive against Axis air forces in Sicily. After the invasion of Sicily and further operations against the mainland, Park was appointed Air Officer Commanding the Middle East Command and left Malta in January 1944.

His final air appointment of the Second World War also saw him, as Allied Commander South-East Asia, exploit the Spitfire with great success over Burma and in the final victory against Imperial Japan.

In a final salute to the Spitfire, Park personally selected one to be donated to the Auckland War Memorial in his native New Zealand. It is still there, along with the Battle of Britain hero's uniforms and decorations.

Park's name also lives on in two quintessentially British memorials. In 2013 the 'Battle of Britain' class steam railway locomotive *Sir Keith Park* (34052) was rededicated at Kidderminster station as part of a preservation effort by the Severn Valley Railway, 66 years after the great man named it at Brighton, just after he was promoted to Air Chief Marshal and retired to his native New Zealand.

At RAF Northolt, which is still a fully functioning Royal Air Force station, there is a major effort to recreate an Operations Room that Park and Dowding used to develop the Dowding system of integrated air defence used in the Battle of Britain. The building, saved from demolition by an enthusiast group at the station, was the original Operations Room of Sector-Z, one of seven such sector control rooms in Park's No 11 Group. Park was station commander at RAF Northolt in the period 1931–32 and during the Battle of Britain used the buried Operations Room at RAF Uxbridge, just two miles way, as his headquarters from where he 'ran' No 11 Group.

Air Chief Marshal Sir Charles Portal KG, GCB, OM, DSO*, MC

Born 21 May 1893
Died 22 April 1971
Commander in Chief, Bomber Command, 1940
Chief of the Air Staff, 1940–45

Portal's role in the Spitfire story has two distinct angles: his support for more junior officers, like Air Marshal Freeman, in their attempts to get aircraft production into high gear, and the championing of important innovations, such as pressurised cockpits for photo-reconnaissance and high-altitude fighters, using the Spitfire airframe and new technical developments, including the Griffon engine.

Understanding the threat posed by a resurgent Germany would have been obvious to Portal in his appointment as Deputy Director of Plans in the Air Ministry's Directorate of Operations & Intelligence in December 1930. In this role he would have received the first real accounts of Hitler's plans for the Luftwaffe and, although that organisation did not become 'public' until 1935, he would have been privy to raw intelligence on developments, including Nazi Germany's relationship with Soviet Russia. He left that job as a Group Captain and was posted to Aden.

After his return, he was promoted to Air Vice-Marshal and appointed Director of Organisation at the Air Ministry on 1 September 1937. This was an important post that allowed Portal to influence events and be seen to influence events. Just in time for the outbreak of the Second World War, he was appointed the Air Member for Personnel, another vital position in the Royal Air Force and, in personal terms, always a key position for further advancement.

On the day the Second World War broke out Portal was promoted to Air Marshal and appointed Commander-in-Chief of Bomber Command. Despite the amazing sacrifice of the light bomber crews in France, Bomber Command had had an inglorious start to its strategic bombing offensive, notably as a result of its inability to hit any targets at night. Portal's appointment to this position was not surprising as he was an advocate of strategic bombing, but his command lasted only a short as Air Chief Marshal Sir Arthur Harris soon took over. It is Portal, however, who deserves credit for pushing for the introduction of Merlin-engined heavy bombers to wage war on German industrial cities.

A dyed-in-the-wool Trenchard advocate of independent air power, Portal fought off the Admiralty's attempt to take over Coastal Command at a time in the Battle of the Atlantic when the Air Ministry would give no funding or priority to long-range maritime patrol aircraft. He also succeeded in fighting off the War Office's move against army cooperation flying, which again was under-resourced, and the British Army was only able to fly assault gliders and to pilot artillery-spotting aeroplanes.

Portal's importance to the Prime Minister is apparent from his inclusion in most of the great leader's trips to Canada, the USA and North Africa for his initial meetings with President Roosevelt.

Portal also foresaw the need for a high-altitude fighter, perhaps spurred on by the success in Egypt of No 103 Maintenance Unit, which created a high-altitude Spitfire to combat German Junkers Ju 86P diesel-engined reconnaissance bombers.

Highly intelligent, elegant and wily, Charles Portal was a late convert to the need for fighters. Brought up in the Trenchard tradition of 'the bomber will always get through', Portal commanded Bomber Command in the first months of the Second World War. As Chief of the Air Staff for the whole of Churchill's term as Prime Minister, he was at the centre of power and relished it. RAF Museum

CHAPTER 6

THE PILOTS

This chapter highlights some of the extraordinary achievements of the Spitfire and its pilots during its service career with the Allied air forces in the Second World War. It is not a complete history by any means, but captures the essence of the Spitfire and its contribution to the eventual victories against the Axis powers.

Dunkirk was the Spitfire's real baptism of fire. Spitfire squadrons along the East Coast had been in action since October 1939 against the occasional raider operating from Germany or, latterly, Occupied Europe. Several secretly modified Mk Is, optimised for photo-reconnaissance, had been flying from forward air bases in France to record images of German preparations before and immediately after the German invasion.

The fighting over the Low Countries and France, where Spitfires met Messerschmitt Bf 109s in air combat for the first time, also showed the Air Ministry and its new successor, the Ministry of Aircraft Production, just how much 'punishment' a Spitfire could take. It was No 66 Squadron, based at RAF Duxford, that was in action first on 12 May 1940, when Spitfires were escorting Defiants sent to help the Royal Netherlands Air Force defend Amsterdam. One Bf 109 and four Junkers Ju 87 Stukas were shot down for the loss of a single Spitfire and five Defiants, showing how useless the Defiants were in daylight.

As the air battles developed, more and more fighter resources were allocated to protect the troops, although this was not always apparent to the soldiers on the beaches, leading to unnecessary and ill-judged resentment of the Royal Air Force back in Britain.

The battles over France reduced the number of Spitfires in the Fighter Command order of battle by 75 lost or written-off and, to replace them, Supermarine delivered only 39 between 19 May and 1 June, according to a note delivered to a meeting of the War Cabinet by Lord Beaverbrook. At the same meeting, on 3 June, Dowding gave the total number of Spitfires available as 280, which, interestingly, was 56 more than the number of Hurricanes in service at that time because of the attrition in France.

This reinforced Beaverbrook's view that the whole of Britain's aircraft industry needed to be mobilised for the coming battles over the Channel and southern England and that a Civilian Repair Organisation would be vitally important in maintaining and repairing the nation's fighter aircraft. Centres for Spitfire repair were set up across the country and they included former aero clubs and small aviation repair businesses, thus ensuring a workforce of a very high and regulated standard.

For many modern historians, the Battle of France's closing stages, including the Dunkirk evacuation, were the opening rounds of the Battle of Britain. Royal Air Force Fighter Command learned many lessons with the loss of 67 Spitfires operating from its English bases. The Germans also acquired some early Spitfires during the Battle of France, including two Mk Is – one from No 74 Squadron made a forced landing at Calais and another crash-landed at Le Touquet – and a Mk PR IB, which was abandoned at Reims. There was even a French Spitfire, delivered before war broke out for evaluation against a possible order, captured intact at Orléans and later investigated in detail by the Luftwaffe. Because it was such an early model, however, the data extracted by the Germans during flight trials at their Rechlin experimental centre was misleading and did not reflect the improvements that Supermarine had made by July 1940 and the opening stages of the Battle of Britain.

The Dunkirk operation coincided with the appointment of Air Vice-Marshal Keith Park as Air Officer Commanding No 11 Group, charged with the air defence of Great Britain from the Thames estuary to the Hampshire border. Immediately before his appointment in April 1940, the then Air Commodore Park had been working with Air Chief Marshal Dowding as his Senior Air Staff Officer to create an integrated air defence system using facilities at RAF Northolt. Park's headquarters was at Hillingdon House, RAF Uxbridge, an administration centre just two miles from Northolt. It was Park's calm control of meagre resources that allowed Fighter Command to give air cover to the troop embarkation, first from the harbour moles and then over the beaches. It is worth recalling that over 100,000 British troops remained in France after Dunkirk in an ill-fated effort to stem the German *Blitzkrieg* and support the French.

For reasons best known to itself, the Air Ministry in London decided that the official start of the Battle of Britain would be 10 July. In the intervening period after the Fall of France on 22 June, Fighter Command was tasked with maintaining its traditional Home Defence and escorting light bombers on reconnaissance and offensive operations, as well as fighting patrols over the Luftwaffe's newly acquired bases in the Pas-de-Calais and Normandy.

Despite lessons learned from seeing the Luftwaffe in action during the previous two months, the Air Tactics Branch of the Air Ministry still persisted in the pre-war basic fighting unit of a 'Vic' of three fighters, making up a section, and later the use of a waiver, known as the 'Tail-End Charlie', which mistakenly was thought to be the best defence against a 'bounce' by enemy fighters attacking from above and behind; in fact a waiver had the highest probability of being picked off first in these circumstances. The deficiencies of this tactic became very apparent during the heavy fighting in August, when the total number of Spitfires lost by Fighter Command is thought to have been 125, many of which were in the hands of inexperienced pilots allocated to the job of waiving behind the formation.

Enlightened squadron commanders disliked the 'Vic' and preferred the German formations based on a 'fighting finger four', which allowed much better mutual support. By mid-August Squadron Leader Douglas Bader's No 242 (Canadian) Squadron and Squadron Leader 'Sailor' Malan's No 74 Squadron (which included New Zealand ace Flight Lieutenant Al Deere DFC) adopted a modified practice of flying a squadron in line astern separated by up to a mile of airspace, but many units continued to follow the Air Tactics directive until the end of the year.

There was enlightenment creeping into the aerial fighting of the summer of 1940. Just as the British Army found later in the Western Desert, experience from the vital air battles over Dunkirk and the opening stages of the Battle of Britain showed that leadership of a formed unit was not necessarily best enshrined in the designated commander. Instead, as exemplified by Royal Air Force Fighter Command, the practice that emerged was to have the most experienced pilot, irrespective of rank, lead battle formations. This was a policy that the Luftwaffe had also found effective during the Spanish Civil War and that the US Navy would adopt in the Pacific naval air battles.

After the combination of weather, fatigue and a change in Hitler's war plans saw the reduction of aerial activity over Britain, Occupied Europe became the focus of Fighter Command's attention. Despite having been the architects of victory in the Battle of Britain, Air Chief Marshal Dowding and Air Vice-Marshal Park were replaced, in November 1940, by Air Chief Marshal Sir Sholto Douglas and Air Vice-Marshal Trafford Leigh-Mallory. Military historians have long debated the wisdom, efficacy and timeliness of these changes in command.

Keen to take the fight across the Channel, the new commanders started daylight operations in late 1940 and early 1941. With hindsight, it seems that the lessons of the Battle of Britain identified by the Germans – that operations over a hostile country were severely disadvantaged with limited fuel and with the waters of the English Channel in the way – were not apparent to their British equivalents.

Leigh-Mallory, the architect of the 'Big Wing' concept at No 12 Group, adopted this method for offensive operations in order to bring the Luftwaffe to combat, which he hoped would favour the Spitfire. By now the front-line squadrons had been re-equipped with uprated Spitfire Mk II airframes with improved light-alloy ailerons, while No 92 Squadron received, in February 1941, the first of the Mk V variants with the Merlin 45 engine, which gave the Spitfire better performance at altitude than the Bf 109F.

Two distinct tactical concepts were initially authorised: the Rhubarb comprised fighter sweeps by Spitfires, Hurricanes and twin-engined Whirlwinds over the Normandy and Pas-de-Calais regions; the Circus involved the escort of Blenheim and Boston light bombers over Occupied France and the Low Countries. It was at this time that Spitfires and other offensive types were repainted with dark sea grey and green upper camouflage to make them less conspicuous during cross-Channel flying, and these schemes were retained throughout the war in Europe.

Such fighter sweeps were commanded in the air by a wing leader with several squadrons under his operational command in what was known as a 'beehive' of squadrons, ready to engage the Luftwaffe at every opportunity. Outstanding Spitfire wing leaders at this time included Douglas Bader (Tangmere) and Bob Stanford Tuck (Duxford, then Biggin Hill). Both failed to return from operations, having been captured and imprisoned until 1945.

On 19 August 1942 Spitfires featured in the Dieppe raid (Operation Jubilee) when 48

Spitfire – the pilot's aeroplane. How many times have its pilots been quoted as saying 'a Spitfire is strapped on'? Or 'it was love at first sight'? As Mitchell's baby grew into maturity through the skill of Joe Smith, Alan Clifton and the Hursley Park team, the Spitfire retained its world-class capability. It is exemplified by Hugh Cowin's portrait of a clipped-wing Mk XII somewhere over Wiltshire on test from High Post. Rex Features (Hugh Cowin)

squadrons supported disastrous amphibious-landing operations that resulted in the loss of 70 fighters to enemy action, and 3,367 men killed, wounded or captured. The Spitfire Mk IX was first flown operationally during the Dieppe period, proving itself against the Focke-Wulf Fw 190 and improved Messerschmitt Bf 109Fs.

A month after the ill-fated Dieppe raid, the three US-manned Eagle Squadrons of Fighter Command were disbanded and transferred to the US Army Air Force. The Eagle Squadrons initially flew Hurricanes but converted to Spitfires in 1941, receiving the Mk IX in 1942 just before the handover to American command. So impressed were the US pilots with their Spitfires that they asked for them to be transferred to US control, and so it was that these aircraft became the 4th Fighter Group, flying with stars and bar markings until replaced by Mustangs in 1944.

A cursory look at the aces' scoreboard in 1942 shows that the top 20 scorers were an international bunch, with only seven of them British. The highest-ranking ace was the Canadian George Beurling (see page 181) and there were another three Canadians in the rankings. In addition there were two American volunteers, a Rhodesian, two New Zealanders and four Australians who scored significantly in Spitfires.

The English Channel was the stage for the début in February 1943 of the first Spitfires powered by the newly developed Rolls-Royce Griffon engine. Two units that flew the first Spitfire to be manufactured for the Griffon, the Mk XII, formed the Westhampnett Wing and today the airfield is known as Goodwood – and still hosts Spitfires. No 41 and No 91 Squadrons found the first Griffon-engined Spitfire excellent at low and medium altitudes but lacking performance above 15,000ft and so adapted their tactics accordingly.

Malta was another theatre where the Spitfire was deployed with skill and aggression. Sea Gladiators and Hurricanes flew the initial defensive operations over Malta but several groups of Spitfires were soon despatched because of the aeroplane's versatility. The first delivery of Mk Vs was by packing case in a freighter, but subsequently the Spitfires were launched off aircraft carriers 700 nautical miles from the beleaguered island fortress. Experienced Spitfire pilots, men who had used the latest tactics in Britain, also arrived, some by Sunderland flying boat.

The first combat was recorded on 10 March 1942 when No 249 Squadron was in action against Junkers Ju 88 bombers escorted by Messerschmitt Bf 109 fighters. Thereafter the action was almost non-stop for about the year. There were 13 carrier-launched groups of Spitfires flown to Malta during 1942 and 385 launches from British and American warships, with 367 safe on Malta. During 1942 and 1943 Malta-based Spitfires claimed some 617 enemy aircraft, until gradually bomb-carrying Spitfires started taking the action back against the Axis forces in Sicily.

In the same Mediterranean theatre of operations, the Spitfire was operated in the Western Desert, in defence of Egypt and its Suez Canal, and was also used for the training of pilots in Palestine and Syria. The first squadron to fly Mk Vs became operational in May 1941 and allowed the slower types of aircraft to be used in the ground-attack role while the Spitfires provided fighter top cover.

Reinforcing the Soviet offensive, 150 Spitfire Mk Vb fighters were delivered to Russian squadrons in 1943, together with spare engines; many were transferred via Iraq and Iran, others via the Arctic convoys. The Russians would never publicly admit to having foreign aid and so the Spitfires were only identified some years after the end of the war. Russian Spitfires were used for air defence and for working with the ground troops in front-line aviation regiments under army control. Although that air/land coordination was lacking in France in 1940, the North African campaign started to show from 1942 how vital it was – and the process has developed through to modern operations over Iraq and Afghanistan.

Developing excellent cooperation and good tactical awareness, the Desert Air Force and the 8th Army created the role of forward air controllers and started using cab ranks of bomb-carrying Spitfires stationed airborne and ready to strike enemy targets when called upon by the ground controllers. The experience gained here (and at Dieppe) was used to

Fighter pilots would not have been able to fly without these gentlemen – riggers, fitters, armourers, instrument mechanics and electrical fitters. It is right and fitting that No 609 Squadron's groundcrew should be showing off the score tally of 103 German machines claimed destroyed in the Battle of Britain. Squadrons always collected memorabilia and many examples are displayed today in the Museum of Army Flying. Museum of Army Flying

good effect by the 2nd Tactical Air Force in the operations before, during and after the D-Day landings in June 1944.

Mediterranean operations were extended to the Balkans in 1944, with Spitfires operated first from Italian airstrips and then from Yugoslavian and Greek ones as the German forces were pushed back towards the Reich proper. In spring 1945 Spitfire Mk IXs marked with improvised 'partisan' markings were operated against enemy aircraft as well as in the ground-attack role.

Egypt was the only operational base of the Spitfire floatplane, which was built at the Folland factory at Hamble and fitted with Supermarine-designed floats in September/October 1942. After trials in Scotland, two Spitfire Mk Vs with the Merlin 45 engine were shipped to Egypt's Great Bitter Lake. The requirement for floatplanes came from the lessons learned during the Norway campaign in 1940, when a lack of suitable air bases hampered air operations, and this same factor was foreseen as a factor in the Mediterranean, especially amid the Greek islands. The audacious plan was to operate Spitfire floatplanes against German transport aircraft, flying without escort until surprise had been lost, and then bring them back to Egypt, ready for another operation. In the event, there was no operation but the expertise gained led to a development of the Mk IX version on floats ready for the Pacific theatre, but that planned operation was also dropped.

Against Japan, the Spitfire was also deployed to protect Australia and to prevent the Imperial Japanese Army from invading India. The initial operations in defence of Darwin in 1942 were plagued with problems, including faulty Merlins in the Mk Vc fighters and a lack of experienced pilots. The Spitfire Mk VIII replaced the unsuitable Mk Vs in February 1944, by which time the Japanese threat to Australia had been all but neutralised.

Desert war veteran Wing Commander Clive Caldwell, commanding No 457 Squadron Royal Australian Air Force, saw extensive operational service and established himself as both an ace and a controversial leader, with victories over German, Italian and Japanese adversaries. The role of Australian aircraft was later scaled back by the publicity-hungry US General Douglas MacArthur, who relegated the Australian Spitfires under his command to ground-attack sorties over the Dutch East Indies rather than taking part in the liberation of the Philippines. Not surprisingly, the Australians rebelled.

In the Burma campaign, the first Spitfires arrived in February 1943. These were Spitfire Mk Vc fighters and they were soon in action with the Royal Australian Air Force, supplemented by Mk VIIIs the following year. A notable air battle over Chittagong resulted in 65 Japanese aircraft being shot down by Spitfires for the loss of only three of the Supermarine fighters.

During and after the D-Day landings on the coast of Normandy in June 1944, it was the pilots of the Royal Canadian Air Force's Spitfires, predominantly Mk IXs, who were the most successful. Based at first in southern England and then across the Channel in the newly liberated areas of France and the Low Countries, the Canadian contingent included such worthies as Wing Commander 'Johnnie' Johnson (see page 175), who, in the air, led the Canadian-manned No 127 and No 144 Wings from RAF Tangmere. Johnson's 41 victories were all claimed with the Spitfire and for a six-month period he flew the same Mk IX, his Salisbury-built EN398, which was his mount for 12 confirmed victories. When he returned to the fight after a staff tour, he again flew a Mk IX, this time a Castle Bromwich-built example, MK392. Both of these Spitfires carried his personal markings of JE-J.

Another Canadian, Flight Lieutenant Don Laubman, became the highest-scoring ace of the 2nd Tactical Air Force in 1944–45. While flying with No 412 Squadron between March and October 1944, he accounted for 16 enemy aircraft before himself being brought down by anti-aircraft artillery and made a prisoner of war. *Spitfire Aces of Northwest Europe 1944–45* by Andrew Thomas shows only three non-Canadians in the top 20 air aces of the campaign and one of those was 'Johnnie' Johnson and another was the Battle of Britain ace, Geoffrey Page, founder of the Battle of Britain Fighter Association.

Canada's highest-scoring ace was Flight Lieutenant George Beurling (see page 181), who achieved great success over Malta in 1942 and continued to fly in Europe until February 1944, when he was posted back to Canada. Beurling achieved 32 confirmed victories over Italian and German aircraft in the Spitfire and his 32nd and final victory was a Fw 190 when flying with No 412 Squadron RCAF.

Despite the speed advantage of the Messerschmitt Me 262, Spitfires also accounted for a

Another Hugh Cowin portrait, this time a Mk F 22 with its characteristic five-blade propeller, still recognisable as a Spitfire. This model first flew in March 1945, too late to see wartime service, but was sent to Malta for No 73 Squadron to operate until 1948. Despite the formidable cannon armament, the Mk F 22 did not fire its weapons in anger. Rex Features (Hugh Cowin)

number of confirmed kills of these German jets over Europe in this period. The last Spitfire victory of the Second World War was a Heinkel He 111 in the Flensburg area on 4 May 1945 and, fittingly, it was Canadian Flight Lieutenant D.F. Campbell of No 411 Squadron RCAF of No 126 (Canadian) Wing who claimed the victory.

Sadly, the Royal Canadian Air Force's other top-scoring ace of the Second World War, Squadron Leader Wally McLeod, with 21 victories, was shot down and killed protecting the Arnhem landing zones.

The Norwegians were also highly effective in the Spitfire Mk IX, even with only two operational squadrons of the newly created Royal Norwegian Air Force within the Royal Air Force order of battle. Two Spitfire squadrons were established in 1942 operating from a number of bases including RAF North Weald, where there is a fine memorial to the sacrifice and dedication of these brave Norwegians. The two Spitfire squadrons were numbered No 331 and No 332, their number plates still being used today by the Royal Norwegian Air Force, as is the wing number, No 132. The bonds between British and Norwegian pilots remain strong. Several Norwegian pilots achieved the status of ace during the Second

World War including those who subsequently, and quite rightly, became national heroes in Norway: Lieutenant Colonel Rolf Arnë Berg (see page 185), Major Martin Gran and Captain Helner Grundt-Spang were among them. The Norwegian wing even boasted a Danish ace, Lieutenant Colonel Kaj Birksted, in its midst.

One of France's great heroes of the air war was Pierre Clostermann (see page 187), whose autobiography *The Big Show* is a must-read for any flying enthusiast. Clostermann was a sports fisherman and engineer, as well as one France's leading aces flying with No 602 (City of Glasgow) Squadron Auxiliary Air Force. He was one of only 3,000 Frenchmen who volunteered to join the battle against the Nazi occupation after the Fall of France but he, and his Free French colleagues, certainly made their presence felt by the Germans through their exploits.

No account of the Spitfire in operational service should be allowed to end without mention of the fighting Poles (see pages 166–167). When the Germans occupied Poland in 1939, some experienced and trained fighter and bomber pilots escaped, first to France and later to Britain. For a few months the Royal Air Force did not know what to do with them, or with the small number of Czech pilots who had also arrived. The first Polish-manned unit in Fighter Command was No 303 Squadron, which became operational at RAF Northolt on 31 August 1940 and, in only two months of service, became the highest-scoring squadron in the Battle of Britain with their Hurricanes. No 303 converted to Spitfires in January 1941 and Polish pilots flew Spitfires of later marks in the Western Desert as a semi-independent Polish Fighting Team.

Keen to fight to liberate their homeland, Poles continued to fly in north-west Europe until the end of the Second World War, particularly in operations over Germany, including escorting Lancasters on the last Bomber Command mission of the Second World War, to Berchtesgaden in April 1945. The Poles achieved a reputation for cool-headed precision and excellent marksmanship, even if fitting into the disciplined Royal Air Force system proved to be difficult.

Spitfire activity continued apace until the German collapse in May 1945. Spitfire Mk XVI units flew this 400mph-plus fighter against V1 flying bombs and later attacked V2 rocket installations. Commanding B Flight of No 602 Squadron at RAF Coltishall, Raymond Baxter – later to become a prominent television presenter – flew many of the squadron's sorties over the Netherlands, mostly on interdiction of targets of opportunity rather than more traditional air-supremacy operations.

By this stage of the war German fighter aircraft were few and far between, and they were often flown by novices. Ground defences, however, remained highly effective right until the last days of April 1945, and many more Spitfire pilots were killed by 'flak' at this time than by enemy fighters.

There is no doubt that the Spitfire was the outstanding defensive fighting aeroplane of the Second World War. It was the only British fighter to remain in production throughout the conflict and maintained its position as the prime defender of the United Kingdom's airspace for the entire duration of the war.

Wing Commander Douglas Bader DSO* DFC*

Born 21 February 1910
Died 5 September 1982
The world's most famous Spitfire pilot

There has never been such a controversial, enigmatic or iconic Spitfire pilot as Douglas Bader. He was a disabled fighter pilot who pursued aerial combat as an intellectual pastime and was a gifted war leader with a relatively short time of operational service in which to make his mark.

Bader was gifted as a sportsman and as a pilot. He learned to fly in the Royal Air Force of the 1920s as a cadet at the Royal Air Force College Cranwell and was commissioned in 1930 as a full-time aviator. His sporting activities were legendary in a service that prides itself on achievement at every level, and at one time there was even the prospect that Bader might play hockey for England.

Bader went solo after a relatively long 11 hours 15 minutes, on 19 February 1929, having learned on an Avro 504K. After passing out of Cranwell, he was sent to No 23 Squadron at RAF Kenley equipped with Gloster Gamecock and later Bristol Bulldog biplane fighters. These relatively slow aeroplanes were excellent for aerobatic training and starred in the many air shows of the period.

The main public event of the era was the dispay at RAF Hendon where front-line fighter squadrons vied for coveted aerobatic and precision-flying trophies. No 23 Squadron was seen as setting the benchmark for such displays and won the pairs trophies in 1929 and 1930, before Bader joined the Squadron. By 1931 Bader was involved, paired with Flight Lieutenant Harry Day, and they won the trophy for No 23 Squadron once again.

In the days before risk assessments and health and safety, the Royal Air Force nevertheless imposed strict rules for aerobatics training on its pilots. These stated that no manoeuvre routine should be entered into below 2,000ft and the 'hard deck' – as naval aviators might say – was 500ft. Low flying and dare-devil aerobatics were seen as unprofessional and highly dangerous, and several fighter pilots were killed every year doing just that.

Bader's aerobatics were evidently better than his marksmanship because the Squadron records show that he was below average for air-to-air gunnery on the ranges in the Bristol Bulldog at the time.

At Woodley aerodrome, home of the Reading Aero Club, on 14 December 1931, Bader seems to have been dared to perform some low aerobatics and the impression given in *Reach for the Sky*, his official biography written by Paul Brickhill, is that he had accepted a challenge simply to show off. Whatever the reason, his low, slow roll caused the Bulldog's port wing tip to strike the ground and catapult the fighter into the ground. Bader survived the crash but both of his legs had to be amputated later that day. It seemed that his flying days were over.

In the film portrayal of his biography, directed by Lewis Gilbert and released in 1956, Bader shows extreme determination to overcome his disability and by the mid-1930s he

Irascible squadron commander and inspirational leader, Douglas Bader served in Fighter Command despite having two artificial legs. He is remembered for licking squadrons into shape, for challenging the norms of aerial combat, and for his magnanimous statement that Fighter Command did not win the Battle of Britain, but 'everyone in this country'. Later he supported service and disabled persons' charities with the same vigour that he unleashed on the enemy. RAF Museum

was playing golf and driving a modified sports car. His affair with Thelma Edwards led to a 40-year marriage.

With war clouds looming, Bader wanted to fly again and the Royal Air Force had no regulation saying that he could, or, indeed, that he could not. Despite being competent to fly an Avro 504K and having the support of influential friends, including Sir Philip Sassoon, Parliamentary Under-Secretary for Air, he was invalided out of the Royal Air Force and took a job with what would become Shell-Mex.

In October 1939 Bader was given an assessment for flying duties by the Central Flying School, then at RAF Upavon on Salisbury Plain. He passed and went solo again on 27 November 1939 in an Avro Tutor and then progressed through the Fairey Battle and the Miles Master, advanced monoplane trainers powered by Rolls-Royce Merlin engines. These aircraft introduced Bader to the technological advances made since his crash.

Bader was posted to No 19 Squadron at RAF Duxford in January 1940. The squadron was under the command of Squadron Leader Geoffrey Stephenson, with whom Bader had been well acquainted at Cranwell. This was reportedly Bader's first acquaintance with the Spitfire and it seems that his disability brought an advantage. Compared with most pilots he could endure more G before passing out because, without legs, his blood was less able to drain away from his head under high gravitational loadings.

After a spell of operational training in air tactics and formation flying, which had not changed much since Bader's first Royal Air Force career, he went on to fly operational sorties over East Coast convoys, but he did not like the section attacks and other tactics that he considered to be outmoded against a fast and agile enemy. Nevertheless, he was promoted to section leader as a Flying Officer in April 1940.

Besides a rather rudimentary flying accident in a Spitfire when Bader suffered a head wound after neglecting to select a fine – rather than coarse – propeller setting (a feature absent from a Bulldog), he continued to perfect his flying and fighting skills.

By May 1940 Bader had moved across the airfield at RAF Duxford to join No 222 Squadron as a Flight Commander with the rank of Flight Lieutenant under Squadron Leader Herbert 'Tubby' Mermagen, with whom Bader had sparred during aerobatic training. Mermagen was a polished performer who had demonstrated his talents for HM King George VI while at the Central Flying School in 1937–38. Mermagen went on to be one of the few pilots to fly the Spitfire floatplane from Great Bitter Lake in Egypt later in the war. He ended the Second World War in Berlin as the Air Officer Commanding the British Air Command in the rank of Air Commodore.

Taking No 222's Spitfires south over the beaches of Dunkirk, Bader had his first combat on 1 June 1940 with the destruction of a Bf 109E and later damaged a Bf 110; his claims for five other enemy aircraft destroyed were disallowed. He claimed further enemy aircraft damaged during these hard-fought air battles but left No 222 at the end of June on promotion, as the squadron moved to RAF Kirton-in-Lindsey.

For a short while Bader left the Spitfire for the Hurricane and command of the Canadian-manned No 242 Squadron, which was just forming at RAF Duxford. On the day that the

Battle of Britain is now deemed to have started, 10 July, Bader claimed his first kill at the controls of a Hurricane against a Dornier Do 17 over the Norfolk coast. During August and early September, No 242 was heavily involved in aerial combat over East Anglia and on 14 September Bader's first Distinguished Service Order was awarded; he had also become an ace by this stage in the fighting and yet he was still only a substantive Flying Officer.

At this stage in what was to become known as the Battle of Britain, Bader became involved in the 'Big Wing' controversy with his criticism of Air Vice-Marshal Park's tactics at No 11 Group and his support for the Air Officer Commanding No 12 Group, Trafford Leigh-Mallory, who wanted massed ranks of fighters to be formed up for attacks on bombers. The problem with the Big Wing was that it took time to launch and assemble large multi-squadron formations, and during that time the bombers and their escorts were head-down for France. Post-war analysis shows that the Luftwaffe was put off balance by the small fighter formations and its difficulty in locating them, yet there were instances when a massed formation would have been useful. On balance, we should conclude that the Big Wing would only have been effective on rare occasions.

After the Battle of Britain, in which Bader had at least 11 enemy aircraft destroyed and for which he was awarded the Distinguished Flying Cross, he was reunited with the Spitfire. This was in March 1941 when he was posted to RAF Tangmere to command one of the first Spitfire Wings, in this case two Auxiliary Squadrons, No 610 and No 616, and No 145, which was just converting to the Spitfire Mk IIa. By this time, Leigh-Mallory had become AOC No 11 Group and Bader's other great supporter, Air Chief Marshal Sholto Douglas, had replaced Dowding as head of Fighter Command.

Bader excelled in the opportunity to take his Spitfires across the Channel to lure German fighters into the air and he flew his own Spitfire marked with his initials, the perk of being the Wing Leader. Because of the 'DB' markings, he made his call sign 'Dogsbody' and his own formation was known as 'Bader's Bus Company'.

German opposition grew and the Spitfire Mk II was becoming outclassed by the latest Messerschmitt Bf 109 model, the F (for *Felix*), which had elliptical wings that gave it a very similar profile to both the Mk II Spitfire and the variant that replaced it in mid-1941, the Rolls-Royce Merlin 45-powered Mk V, which appeared to counter the *Felix*. The Mk V had two European theatre variants, the Va with eight Browning machine guns (preferred by Bader and of which only 94 were built) and the cannon-armed Vb. The Spitfire's supremacy over contemporary German fighters was short-lived, however, as production was shifting from the Messerschmitt design to the Focke-Wulf Fw 190, a superior fighter in almost every aspect of aerial combat.

Bader added to his personal score of enemy aircraft destroyed during this period when combat was mostly against Bf 109s and the occasional medium bomber caught in the air over its French base. It was during this time that Bader's formation duelled with one led by *Oberstleutnant* Adolf Galland, perhaps the best-known German pilot of the Second World War. After the war, Bader and Galland often appeared at events together, signing prints and talking of combat between Spitfire and Focke-Wulf over France and the Channel.

Controversy has always surrounded Douglas Bader's last operational flight. In August 1941, while leading the Tangmere Wing on a fighter sweep in a Spitfire Mk Va with Flight Lieutenant (later Sir) Alan Smith as his No 2, a gaggle of Bf 109s from Jagdgeshwader 26 was encountered at over 25,000ft. It seems that Bader was not the victim of a collision but rather that his Spitfire was disabled by fire from another Spitfire. On landing in France, Bader was captured and treated with great respect (including a staff car ride to hospital) but his persistent escape attempts put him into Colditz.
RAF Museum

These 'leaning over the Channel' operations, pushed so heavily by Leigh-Mallory, were ineffective and caused more losses than the Battle of Britain in terms of pilots lost to the enemy or the sea, and in terms of the number of Spitfires destroyed. Bader's Wing was in action along the coast from Gravelines to Abbeville particularly, and Bader himself increased his personal combat tally to 20, winning a bar to his DSO on 2 July 1941.

Bader was now the leading exponent of operations over France and, despite having a tired group of pilots, he wanted to keep hitting back at the enemy. Several times during this period Leigh-Mallory considered taking Bader off combat and moving the squadrons in the Wing north for a rest. Each time it was raised, Bader objected. The strain even on a star like Bader was immense, with 62 fighter sweeps in his logbook from 24 March to 9 August, when Bader's Spitfire was so badly damaged that he was forced to bail out over France and was subsequently captured and imprisoned.

Exactly what happened between Abbeville and Wissant on 9 August 1941 remains the subject of controversy, but Bader himself believed that a Bf 109 rammed him. *Feldwebel* Max Meyer, the only Luftwaffe pilot to claim a Spitfire destroyed that day, thought that

Post-war, Bader worked for Shell and then devoted his life first to his wife Thelma, who died in 1971, and then to the British Limbless Ex-Servicemen's Association. He is seen here in 1982, shortly before his death, in conversation with Wing Commander Peter Squire DFC, OC No 1 Squadron. Squire, another born leader, went on to be Chief of the Air Staff and is President of the Royal Air Force Club. **RAF Museum**

he might have taken the tail off Bader's Spitfire with his cannon, while a well-researched television documentary by Andy Saunders, author of *Bader's Last Flight* and the founder of the Tangmere Aviation Museum, points to a case of 'blue-on-blue', citing the difficulty pilots found in distinguishing between the Spitfire Mk V and the Bf 109F in combat. Flight Lieutenant 'Buck' Casson of No 616 squadron claimed a fighter destroyed with its tail blown off and the pilot struggling to leave the stricken fighter, an account that tallies with Bader's – so this does seem to be the most plausible explanation. As Bader's Spitfire Mk Va, serial number W3185, has never been found, it seems unlikely that this small but significant episode in the history of the Spitfire will ever be confirmed.

In 1942, after a period in hospitals and prison camps, Bader arrived at Colditz and remained there until liberatation by the Americans in April 1945. He was soon reunited with the Spitfire, for in June 1945 he led the Victory Flypast of London in a Spitfire Mk IX marked 'DB'. His final logbook is in the RAF Museum and even a cursory glance shows his professionalism as a pilot; his first logbook is in a private collection. On his return from imprisonment in Germany he immediately undertook recurrency training on a Miles

Master two-seater and, within an hour, was authorised to fly the Spitfire – a remarkable achievement for someone who had not flown for three years.

Bader will forever be associated with the Spitfire and his legacy also lives on in the tireless charity work he performed after leaving the Royal Air Force and joining Shell. His advocacy for limbless pilots and disabled flying in particular has won him even greater respect than did his flying skills.

Flying Officer Eric Stanley Lock DSO DFC* RAFVR
Born 19 April 1919
Died 3 August 1941
Highest-scoring Battle of Britain Spitfire ace

Eric Stanley Lock has been acknowledged as a Spitfire hero only relatively recently. His short career was fast and furious with 26 enemy aircraft confirmed destroyed in combat between May 1940 and 3 August 1941, when he was posted missing. He was the highest-scoring Spitfire pilot of the Battle of Britain.

During his tenure with No 41 Squadron at RAF Catterick, 'Sawn-Off Lockie', as he was known to his comrades because of his limited stature, was a Spitfire pilot in the rank of Acting Pilot Officer. For several months, during which time he married, Lock patrolled the North Sea protecting coastal convoys from attacks from German bombers that never seemed to materialise.

Lock's quiet life changed on 15 August when a large formation of Junkers Ju 88 medium bombers, with their long-range escorts of Messerschmitt Bf 110Cs, appeared over the North Sea from Norway. This was part of a carefully calculated move by the Luftwaffe – one of the few they achieved in the Battle of Britain – to split Fighter Command's assets. Following the classic formation attacks that had been taught in the 1930s and that No 41, not used to the combat over the Channel, still flew, Lock's section went into line-astern formation. This tactic had already been discredited 'down south' as it wasted time and could be dangerous when facing the big twin-engined Messerschmitt fighter. During the combat, Lock attacked the escorts, hitting a Bf 110's starboard engine and downing it. Then he took his Spitfire Mk I into the bombers and claimed a Junkers Ju 88 as well.

On 3 September No 41 went south to RAF Hornchurch, the section station to the east of London and right in the thick of it. Two days later, Lock was flying Red Two to the Squadron commander, Squadron Leader Hilary Hood DFC, on patrol to the east when Hood suffered a mid-air collision with Red Three, Flight Lieutenant 'Terry' Webster, and was killed. Now alone, Lock promptly engaged two Heinkel He 111s over the Thames estuary and brought them both down. Then he was bounced by a Bf 109 and, although wounded, Lock shot that down too. He was an ace.

On 6 September, Lock was airborne again, despite his bandaged leg, and claimed his seventh enemy aircraft, a Ju 88 over Dover. By 11 September Lock and his Spitfire had

'Sawn-off Lockie' was the most successful Spitfire pilot of the early years of the war with 21 confirmed victories. This is the last photo of him, taken on 31 July 1941 at RAF Hornchurch, where he was a flight commander with No 611 (West Lancashire) Squadron with 26 victories on his Mk Vb's fuselage side. The dog's name is not recorded. Getty Images (Hulton Archive)

destroyed eight enemy aircraft in seven days. A Distinguished Flying Cross followed.

His leg now recovered and his fighting spirit unquenched, Lock continued to scramble and patrol over Essex, Kent and Sussex. His citation said that he had displayed 'great vigour and determination' and that can easily be seen by his further tally of enemy aircraft destroyed, both fighters and bombers.

A bar to the DFC followed in recognition of the 15 victories in 16 days. His third OC in as many weeks was Squadron Leader Donald Finlay, who was also an aggressive Spitfire pilot and led very much by example. Finlay survived the war, having transferred, unusually, to the Engineering Branch of the Royal Air Force rather than remain a pilot.

Lock had now added a Henschel Hs 126 to his tally and before the end of the Battle of Britain he had claimed and been awarded 21 victories against the Luftwaffe, making him the most successful fighter pilot in the Royal Air Force at that time.

On 8 November, the Battle officially over, Lock's luck began to run out when he was wounded in a duel with a Bf 109 over Beachy Head, crash landing into a field. On 17

November, again in combat with Bf 109s, he was badly wounded and crashed near RAF Martlesham Heath. Found unconscious, the now further decorated and promoted Lock was in hospital at RAF Halton for three months and later went to the Royal Masonic Hospital, where he got to know Richard Hillary (see page 174), the ace and author, who was writing *The Last Enemy* at that time.

In June 1941 Lock was back flying with No 41 Squadron before being posted to No 611 Squadron in command of B Flight. In July three more Bf 109s were destroyed by the new combination of ace pilot and Spitfire Mk V. His last mission was on 3 August 1941 over Pas-de-Calais when he fell victim to light flak, as did so many at the time. Neither his body nor the wreckage of his Spitfire was ever found.

Flight Lieutenant Adolph 'Sailor' Malan DSO* DFC

Born 24 March 1910
Died 17 September 1963
Second Spitfire ace
OC No 74 Squadron, 1940–41
Station Commander, RAF Biggin Hill, 1944

Adolph 'Sailor' Malan was the second Spitfire ace. An inspiring leader, excellent shot and natural pilot, he was a South African whose first career was with the Union Castle Line in the Merchant Navy, hence his nickname in the Royal Air Force.

'Sailor' Malan's route to 'acedom' started in 1935 when he joined the Royal Air Force on a short service commission. He was commissioned as an Acting Pilot Officer on 2 March 1936 during an elementary flying course on Tiger Moth biplane trainers. He was a natural pilot and showed good leadership potential when in December that year he joined No 74 (Tiger) Squadron then flying the Hawker Demon biplane fighter. By April 1937 the squadron, based at RAF Hornchurch, was equipped with the Gloster Gauntlet III, resplendent in 'tiger-skin' markings.

Already confirmed in the rank of Pilot Officer, Malan honed his flying skills on the Gauntlet and was made an acting Flight Commander as No 74 prepared to receive Spitfires in February 1939. The other two fighter squadrons in the Hornchurch Wing, the Gloster Gladiator-equipped No 54 and No 65, had to wait a month after No 74 to become equipped with the Spitfire Mk I, and that no doubt added to the rivalry and banter.

On 2 March 1939, having now risen to Acting Flight Lieutenant, Malan was already a master of the art of flying the Spitfire but had yet to show his skills in combat. His gunnery reports were very good and Malan was probably what would be called a 'natural shot', having been brought up with rifles and shotguns at his parent's home in the Western Cape.

No 74's first action was on 6 September when A Flight, led by Malan, was scrambled to identify potential bandits flying towards London. The 'enemy' turned out to be Hurricanes of No 56 Squadron and sadly two were shot down by No 74's Spitfires before the mistake

Every inch a pilot and commander, 'Sailor' Malan was the second recorded Spitfire ace and Spitfire formation leader in the Battle of Britain. Seen here as a Group Captain when commanding RAF Biggin Hill, in 1942–43, Malan believed in teamwork and discipline in the air and on the ground.
RAF Museum

was realised. Dubbed the Battle of Barking Creek, the incident led to the pilots being court-martialled and Malan, the flight commander, was involved in fierce debate during the cross-examination. In the end the Court ruled that it was an unfortunate error and no blame was attached to Malan.

No 74 was commanded at this time by Squadron Leader C.E. Sampson, who took the unit forward to RAF Rochford (now Southend airport) in November during the inaction of the Phoney War. No action was forthcoming and after several moves the Spitfires returned to Hornchurch again for the Dunkirk air battles that heralded the Battle of Britain.

As the German forces smashed through the Low Countries and France, Fighter Command was operating at range across the North Sea and the English Channel. Malan started his score of enemy aircraft on 21 May with the destruction of a Junkers Ju 88 bomber and the probable shooting down of a Heinkel He 111 bomber. The 'probable' nomenclature would most likely have been because the Heinkel's destruction had not been witnessed by a third party. On 22 May Malan damaged another Ju 88 and shared a Dornier Do 17 bomber, and then on 24 May he destroyed an He 111.

Over the Dunkirk salient, Malan's first success against the outstanding German fighter of the period, the Messerschmitt Bf 109E, was achieved on 27 May when he claimed one shot down, as well as sharing a Dornier Do 17 and damaging two others as the Luftwaffe tried to stop the embarkation of the British Expeditionary Force from Calais and Dunkirk.

Malan's flying skill, dedication and fearless fighting spirit were recognised on 11 June with the award of the Distinguished Flying Cross. In a rare night-flying moonlight action on 19/20 June, he destroyed two He 111 bombers and became an ace, recognised by a bar to his DFC, and he confirmed it on 12 July, two days after the official start of the Battle of Britain, by sharing another He 111.

As the leading flight commander and now an ace, Malan was the obvious choice to lead the squadron when Sampson was posted and for this he attended the rank of Acting Squadron Leader. A date well remembered on No 74 Squadron is 11 August, when its Spitfires started the day with an interception over Dover at 07.00 and continued fighting all day with four major engagements. The squadron claimed 38 German aircraft destroyed, perhaps somewhat optimistically, and the feat brought a Distinguished Service Order for Malan. Perhaps because of his naval background, 'Sailor' Malan was said to run 'a tight ship', with discipline and fighting spirit counting for almost everything.

As No 74 had been in the front line at Hornchurch and Rochford during the initial heavy fighting in the Channel, it was withdrawn north to rest in August and it was here that Malan perfected a new style of fighting formation in the combat area – a loose four rather than the textbook tight 'Vic' of three that was already becoming the cause of many a young man's death. The Luftwaffe had been using the mutually supportive 'finger four' to great effect over France and in the Battle of Britain, having developed the concept in the Spanish Civil War. This fundamental formation is still used by fighter pilots today.

Malan's ten rules for air fighting still hold true today: (1) wait until you see the whites of his eyes – fire short bursts of one to two seconds only when your sights are definitely 'ON'; (2) whilst shooting think of nothing else, brace the whole of your body; have both hands on the stick; concentrate on your ring sight; (3) always keep a sharp lookout – 'keep your finger out'; (4) height gives you the initiative; (5) always turn and face the attack; (6) make your decisions promptly – it is better to act quickly even if your tactics are not the best; (7) never fly straight and level for more than 30 seconds in the combat area; (8) when diving to attack always leave a proportion of your formation above to act as a top guard; (9) *initiative, aggression, air discipline* and *teamwork* are words that mean something in air fighting; (10) go in quickly – punch hard – get out!

These watchwords also worked well for Malan and his pilots in 1941, when the air fighting was taken to the skies of France when he was Wing Leader at Biggin Hill, a station that he later commanded. And during D-Day he commanded the Free French squadrons, having added a bar to his DSO by then.

It is widely believed that writers James Kennaway and Wilfred Greatorex based the Robert Shaw character in the film *Battle of Britain* on Malan. Shaw plays an unnamed squadron commander at an unnamed airfield and is known only as 'Skipper' to the squadron

POLISH PILOTS

No account of the Spitfire is complete without mention of the pilots and groundcrew of the Polish Air Force who escaped from Occupied Europe and joined the Royal Air Force. Initially operational on Hurricanes in the Battle of Britain and achieving high-scoring rates despite their late start, it was in the Spitfire that the top aces made their names. This symbiotic relationship between dedicated fighter pilot and superb fighting aeroplane is particularly exemplified by the Polish Fighting Team in the Desert Air Force.

Modern Poland is rightly proud of these men. Initially the Royal Air Force was sceptical of the Poles' abilities and then of their perceived lack of discipline in the air, despite their skill and bravery in the Battle of France. This delayed the operational status of No 302 and No 303 Squadrons, which were both equipped with Hurricane fighters.

During the Battle of Britain 145 Polish pilots served with Fighter Command, No 303 becoming the highest-scoring unit. Eager to fly the Spitfire, Polish pilots had to wait until January 1941 before No 303 received the Mk I, with Mk II fighters following in March and the Mk Vb in July. Polish airmen were masters of the Mk IX from June 1943, often

Seldom has a nation in exile captured the imagination of its hosts more than the Poles, who fought with great bravery and skill in the Battle of Britain. Nothing typifies this more than the Polish Fighting Team raised in 1942 and led by Squadron Leader Stanisław Skalski (left), seen with Air Marshal Arthur Coningham in the desert. RAF Museum

Stanisław Skalski (left) had many accolades: the first and highest-scoring Polish ace in Britain; the only Pole to command a Royal Auxiliary Air Force fighter squadron; and he survived the death sentence at home in Poland in 1948. Refugee pilots from other occupied nations also came to fight in Britain in 1940, including the Czech Karel Mrázek (right), who was awarded the DSO and DFC, and led the Czech Spitfire Wing in 1942–43.
The Polish Institute and Sikorski Museum – London

being posted into other units to bring combat experience to help newly trained pilots.

The Polish Fighting Team consisted of 15 second-tour Polish pilots and was formed in 1943. It was attached to No 145 Squadron but became known as 'Skalski's Circus', after its leader **Squadron Leader Stanisław Skalski**. The unit was actually raised at the request of the Polish Government in Exile, which wanted Polish pilots to go to the Desert Air Force and gain tactical fighter experience for the forthcoming invasion of Europe. In the six months or so of its existence, until it was disbanded when the Germans surrendered in North Africa, its Spitfires of Mk Vb and Mk IX types accounted for 25 enemy aircraft. Skalski was the highest-scoring Polish ace of the Second World War with 21 victories and retired with the rank of Wing Commander.

Despite being South African by birth, 'Sailor' Malan was a lifelong campaigner for equal opportunity. At RAF Biggin Hill in January 1943, he is in conversation with Flight Sergeant (later Pilot Officer) Vincent Bunting, a Jamaican who flew Spitfires with No 611 and No 132 Squadrons, and one of 300 West Indian volunteers with the Royal Air Force. RAF Museum

or 'Rabbit Leader' to his sector controller at 'Cowslip'. The analogy is reinforced by the domestic scene in the film where 'Skipper' is seen leaving his house, a parallel to Malan's own family arrangements where his wife and children lived near the air stations at which he served. As depicted in the film, the use of codenames for both squadrons and controlling stations during the Battle of Britain was required because the Germans were able to listen in to VHF radio transmissions.

Despite the many historical flaws in Guy Hamilton's film *Battle of Britain*, it remains a firm favourite with many as it captures the spirit of the Battle of Britain and those who fought it, in the air and on the ground. It is not unusual for aviation enthusiasts, young or old, pilot or spotter, to be able to quote whole sections of the film's script, especially on Twitter and other social media. So, 'Don't you yell at me, Mr Warwick!'

'Sailor' Malan retired from the Royal Air Force in 1946 and returned to South Africa, where he worked tirelessly against racism as well as the ruling National Party. One of the great exponents of the Spitfire and an exemplary fighter pilot, he died of Parkinson's Disease at the age of only 53.

Group Captain Wilfred Duncan Smith DSO* DFC**

Born 28 May 1914
Died 1 December 1996
Spitfire ace and last operational Spitfire sortie

Wilfred Duncan Smith was a Spitfire ace, squadron commander and noted author on Spitfire operational flying. Born in India, he had already spent his boyhood and teenage years full of adventure, including such *Boy's Own Paper* activities as shooting rogue tigers and being tucked away in a Scottish boarding school.

'Smithy' joined the Royal Air Force as a Sergeant Pilot after returning to Britain from India, and following a spell as an apprenticed car mechanic by day and Royal Air Force Volunteer Reserve cadet at weekends. After pilot training at No 7 Operational Training Unit, he was posted in October 1940 to No 611 (West Lancashire) Squadron, then a training unit on Spitfire Mk Is at RAF Tern Hill. This posting to a non-operational squadron meant that Duncan Smith did not qualify for the Battle of Britain clasp.

Duncan Smith was awarded the first of his Distinguished Flying Cross gallantry medals on 22 July 1941. No 611 was then based at RAF Hornchurch and the forward airfield of RAF Rochford during offensive operations over Occupied France and the Low Countries. With the DFC on his tunic, Duncan Smith went to the Hornchurch-based No 603 (City of Edinburgh) Squadron of the Auxiliary Air Force on promotion to Flight Lieutenant. His leadership role at the squadron brought him another DFC and the Spitfire Mk Vb to fly.

After a short illness, he returned to operations in March 1942 with No 411 Squadron, to regain experience, and was then given command of No 64 Squadron, part of the Hornchurch Wing and the first unit to receive the Spitfire Mk IX. During that summer's Dieppe raid, on 19 August, Duncan Smith's Spitfire Mk IXc was shot down over the English Channel by return fire from a Dornier Do 217 but he was rescued by a Supermarine Walrus, having survived in the water without a dinghy for several hours and despite having suffered double pneumonia just a year before.

Later, in August 1942, Duncan Smith was promoted to Wing Commander and posted away from the front line to the School of Tactics at RAF Charmy Down near Bath. This station also hosted Douglas Turbinlite Havoc 'night fighters' and a Spitfire operational conversation unit at which Duncan Smith was able to 'keep current'. He had recently received his first Distinguished Service Order for his leadership in the offensive operations over Occupied France.

Back to operational flying in 1943, he was posted to take over a Luqa Fighter Wing in Malta but this was a short period before his talents were needed to fly Spitfires with the Desert Air Force, leading No 244 Wing. Baling out into the sea, Duncan Smith survived for five hours without the benefit of a dinghy before he was rescued, and then the rescue boat endured attack by German aircraft on the way back to Malta.

Between November 1943 and March 1945, Duncan Smith was active in the Mediterranean as a Group Captain commanding No 324 Wing. Leading the unit during the invasion of

Group Captain Wilfred Duncan Smith – Battle of Britain veteran, Spitfire ace and noted author – is pictured briefing pilots from No 324 Wing, possibly for a sortie to provide cover for the invasion of southern France. Duncan Smith remained in the Royal Air Force after the war and served in the Malayan Emergency, where he flew the last operational Spitfire sortie in 1951. RAF Museum

southern France, he was possibly the first to land there in a Spitfire Mk LF IX, marked with his initials (a privilege of a flying Group Captain), in August 1944.

During the Second World War and exclusively flying the Spitfire, rising from Sergeant to Group Captain, Duncan Smith had 17 confirmed kills, two shared, six probable, two shared probable and eight damaged enemy aircraft in aerial command.

Spitfires were still operating in the Far East when communist terrorists attacked and killed British rubber plantation workers at Sungai Siput in Perak state, Malaya, in 1948. For three years British aircraft, including late-model Spitfires, were actively engaged with rockets and cannon against known terrorist camps and hide-outs. By 1951 over 1,800 sorties had been flown by the 16 Spitfire Mk XVIII fighter-bombers of No 60 and No 81 Squadrons. Duncan Smith led No 60 Squadron in a four-ship strike against terrorists near Kota Tinggi on New Year's Day 1951 and thus made history, together with his wing man, Flying Officer

Frank Walters, by completing the last Spitfire armed operational sortie. His leadership and gallantry in Malaya were further recognised with a second bar for his DFC.

Duncan Smith left the Royal Air Force in 1960. His son, Iain Duncan Smith, was Conservative Party leader in 2001–03, having been in industry prior to politics. His office wall is always decorated with a painting of his father's Spitfire.

Wing Commander Bob Stanford Tuck DSO DFC**AFC
Born 1 July 1916
Died 5 May 1987
First Spitfire ace and Wing Leader

Bob Stanford Tuck was a larger-than-life character before, during and after he flew the Spitfire. He was a true exponent of the fighter pilot's art and he was a skilled test pilot. He described being a Spitfire pilot as 'cold, calculating and a "cat and mouse" affair'.

Tuck was commissioned into the Royal Air Force on a short service commission in September 1935 at the age of 19, having given up his first career as a Merchant Navy cadet. His training was on the Avro Tutor and Hawker Hart, moving to the biplane fighters of the era – Hawker Fury and Bristol Bulldog – at No 3 Flying Training School, Grantham. He passed out with 'exceptional' noted in his logbook; there is no finer endorsement.

His first operational squadron in July 1936 was No 65 based at RAF Hornchurch, flying first Hawker Demons, then Gloster Gauntlets, only to see those replaced by Gloster Gladiators. His introduction to the Spitfire came at RAF Duxford in December 1938 when Squadron Leader Henry Cozens, the Officer Commanding No 19 Squadron, the first unit to receive production Spitfires, invited him to go flying and help with the Spitfire's service introduction. In the space of two years Tuck saw Fighter Command go from fighters little better than those of the First World War to the Spitfire Mk I, such was the pace of change once Hugh Dowding had taken over.

In interviews Tuck characterised the Spitfire as 'revolutionary' for its speed, monoplane appearance and firepower, and his introduction to the fighter at RAF Duxford served both him and the Royal Air Force well when he was asked to test a Spitfire again prior to the Battle of Britain. Included in the test were new two-step auxiliary rudder pedals that Tuck found, after an extended trial, to enable even better combat flying and provide more comfort for the pilot at 350mph and pulling G.

By now at No 92 Squadron and a Flight Lieutenant, Tuck led the three-ship escort for Winston Churchill's epic trip to Paris on 16 May 1940, just after the Germans had broken through French defences at Sedan. Tuck took the flight to RAF Hendon and provided close escort for the Prime Minister's De Havilland Flamingo to Le Bourget, where they stayed overnight. These were the first Spitfire fighters to be deployed operationally outside Britain.

Soon after that Tuck was in action over Dunkirk supporting the evacuation of the British Expeditionary Force and claiming three Messerschmitt Bf 109Es downed on 23 May,

Bob Stanford Tuck was the first Spitfire ace. His early 'bonding' with the Spitfire included operational test flying, escorting Churchill to France, and aerial combat in defence of the Dunkirk beaches. Like many veterans of the Battle of Britain, his career was cut short by the controversial fighter sweeps over northern France, ignoring the lessons that the Germans must have learned about fighting at extreme range mere months before.
RAF Museum

followed by two German bombers the next day. The fighting was fierce and No 92 lost its commanding officer and the senior flight commander, causing Tuck to assume command and lead the remaining eight Spitfires for the next 24 hours.

By 2 June Tuck was an ace – the first Spitfire ace. His contribution was considerable, with four Dornier and Heinkel bombers, and four Bf 109 fighters, destroyed over Picardy out of sight of the beaches while the enemy was en route to attack the Dunkirk evacuation. Not surprisingly, this fine leadership was recognised by the award of the Distinguished Flying Cross on 11 June, and the honour was presented by HM King George VI on 28 June, just before the Battle of Britain officially started.

During July and August No 92 Squadron was in the thick of the aerial battles over Kent and the English Channel, with Tuck using a bold tactic of head-on engagement against bomber formations that often outnumbered the defending fighters 10 to one. Tuck 'took to the silk' – baled out – twice in quick succession, on 18 August and 25 August, when fighting

Dornier Do 17 and Junkers Ju 88 bombers respectively, proving that even the Spitfire could be vulnerable to return fire from a determined enemy. His score increased to include more Bf 109s and their larger, twin-engined brother, the Bf 110. This resulted in a bar to his DFC.

His leadership qualities were well known and Dowding moved Tuck to RAF Coltishall, where on 11 September he took command of No 257 (Union of Burma) Squadron, which, flying Hurricanes, had been badly mauled in earlier fighting. He brought the unit back to scratch, adding four more enemy aircraft to his tally and scoring at least 18 by January 1941, when he was awarded the Distinguished Service Order.

In June 1941 Tuck again had to 'take to the silk' over the Thames estuary. The next month he was posted to RAF Duxford and then RAF Biggin Hill as the Wing Leader, back on Spitfires. He led formations across the Channel on Rhubarb sorties and it was over Occupied France that his wartime flying career ended, when he was forced to crash land near Boulogne. Captured, he escaped several times before ending up at Stalag Luft III.

Eventually, in February 1945, he managed to get away to the Soviet lines, where, by continued good fortune, his childhood Russian language skills helped secure his eventual repatriation to England. Over the duration of the war he had been accredited with 27 kills in aerial command and a host of damaged, 'probables' and shared victories.

Tuck's final years in the Royal Air Force included command of RAF Coltishall and a staff tour in Singapore. After test flying the English Electric Canberra jet bomber, the world's first, Tuck retired in 1949 into relative obscurity, although he was still called upon from time to time to comment on the Spitfire and the Battle of Britain.

BATTLE OF BRITAIN SPITFIRE ACES

During the Battle of Britain some 40 per cent of pilots achieved Spitfire combat success. A select few became aces, the Royal Air Force definition of an ace being a pilot who achieved five victories confirmed by an eyewitness. These include:

Flying Officer Brian Carbury from New Zealand became an ace in a single day by destroying five enemy aircraft in 24 hours. In total, he achieved 15.5 victories with No 603 Squadron Auxiliary Air Force and his fellow countryman, **Pilot Officer Colin Gray**, was close behind with 14.5 while on No 54 Squadron.

Pilot Officer Bob Doe scored 14 with No 234 Squadron on Spitfires and then No 238 Squadron on Hurricanes.

Flight Lieutenant Paterson Hughes from Australia also scored 14 on No 234 but had fewer shared victories. He perished during the Battle of Britain.

Pilot Officer Eric Stanley Lock (see page 161) of No 41 Squadron was the highest scorer in the Battle of Britain with 21 confirmed kills.

The total number of British, Commonwealth and Allied pilots who took part in the Battle of Britain was 2,332, of whom 20 per cent were dead by 31 October.

Flight Lieutenant Richard Hillary

Born 20 April 1919
Died 8 January 1943
Spitfire pilot and wartime author

There have been many accounts of the Battle of Britain but only a few are truly outstanding. One written at the time with the immediacy of action is Richard Hillary's *The Last Enemy*, published in 1942. Hillary lived a mere seven months after the book was published, dying in a night-flying accident while piloting a Blenheim.

He was educated at Oxford, where he was Secretary of Boats in 1938 and a member of the University Air Squadron. He was called up to the Royal Air Force in October 1939 and by the following July, having completed his training, he was posted to fly Spitfires with No 603 (City of Edinburgh) Squadron Auxiliary Air Force, then based at RAF Montrose. Hillary was a natural.

Richard Hillary was the classic Spitfire pilot – good looking, bright, well educated and naturally gifted as a pilot. The Battle of Britain changed much of that and the anxiety about aerial combat is captured in his autobiography, The Last Enemy, *which remains a must-read.* TopFoto

Before he joined the Squadron, it had converted from Gloster Gladiators to Spitfire Mk Is and been declared operational just in time to intercept the first German air raid on Britain on 16 October 1939. No 603 has the credit for destroying a Junkers Ju 88 that was attacking warships in the Moray Firth. This was the first German aircraft to be shot down over Britain since 1918 and was achieved by an Auxiliary Squadron manned by reservists.

As the Battle of Britain hotted up, the Squadron completed its training and moved south to RAF Hornchurch in Essex, close to London and in the thick of the battle. Arriving on 27 August 1940, the Squadron immediately saw combat, and Hillary's tally in the first week made him an ace. No 603 was tasked to engage the Luftwaffe fighter cover of Bf 109s and Hillary destroyed five with two probable victories and one damaged.

Unfortunately, his fifth kill left him exposed to another Bf 109 that all but destroyed his Spitfire. Unable to leave his burning Spitfire until very low and very late, Hillary was badly burned when picked up by the Margate lifeboat. He was taken to Queen Victoria Hospital, East Grinstead for pioneering plastic surgery by Archibald McIndoe, thereby becoming a member of the so-called Guinea Pig Club of pilots who had received reconstructive surgery. In Hillary's case it was his face and hands that needed this attention; he was determined to return to flying and needed both to function. He wrote *The Last Enemy* during his prolonged convalescence.

Group Captain J.E. 'Johnnie' Johnson DSO DFC
Born 9 March 1915
Died 30 January 2001
Leading Spitfire ace

Johnnie Johnson was perhaps the greatest exponent of the Spitfire and the leading Spitfire ace with 34 confirmed victories from 57 engagements and 700 operational sorties. He was the master of the air against the Focke-Wulf Fw 190, destroying 20 of these deadly German fighters in combat over Occupied Europe.

Johnson was an engineer by education before he joined the Royal Air Force and learned to fly at the Marshall of Cambridge flying school – then No 22 Elementary Flying Training School. By August 1940 Sergeant Johnson RAFVR was converting to the Spitfire with No 19 Squadron so he missed the air battles over Dunkirk because he was still in training. He was awarded the Battle of Britain clasp despite only doing a single patrol, with No 616 Squadron Auxiliary Air Force, before a landing accident exacerbated an old rugby injury to his collarbone. Rather than give in to the threat of being an elementary flying instructor for the rest of the war, Johnson chose to have an operation to repair the collarbone, which had been badly set before the war.

Once fit again in December 1940, Johnson returned to No 616 Squadron, which had moved from RAF Coltishall to the Tangmere Wing in Sussex, where Douglas Bader was fully established as the *primus inter pares*. Johnson threw himself into the fray and was an

When making a film, as with Reach for the Sky, *it is good to get expert help, such as how to climb in and out of a Spitfire. In 1956, at RAF Kenley, Kenneth More (playing Douglas Bader) gets such advice from 'Johnnie' Johnson (right) under the gaze of another advisor, Wing Commander Ronald Adams (centre) and Danny Angel, the producer.* Rex Features (Moviestore Collection)

enthusiastic pilot in the 1941 Circus operations over Occupied France and the Low Countries but he thought the Rhubarb ground-attack sorties foolish and too dangerous for pilots. He was right as the death of Eric Stanley Lock and the capture of Bob Stanford Tuck showed.

Johnson's first confirmed victory came on 28 June 1941. He was there in Bader's section in August when the legless legend was shot down and captured. Johnson kept flying from Tangmere and was an ace by September. He pursued the adoption of the 'finger-four' tactical fighting formation against the official policy and was successful against Fw 190s over Dieppe, noting the lack of performance in his Mk V.

When he took command of the Canadian No 144 Wing at RAF Tangmere – with the personal call sign 'Greycap leader' – his confirmed victories topped 20 and he continued in the front line covering the D-Day beaches and the Rhine crossing. His last flying appointment was a Group Captain and in command of RAF Wildenrath in Germany. Before he left the Royal Air Force, he wrote two outstanding personal accounts of the Spitfire war: *Wing Leader* and *Full Circle*.

Leaving the Royal Air Force as an Air Vice-Marshal, Johnson was personally astonished that he managed to achieve so much, having been rejected by the Royal Air Force twice and almost losing his flying medical after playing rugby.

Johnson's uncanny ability to judge a deflection shot against a fleeing enemy aircraft has often been put down to his youth in Leicestershire where he learned to shoot rabbits and game birds. Post-war, he was often invited to discuss the Spitfire and its capabilities, sometimes with retired Luftwaffe fighter pilots. He believed that the Mk IX was the finest version of the great design and one particular Spitfire, EN398, built at Salisbury and test-flown at Chattis Hill, was the highest-scoring aircraft flown by the highest-scoring pilot.

Squadron Leader Tony Martindale AFC RAFVR

Born c1910
Died c1946
Spitfire test pilot and speed record holder

A true professional and an outstanding pilot, Tony Martindale is another unsung hero of the Spitfire's evolution. Described by Captain Eric Brown as one of the finest test pilots with whom he ever worked, Martindale holds the record for the maximum speed attained by a Spitfire.

As the Second World War progressed, the Spitfire was redesigned and modified as technology advanced. Even a cursory glance at the profile of the later marks of Spitfire compared with the shape of the Mk I shows how much Joe Smith and his team at Supermarine developed their thinking and production techniques.

Martindale was a test pilot at Rolls-Royce before the war and was called up for service on the outbreak of hostilities. His test-flying skills recognised, he was posted to the Royal Aircraft Establishment at Farnborough where high-speed trials commenced in 1943. The aim of the trials was to investigate the limiting Mach number as conventional aircraft neared the speed of sound – something that the Germans understood because they had supersonic wind tunnels in which theories could be tested.

The British government did not invest in such technology and as a result Martindale, Lieutenant Eric Brown RN and Squadron Leader J.R. Tobin AFC, the then Officer Commanding the Aerodynamics Flight, used a Spitfire Mk IX (EN409) to test speeds and angles of attack. Tobin reached 606mph (Mach 0.891) in a 45-degree dive in late 1943 but left Farnborough almost immediately after the trial, handing over to Martindale and Brown. Tobin was posted to Blackburn Aircraft as a loan test pilot where he sadly died in a flying accident the following year.

Martindale continued the high-speed trials, slowly increasing the speed until April 1944, when he took the same Mk IX to altitude only to have the Rotol propeller break off (even though it was feathered) and take the engine reduction gear with it. In the dive that caused the break-up, Martindale reached a recorded Mach 0.92, the fastest speed ever for a Spitfire and for any propeller-driven aeroplane. He showed great courage and did not try to bale out as the Spitfire, now tail-heavy, zoom-climbed to altitude with considerable gravitational loading – 11 times that at ground level – and not surprisingly he blacked out. Regaining consciousness at 40,000ft, he succeeded in bringing the 'glider version' of the Spitfire back some 20 miles to Farnborough – an almost unparalleled feat of airmanship that led to the award of the Air Force Cross.

On landing, the Spitfire was inspected and the wings were found to be intact but no longer straight: they had a backwards sweep of several degrees as a result of the exceptional speed and acceleration. It is little wonder that a team from Supermarine, including chief designer Joe Smith, hastened to Farnborough.

Martindale survived the war but died from cancer not long afterwards.

Squadron Leader Mahinder Singh Pujji DFC

Born 14 August 1918
Died 18 September 2010
India's Spitfire hero

India contributed many millions of volunteers to the British armed forces in two World Wars. Born in British India, Mahinder Singh Pujji was a lawyer by training who learned to fly at the Delhi Flying Club before the Second World War. He volunteered with other Indian private pilots and was accepted, arriving in Britain by ship at Liverpool on 1 August 1940 at the height of the Battle of Britain.

After training, he was posted to RAF Drem and No 43 Squadron on Hurricanes at RAF Martlesham Heath. He arrived just after the Battle of Britain so did not receive the Battle of Britain clasp, having not flown operationally during the official dates. In fact his 'wings' were not awarded until April 1941.

In a rare exception to King's regulations, Pujji was allowed to fly wearing his traditional Sikh head-dress of wrapped cloth, known as a *dastar*. Because an oxygen mask would not fit around his *dastar*, he frequently flew without one in both Hurricanes and Spitfires. Having been brought up in the high-altitude foothills of the Himalaya, he was able to manage but nevertheless suffered lung damage that affected him in later life.

After flying in Scotland, Pujji was posted to No 258 Squadron at RAF Kenley and, on promotion to Flight Commander, converted to the Spitfire Mk V, claiming two Messerschmitt Bf 109s destroyed and three damaged. His view of the Spitfire seems to have been divided between fighting it (which he loved) and landing it (which he did not); he always said that the Hurricane was easier to land and he was probably right.

In September 1941 he was posted to the Middle East, then the Royal Indian Air Force serving on the North-West Frontier, back on Hurricanes. A spell at No 4 Squadron in the Army Co-operation Role followed for the acting Squadron Leader and the award of the Distinguished Flying Cross.

After his war service Pujji did not return to Britain until 1973, when he decided to live in the Darent Valley near Gravesend in Kent. During these last years, he became a well-known and fervent advocate for both the Indian contribution to the Allied victory in both world wars and for piston-engined fighters, notably the Hurricane and Spitfire.

In two world wars the British cause was blessed by support from volunteers from the Dominions, Colonies and the Commonwealth. Such men and women are exemplified by Mahinder Singh Pujji (right), who is best remembered for his exploits in Hurricanes but who also flew the Spitfire. His fellow countryman seen here died on operations in 1941 but his identity is unknown. Rex Features (Associated Newspapers)

Air Commodore Al Deere DSO, OBE, DFC*

Born 12 December 1917
Died 21 September 1995
New Zealand Spitfire ace

The best-known New Zealander in the Battle of Britain, Al Deere was a Spitfire pilot with No 54 Squadron who took part in the early operations over Occupied France, the English Channel and southern England. He made his reputation as a skilled pilot and born leader very early on and kept it throughout his service life.

Born in New Zealand and smitten with aeroplanes from the age of eight, he was selected for the Royal Air Force in 1937 and, during training on Tiger Moths at White Waltham, found himself playing rugby and boxing. His initial Fighter Command experience was in the Gloster Gladiator at No 54 Squadron with Colin Gray, who went on to be the highest-scoring New Zealander – but it was Deere who achieved recognition through his leadership.

On 23 May 1940, as British troops were withdrawing to Dunkirk, Deere and Pilot Officer

New Zealand not only produced the senior commander Keith Park for the Battle of Britain, but also an outstanding fighter pilot and leader in Al Deere. Right from the first days of Spitfire operations, Deere was writing the rule book and the operational protocols. He learned the lessons of Dunkirk quickly and passed them on to other pilots throughout the war. RAF Museum

Johnny Allen flew Spitfires across the Channel, escorting Flight Lieutenant James Leathart in a Miles Magister trainer to Calais-Marck airfield. There, Squadron Leader Francis White, Officer Commanding No 74 Squadron, was on the ground with a wrecked Spitfire, having made a forced landing after the Henschel Hs 126 he was chasing damaged his fighter with return fire. On the way home, Deere claimed his first combat victories when he shot down two Bf 109s, and he added a third later the same day.

Deere and the Spitfire had truly bonded. He describes the Spitfire in his autobiography, *Nine Lives*, as 'the most beautiful and easy aircraft to fly'. Deere christened his Spitfires 'Kiwi' and there were more than a few of them, as he explained in his book.

He commanded No 602 Squadron Auxiliary Air Force in 1941 and was given command of the Kenley Fighter Wing in 1943, and then posted to the Central Gunnery School. After the war he was Station Commander RAF North Weald and he led the Battle of Britain pilots in Winston Churchill's funeral cortège in 1965. He was a consultant for the film *Battle of Britain* and retired from the Royal Air Force in December 1967. When he died in 1995 his ashes were scattered from a Spitfire over the Thames estuary.

Flight Lieutenant George Beurling DSO DFC DFM*

Born 6 December 1921
Died 20 May 1948
Canadian Spitfire pilot

George Beurling is probably the most famous Canadian Spitfire pilot and a highly acclaimed Malta ace who was nicknamed 'Buzz' and 'Screwball'. During a glittering career, not without its controversy, Beurling is credited with destroying 27 German and Italian aircraft in a 14-day period over Malta and he ended the war with 31 claims, exclusively on the Spitfire. He was described by the high-scoring ace James 'Ginger' Lacey as 'a wonderful pilot and an even better shot'.

V for Victory and a supercilious grin seem to sum up George 'Buzz' Beurling's attitude to the celebrity that followed his outstanding performance as a Spitfire pilot defending Malta. His carefully thought through air gunnery was at first not recognised and his claims were ignored, but soon it became apparent that he was an exceptional shot. Getty Images (Toronto Star Archives)

Sergeant Pilot Beurling's first Spitfire unit was No 403 (Canadian) Squadron but then in 1941 he had to be transferred to a British-manned unit, despite being a Canadian by birth, and was posted to No 41 Squadron. Finding life more restrictive with No 41, Beurling volunteered for Malta and was posted to No 249 Squadron, a journey that involved flying a Spitfire Mk Vc from the deck of HMS *Eagle*.

Commissioned in July 1942, he earned a fine reputation for his skill in close combat, with his exceptional eyesight and mental arithmetic allowing him to score almost every time he opened fire.

After leaving Malta in October 1942 and surviving an air accident in a Liberator in which he was being transported, Beurling transferred to the Royal Canadian Air Force and was posted back to No 403 Squadron, but he could not fit in with European operations. He was discharged in April 1944 but, missing combat, he volunteered to fly for the newly established Israel Defence Force. He did not make Israel as the Norseman transport in which he was being transported crashed at Rome, with no survivors.

Don Blakeslee
Born 11 September 1917
Died 3 September 2008
American Spitfire pilot

Donald Blakeslee was a keen aviator before the Second World War and volunteered to join the Royal Canadian Air Force in 1940, slipping across the border into Canada from his native Ohio.

Blakeslee went on to achieve cult status as a leader in the Royal Canadian Air Force in Britain and later with the US Army Air Force's newly created 4th Fighter Group. A self-confessed 'bad shot' with only three victories claimed in 200 combat hours over Occupied France, Blakeslee first flew the Spitfire with No 401 Squadron from 15 May 1941 and then transferred to command No 133 (Eagle) Squadron in time for the air operations covering the Dieppe raid in August 1942.

In September 1942, after the transfer of all the Americans in the Eagle Squadrons to the USAAF, Blakeslee continued to fly Spitfires, now marked with a US white star on a blue background, until the redesignated 336th (Pursuit) Squadron converted to the P-47 Thunderbolt in March 1943 and then the Mustang. Blakeslee's style of command, acting as the air boss rather than ploughing and looking for kills, is attributed to his experience of flying Spitfires with Fighter Command, where he realised the necessity for a tactical leader to direct his fighters.

Colonel Blakeslee flew fighters in Korea and wrote an outstanding book, *Tumult in the Skies*, which recalls his combat with the USAAF over Germany and being taken prisoner. He died at the age of 90 with the accolade 'the most decorated USAAF fighter pilot of the Second World War'.

American volunteers went north to Canada to train to fight Nazi Germany and among them was Don Blakeslee. He is seen here (right) in 1944 after he transferred to the US Army Air Force, where he led the 4th Fighter Group and completed 500 combat sorties on Mustangs. It was the Spitfire, he said, that made him a fighter pilot. Getty Images (Popperfoto)

Eugene 'Red' Tobin

Born 4 January 1917
Died 7 September 1941
American Spitfire pilot

Born in Los Angeles, Eugene Quimby Tobin was a legendary figure in barnstorming – daring circus-type flying – even before he joined the Royal Air Force in 1940. Known to his friends as 'Red' on account of his hair colour, Tobin learned to fly in California and, thirsting action, came to Europe as a volunteer.

In March 1940 Finland and the Soviet Union ceased hostilities and Tobin found himself without employment before he had even set out, so he took passage to France (via Canada)

When Eugene 'Red' Tobin came to Britain as a 'Canadian' via a circuitous route, he initially flew Spitfires before moving on to the first Eagle Squadron on Hurricanes, as pictured here in March 1941 just after his transfer. He died six months later on a fighter sweep over France. Getty Images (Hulton Archive)

and volunteered to fly fighters for *L'Armée de l'Air*. Again the swift German advance and the equally quick French capitulation defeated him, so in June 1940 he crossed the Channel to Britain from the Biarritz area.

Commissioned as a Pilot Officer in the Royal Air Force, Tobin and two American friends, Andrew Mamedoff and Vernon Keough, converted to the Spitfire Mk I at No 7 Operational Training Unit at RAF Hawarden. Soon the three Americans joined No 609 Squadron Auxiliary Air Force at RAF Middle Wallop and began operations in defence of Portsmouth and Portland, often flying from the forward base at RAF Warmwell, near Dorchester.

Tobin destroyed two Messerschmitt Bf 110s on 25 August and shared in the destruction of a Dornier Do 17 on 15 September. He flew his last sortie with No 609 Squadron on 18 September, a date the squadron war diary records as 'patrol Brooklands – Northolt'.

Keen to establish an American unit within Fighter Command for political purposes, the Air Ministry reformed No 71 Squadron (which had been established in 1917 as an Australian-manned unit) and designated it an 'Eagle Squadron'. The three Americans from No 609 were the first pilots to join, at RAF Church Fenton in October 1940.

The following year Tobin was killed on No 71 Squadron's first sweep over France, after an attack by Bf 109s. Sadly his friends also perished that year: Keough was reported missing in the North Sea, off Flamborough Head, and Mamedoff was killed on a ferry flight to Northern Ireland.

Lieutenant Colonel Rolf Arnë Berg

Born 27 November 1917
Died 3 February 1945
Norwegian Spitfire pilot

Rolf Arnë Berg was Norway's Spitfire Ace of Aces. Norway was invaded in 1940 and its small army air arm was quickly overwhelmed. In London, the Norwegian government-in-exile started negotiations with the Allies to form an air force and by 1942 pilots were being trained in Canada in Little Norway, Ontario, and in Britain at RAF Catterick and RAF North Weald. The Royal Norwegian Air Force itself came into being in November 1944, mainly flying Spitfires, and No 331 and No 332 Squadrons quickly established reputations as motivated and effective fighters.

The greatest of the Norwegian Spitfire pilots in the Royal Air Force was Rolf Arnë Berg. He was born at Trøndelag and volunteered for the army air arm in 1939, escaping to Britain after the German invasion. When the Norwegian squadrons were formed in 1941, he joined No 331 Squadron and his tally started there in 1942. In late 1944 he was appointed Wing Commander Flying of No 132 Wing and led its formation as part of 2nd Tactical Air Force to a forward base in Belgium at Grimbergen, from where he flew his personally marked Spitfire Mk LF IX with the call letters 'RAB'.

In total Berg scored six enemy aircraft destroyed, two probables, three shared and six destroyed on the ground. He became a great friend of Wing Commander Wilfred Duncan Smith, who recognised Berg's talents as a leader and a pilot by mentioning him in some detail in his autobiography.

Sadly Berg did not live to see his country liberated nor take part in the triumphant return of the Royal Norwegian Air Force – which did not exist in 1940 at the time of the invasion – to Sola with a massed approach of Spitfire Mk IXs. Berg was another victim of the highly effective German flak when, on 3 February 1945, he was brought down over the Netherlands/Germany border while attacking, as it happened, a dummy airfield. When he

Norway produced some outstanding soldiers, sailors and airmen in the Second World War. None better exemplifies the spirit of occupied but undefeated Norway than Rolf Arnë Berg, the Spitfire ace and wing leader. Trained in Canada, Berg flew extensively in north-west Europe, mastering the Spitfire Mk IX to take the fight to the enemy. Cato Guhnfeldt Collection

elected to fly that last mission, he was 'tour-expired' and he knew he would not fly a Spitfire again in combat. On the pull-up from a strafing run, his Spitfire was hit, a wing broke off and the crash was not survivable.

Other leading Norwegian aces included Lieutenant Colonel Kaj Birksted (11 victories), Captain Helner Grundt-Spang (11 victories), Major Kåre Bolstad (OC No 332 Squadron), Major Werner Christie, Major Björn Björnstad and Captain D.G. Ånjsen. Today, Norway has another Spitfire pilot: Major Eskil Amdal is an experimental test pilot on the F-16AN and F-35A but also instructs at the Boultbee Flight Academy in England.

THEY ALSO SERVED

Many thousands of young men flew the Spitfire in combat during and after the Second World War. This selected series of biographies is intended to give a little more insight into the breadth of experience, nationality and abilities of Spitfire pilots.

Group Captain Clive Caldwell DSO DFC* was the leading Australian fighter ace of the Second World War with more than 28 victories in the Western Desert and in the defence of Australia. Initially his fighting skills were honed on various models of the Curtiss P-40 where he was nicknamed 'killer' for his dogfighting skills. He converted to the Spitfire in Australia when he transferred to the Royal Australian Air Force to command a Wing in the defence of Darwin.

Following the Wing's move to the Dutch East Indies, Caldwell was court-martialled for his part in a 'mutiny' of airmen after the US commander designated the Spitfire force as ground attack, which was dangerous and to which the Mk VIII was not suited. He was cleared but eventually left the Royal Australian Air Force under a cloud in 1946. He died in 1994.

Wing Commander Pierre Clostermann DSO DFC* was France's greatest exponent of the Spitfire. After the Fall of France, he travelled from his native Brazil to the USA and then to Britain, where he trained with the Royal Air Force. After operational conversion to the Spitfire, in January 1943 he joined No 341 (Free French) Squadron, known as *Groupe de Chasse 'Alsace'*, the birthplace of his father.

He served with No 602 Squadron of the Auxiliary Air Force in operations over Occupied France and was commended by Général Charles de Gaulle, leader of the Free French. He was also dubbed 'France's First Fighter' in the Free French press. After an air war in which he is credited with 11 kills, he went into French civil aviation manufacture and wrote a highly acclaimed autobiography entitled *The Big Show*.

Wing Commander Bob Doe DSO DFC* was a Battle of Britain ace who joined the Royal Air Force Volunteer Reserve in March 1938 and went solo five months later. A natural pilot and cheerful, confident leader, he flew first with No 234 Squadron on Spitfires and became an ace in August 1940. The following month he transferred to No 238 Squadron, also at RAF Middle Wallop, but now flying the Hurricane.

His personal score during the Battle of Britain was 14 confirmed victories. He suffered two accidents and spent some time in the Park Prewett Hospital at Basingstoke for plastic surgery. When he recovered, he was sent to teach fighter tactics and skills at the Fighter Leaders School, and he completed his war service in Burma in a series of command appointments. He retired in 1966 and died on 21 February 2010.

Flying Officer the Prince Emanuel Galitzine was a White Russian émigré who achieved the highest-ever Spitfire interception at 40,000ft when he was serving with the Special Service Flight of modified high-altitude Spitfire Mk IXs at RAF Northolt.

The Special Service Flight had been formed to counter the high-altitude raids by single Junkers Ju 86R bombers that caused air-raid sirens to be sounded over a wide area even though each aircraft only dropped a single 500kg high-explosive weapon on each trip. As a result of Galitzine's action on 12 September 1942, the Luftwaffe perceived that the Junkers was no longer invulnerable to the Spitfire and the raids ceased. Even though the Junkers was not shot down, Galitzine had taken his Spitfire into combat at a higher altitude than any other aircraft in the Second World War.

Squadron Leader James Lacey DFM* is better known as 'Ginger' Lacey. He was the third highest-scoring ace of the Battle of Britain with 18 confirmed victories. Even before hostilities began on 3 September 1939, he had more than 1,000 hours in his logbook and, when called to the front line, joined No 501 Squadron, flying Hurricanes in the Battle of France and the Battle of Britain.

Lacey converted to the Spitfire in 1941 and joined No 602 Squadron at RAF Kenley in March 1942. In April 1946, when serving with No 17 Squadron, he flew the first Spitfire over Japan. Lacey achieved the notable distinction of serving with an operational squadron on both the first day of the Second World War and the last.

Pilot Officer John Gillespie Magee was a pre-war schoolboy poet, born in China of British and American parents, and educated at Rugby School. He joined the Royal Canadian Air

A natural pilot and Spitfire ace, George Unwin does not represent the public image of a Battle of Britain pilot. He was a gruff Yorkshireman with the deserved nickname of 'Grumpy'. Yet, in the Spitfire, he was outstanding and his anecdotes about pre-war RAF Duxford were spellbinding. He is seen here at RAF Fowlmere in 1940 with his ever-alert German Shepherd, Flash. Rex Features (Sarkar Collection)

Force and died in a flying accident in 1941. He will always be remembered for the most moving poem ever written about aviation, *High Flight*, crafted after he took a Spitfire Mk I to 33,000ft.

The original copy of Magee's poem is in the Library of Congress and President Reagan used part of it in his address to the American people after the *Challenger* disaster in 1986. It was also the reading at the author's wedding in 2006.

Oh! I have slipped the surly bonds of Earth
And danced the skies on laughter-silvered wings;
Sunward I've climbed, and joined the tumbling mirth
of sun-split clouds – and done a hundred things
You have not dreamed of – wheeled and soared and swung
High in the sunlit silence. Hov'ring there,
I've chased the shouting wind along, and flung
My eager craft through footless halls of air...
Up, up the long, delirious, burning blue
I've topped the wind-swept heights with easy grace.
Where never lark, or even eagle flew –
And, while with silent, lifting mind I've trod
The high untrespassed sanctity of space,
Put out my hand, and touched the face of God.

Wing Commander George Unwin DSO DFM* was a natural pilot who was one of the first to evaluate the Spitfire when No 19 Squadron received the very first Mk I from the production line in August 1938. Sergeant Pilot Unwin is thought to have tested 15 different Spitfires in 1938–39.

His first combats were over the Dunkirk beaches, where he claimed a Henschel Hs 126 and two Messerschmitt Bf 110s destroyed. His score rose to 12 enemy aircraft destroyed by the end of 1940, including eight Bf 109s. Commissioned and posted to training in 1941, then Mosquito fighter-bombers, Unwin did not fly Spitfires again and retired from the Royal Air Force in 1961 after 32 years of service. He died in 2006.

A veteran of the Battle of Britain and the Battle of Malta, and Vice Chairman of the Battle of Britain Fighter Association, **Squadron Leader Geoffrey Wellum** is the author of the highly acclaimed *First Light*, an autobiographical account of the Battle of Britain. Flying with No 92 Squadron from RAF Biggin Hill, Wellum described his war as 'average', but what makes him special is the fact that his prose has been read and talks listened to by a new generation of young people.

Without Wellum's memories of the Spitfire, there would be fewer enthusiasts. Today he maintains his public service by supporting the fly2help charity as a Patron.

CHAPTER 7

THE WOMEN

The need for trained pilots to carry out 'second-line' duties, which required plenty of experience but not the physical fitness and youth of a military pilot, was apparent to Whitehall planners early in the build-up to war after the Munich Crisis of 1938. There would be too few service pilots available even with the ramped-up training programmes for the Volunteer Reserves of the Royal Air Force. In response, Gérard d'Erlanger, a banker, aviation enthusiast and director of British Airways Ltd, developed the plan for the Air Transport Auxiliary (ATA).

Air Vice Marshal William Welsh DSC AFC, the newly appointed Air Member for Supply & Organisation, took over the administration of what was to be an organisation within RAF Reserve Command as the ATA was formed, initially as part of No 41 Maintenance Group. This fledgling unit comprised men who were too old or too incapacitated to fly in the front line but still had much to offer as ferry pilots.

The ATA structure was completed with the formation of a civilian ferry unit at White Waltham, the home of the West London Aero Club, on 15 February 1940. Initially a ferry unit for medical supplies, personnel and priority mail, the role soon encompassed also the ferrying of aircraft as the Royal Air Force Ferry Pools were finding it hard to cope.

A far more pressing problem developed where there was an immediate need to ferry newly built service aeroplanes between factory and front line, as well as to collect damaged aeroplanes for repair units (some to be broken up for spares). As these included bombers and high-performance fighters like the Spitfire, the initial recruitment was male (usually men unfit for active service through age or disability) and training was carried out at the Royal Air Force's Central Flying School at RAF Upavon in Wiltshire.

Control of this unique organisation was placed in the hands of Gérard d'Erlanger and staffed by the British Overseas Airways Corporation, where he was still a director. He ensured that there were pilots, flight engineers, radio officers and competent ground staff. D'Erlanger enjoyed the support of Winston Churchill and had family connections with the Prime Minister through marriage.

This was obviously a civilian job but the airlines still needed those pilots not called up to the Royal Air Force to maintain essential air routes and there were also factories that did not have enough production test pilots. It would need a uniformed civilian organisation with a rank structure and discipline to open up access to an additional pool of pilots. The ATA

Nothing exemplifies the role of women in aviation in general and the relationship with the Spitfire more than this photo of 27 female ATA pilots, taken on 1 January 1944 at No 15 (Women's) Ferry Pool at Hamble. Of course, there were more male pilots than female in the ATA, and not all female pilots were 'Spitfire Girls'. Rex Features (Bill Cross)

started out with these aims in mind and became the first organisation in the world to employ civilian pilots to fly military aircraft, to pay women to ferry military aircraft, and to allow women civilians to fly fighters and four-engine aircraft.

There was already a notable group of female pilots in the UK and some high-profile exploits had brought them fame between the wars. There was an obvious source, therefore, for additional pilots. As early as November 1939, Pauline Gower, a young, prominent and well-placed aviatrix, was asked to form a women's section of the ATA, which would ultimately lead to 164 female pilots being recruited and trained during the course of the war. The women of the ATA were not only notable for their flying skills and bravery but also because in 1943, after some negotiation, they were awarded equal pay with male pilots – a 'first' in British government service.

By July 1940 it was clear that the ATA was working well as an organisation and that female pilots were as good as men. As there was a shortage of skilled male pilots, so it was natural that the ATA would expand by taking on more women to fly. The new intake included the renowned long-distance flyer, Amy Johnson, who was by then divorced from the US aviator Jim Mollison. She was one of the first ATA women to die as she flew into bad weather in the Oxford she was ferrying and is believed to have baled out over the Thames estuary. She never flew a Spitfire.

As the role changed, so did the ATA. It developed its own training programme and increasingly handled more complex aircraft, progressing with training aircraft through to heavy bombers. The key discriminator was skill. It was obvious that production ferry flights were the most important aspect of the ATA's daily routine, so it came under the remit of the Ministry of Aircraft Production and, from 1 August 1941, was given responsibility for all ferry flights from factories, Maintenance Units and the Civilian Repair Organisation.

At its peak in 1944 there were 22 ferry pools, bases or stations. There were 1,154 male pilots and 164 female pilots who between them flew more than 742,000 hours. Over the course of five years the ATA flew 87 types of single-engine aircraft, 46 types of twin-engine aircraft and 11 types of four-engine aircraft, as well as four types of flying boat. The ATA was disbanded on 30 November 1945 having delivered more than 308,000 aircraft of 148 types and variants as well as carrying people and equipment domestically and overseas.

Due to the difficult conditions they flew in and the pressures they were under to deliver as many aircraft as possible, 173 ATA personnel lost their lives, of whom 14 were women. In total 86 ATA pilots received honours including CBE, OBE, MBE and the King's Commendation for Valuable Services in the Air. While there were many more male than female ATA pilots, not to mention the engineers, ground crew, trainers and administrators, much of the renown of the ATA has come from its forward-thinking approach to women pilots, and the personalities who made their role possible.

Commandant Pauline Gower MBE

Born 22 July 1910
Died 2 March 1947
Head of Women's Section, Air Transport Auxiliary

Pauline Gower was the founding figure of the women's section of the Air Transport Auxiliary whose pilots made a huge contribution to the progress of the Second World War. Like many of the women who volunteered for flying duties, and then had to undergo a stringent medical as well as other examinations, she flew Spitfire delivery flights across the length and breadth of Britain.

Miss Gower caught the flying 'bug' as a child when she was able to fly with Sir Alan Cobham, the famous pioneer of long-distance aviation, during his promotional tour of the country. As soon as she was old enough she trained as a pilot and in August 1931 she established her own air taxi service in Kent, taking people for flights – very often their first – from pleasure grounds and beaches in south-east England.

Keen to promote flying herself, she contributed pieces to *Girl's Own Paper and Chatterbox* besides having her poetry published in 1934 under the title *Piffling Poems for Pilots* and writing a factual book, *Women with Wings*, which was published in 1938. When Captain

Britain had a notable aviatrix community before the Second World War. Here are two such ladies at the Southampton Air Show of 1932: Pauline Gower (right) became the driving force behind having women in the ATA, while Dorothy Spicer, a ground-breaking engineer, became a technical officer in the Air Ministry. Rex Features (Roger-Viollet)

W.E. Johns came to write the *Biggles* series, the female pilot spin-off, *Worrals*, is said to have been modelled on Miss Gower and another prominent aviatrix of the time, Amy Johnson, who herself became an ATA pilot.

With a European war on the horizon, Miss Gower was keen to play her part. She was appointed a civil defence commissioner for the Civil Air Guard, an organisation that was set up in July 1938 by the Secretary of State for Air, Sir Kingsley Wood, a Conservative Party colleague of Miss Gower's father, Sir Robert Gower, the Member of Parliament for Gillingham in Kent. Wood wanted to create a pool of pilots who could assist the Royal Air Force in a time of emergency.

Membership of the Civil Air Guard, established in conjunction with local flying clubs, was open to any person between the ages of 18 and 50. Within a few weeks, more than 13,350 people enquired about joining and 6,900 enrolled in a flying club that would be entitled to government subsidy.

At first the Air Ministry restricted training to British-made aeroplanes but, with the need for pilots, the rules were relaxed in 1939. The Civil Air Guard created a system, which would also be adopted by the ATA, of categorising pilots by skill and sex, and creating the role of 'auxiliary instructor' so that more people could be taught to fly. This pool of pilots served the armed forces and the civil industry well throughout the war.

Pauline Gower was keen that women should also be part of the ATA and that, once accepted, they should have equal pay with the men. Her father's connections in Whitehall and Westminster undoubtedly helped the 164 female pilots achieve parity with the 1,154 males in 1943.

Miss Gower's network of pilots stretched across the globe and soon there were applications from Argentina, Australia, the Netherlands, Poland, South Africa and the USA. An American equivalent was organised under the title Women Airforce Service Pilots (WASP) but, interestingly, the types flown were limited and the women were paid only 65 per cent of a male ferry pilot's salary.

Miss Gower's dogged determination also resulted in the women pilots of the ATA being allowed eventually to fly high-performance fighters, like the Spitfire, and then heavy bombers, such as the Stirling, under A.R.O. MacMillan's simple but effective training system. This categorised aeroplanes (other than flying boats and carrier aircraft) with similar characteristics into five classes for authorisation so that pilots trained on one type of aircraft could fly all other aircraft in the same class without additional training. This meant that ATA pilots often flew aircraft they had never seen before let alone flown.

Pilots, both male and female, progressed up the class structure, and flew increasingly complex aircraft with the help of their 'Ferry Pilots' Notes', which gave them everything they needed to know about a specific type of aircraft on, usually, just one side of card measuring four inches by six.

A passionate believer in aviation, Miss Gower set high standards and ensured that these were met in flying as well as in her personal life. Very sadly she died only two years after the war when giving birth to twin boys.

Flight Captain The Hon Margaret Fairweather

Born 1902
Died 4 August 1944
First female Spitfire pilot

ATA women achieved great things but perhaps it is Margaret Fairweather who stands out for the purpose of this book. Not only was she one of the First Eight (see pages 196–198) to be selected for the ATA but she was also the first woman to fly a Spitfire.

Margaret – or Margie as she preferred to be called – gained her first flying certificate at the Royal Aero Club in 1937 and her first aeroplane was a De Havilland Puss Moth that her brother, Walter (later Director-General of British Overseas Airways Corporation), had flown in two King's Cup air races. With her trips to mainland Europe in the late 1930s, including as far as Sweden, Germany and Italy, she was awarded a French international pilot's licence and added several more types to her logbook. In fact, prior to being invited to be one of Pauline Gower's first female pilots, Margie had accumulated about 1,000 hours

The first eight ATA female pilots were the trailblazers for 164 pilots and four flight engineers. Here are seven of the first eight (from left): Winifred Crossley, Margaret Cunnison, Margaret Fairweather, Gabrielle Patterson, Mona Friedlander, Joan Hughes and Rosemary Rees. In all, the ATA had 1,246 aircrew members, of whom 173 died in service. ATA Museum/Maidenhead Heritage

THE FIRST EIGHT

Led by the indomitable Pauline Gower, the First Eight, as they were always known, played an important part not just in achieving the equality of women flyers in the Air Transport Auxiliary but also in establishing the organisation's worth in the eyes of Whitehall mandarins.

Their pay was set at £230 per annum with 'flying pay', but because the home base was close to London, at Hatfield, no subsistence grant was paid and the pilots were billeted on families in the surrounding area. Officially inducted into the ATA on 1 January 1940, the First Eight were all qualified flying instructors and their skill certainly showed from the very beginning: by the Fall of France they had delivered 2,000 service aeroplanes without loss or reportable incident.

Framed by a De Havilland Dominie transport, the first eight Air Transport Auxiliary female pilots pose for the camera at the White Waltham headquarters in the late spring of 1940. By 1943 there were Americans as well as British and Commonwealth citizens among the ATA's female pilots, and at least three came to Britain from South America to help in the war effort. ATA Museum/Maidenhead Heritage

Second Officer Winifred Crossley was an early Spitfire ferry pilot who had made her living for several years from flying activities before the Second World War, towing banners for aerial advertising and working as a stunt pilot in a flying circus. By the time war broke out, she already held an instructor's rating and had an impressive 1,860 hours in her logbook, so she was a natural for the ATA. Passing quickly from Class 1 (light aircraft) to Class 2 (single-engine fighters), she became one of the first four Spitfire pilots from the women's section.

Flight Captain Margaret Cunnison was the leading instructor and check pilot of the First Eight. With a career in flying instruction at Hatfield and other airfields around Britain, Miss Cunnison was tasked with evaluating the American volunteers for the ATA in 1942 and had to cope with some very headstrong and direct women. She retired from the ATA in 1943 to marry.

Signing for a Mk I at Eastleigh after its test flight in the hands of Jeffrey Quill (left), Winifred Crossley is about to pilot this brand-new Spitfire to a Maintenance Unit for its war equipment to be fitted. Solent Sky

The first woman to have flown a Spitfire is recorded as **Flight Captain The Hon Margaret Fairweather** and as such she has been singled out for a more lengthy 'main' entry in this book (see page 195).

Flight Captain Mona Friedlander was an international hockey star who also flew for fun. A qualified flying instructor, she flew Tiger Moths and other light aeroplanes in the Civil Air Guard during the build-up to the Second World War, mainly to provide 'targets' for the British Army's Anti-Aircraft Command and the searchlight batteries around London. When Hatfield closed in 1943 and the ferry pools moved closer to Supermarine at Southampton and Vickers Armstrong at Castle Bromwich, she left the ATA and married.

Flight Captain Joan Hughes MBE was the youngest female pilot in Britain when she received her licence in 1933 when aged 15, and she was also one of the youngest Spitfire pilots in the ATA. She became a legendary figure in the ferry pools, being the only female instructor on all types and one of the first to fly heavy bombers, initially the Short Stirling; an iconic photograph in national newspapers in 1943 showed her dwarfed by a Stirling. She still only had 800 hours in her logbook then but she kept flying throughout the Second World War.

Post-war she flew replica aeroplanes in films such as *Those Magnificent Men In Their Flying Machines* and *The Blue Max,* her combination of skill and very light weight making her ideally suited to this work. She retired from flying in 1985 after 11,800 hours and with one of the most interesting logbooks of all time. Miss Hughes never married, telling friends that she could not put a husband before flying.

Flight Captain Gabrielle Patterson was the oldest pilot in the First Eight and was married with a small son and living in Walsall in the Midlands when, in 1935, she qualified as the first female chief flying instructor at a British aero club. During the war she became the head of the Women's Corps of the Civil Air Guard in Romford, Essex.

Deputy Commandant Rosemary Rees (Lady du Cros) was another qualified flying instructor and a keen aviation adventurer as well as being an accomplished ballet dancer and linguist. Taking a Miles Hawk light aircraft for a world tour, she ended up in Germany in 1939, but departed just in time and joined the ATA at the earliest opportunity, remaining in it throughout the war. When the Hamble Ferry Pool was established, she became the Deputy Commandant. Post-war, she returned to private flying and set up an air taxi business with a surplus Percival Proctor. She passed away in 1994, aged 92.

Deputy Commandant Marion Wilberforce was another life-long pilot who joined the ATA as soon as the doors were opened. Miss Wilberforce had considerable pre-war experience as an instructor on a Gypsy Moth and then post-war private flying in a Hornet Moth. Among her accomplishments was an early appointment as Deputy Commandant of the Hatfield Ferry Pool and then command of the Cosford Pool.

of private flying and instructing at the Scottish Flying Club, making her one of the most experienced female pilots.

With war on the horizon, the Scottish Flying Club became part of the Civil Air Guard and naturally Margie was an instructor. It was through this organisation that she got to know Pauline Gower, although there were also social links between the two women as both had fathers in Parliament, Margie's (Lord Runciman) in the Lords, Pauline's in the Commons.

Flying and skill at flying dominated the Fairweather household as Margie's husband Douglas was one of the first pilots to join the ATA, where he set up the Air Movements Flight at White Waltham in 1942. Both were rated on four-engine bombers, Margie being one of fewer than 12 women to be so classed.

Sadly both died before the end of the Second World War. Douglas was lost over the Irish Sea when operating from No 4 Ferry Pool at Prestwick, where they were both stationed. Margie perished when her Proctor ferry aircraft ran out of fuel and she force-landed in a field, hitting an unseen ditch at the end.

First Officer Diana Barnato-Walker

Born 15 January 1918
Died 28 April 2008
Spitfire pilot and supersonic aviatrix

First Officer Diana Barnato-Walker joined the ATA in 1942. From an early age she set out on a quest of adventure and aviation thanks in large part to the pedigree of her father – Woolf Barnato, chairman of Bentley Motors and three-times winner of the Le Mans 24-hour race – and his first wife, Dorothy, from New York State.

Courtesy of her father's position and wealth, Diana spent much time during her teenage years at the Brooklands circuit in Surrey, where the proximity to the Brooklands Aero Club made it the natural place for her to take lessons in one of the black and maroon Tiger Moths. She learned to fly by the time she was 20 and she seems to have been a natural, going solo in six hours and excelling in handling and navigation. These two skills would make her a ideally suited for the Air Transport Auxiliary just two years later.

Before applying to the ATA in 1941, Diana volunteered to be a nurse with the Red Cross, serving with the British Expeditionary Force in France in 1939–40; she may have been evacuated through Calais in the last days before the Germans overran the port. Undeterred, she drove a Red Cross ambulance in the London Blitz during the winter of 1940–41.

When the ATA started a second expansion of female pilots, Diana was called to interview at White Waltham and on 9 March 1941 was given a check ride in a Tiger Moth with the chief flying instructor, A.R.O. MacMillan. She passed and, after a medical, was posted in November to the ATA Elementary Flying Training School, also at White Waltham. By May 1942 she was a ferry pilot at No 15 Ferry Pool at Hamble. Her initial training allowed her to fly light single-engine aircraft, including Tiger Moths and other trainers. She was again

THE LADIES OF THE PRODUCTION LINE

Britain suffered a considerable skills shortage in the Second World War. With so many men called away to fight and a scarcity of skilled people familiar with the new technologies in aero engineering and design, it was natural that women would be recruited by many firms in the aviation industry.

By 1944 most production lines had at least a 60 per cent female workforce who were found to be quicker to train and could concentrate for longer. The Supermarine dispersed factories at Salisbury and Trowbridge and the huge Vickers plant at Castle Bromwich particularly benefited from this influx of new talent.

Before the war, in 1938, Supermarine had already employed women on the Spitfire production line at Woolston and after the Luftwaffe bombed the factory, on 26 September 1940, many were sent to small workshops around the Southampton area to become involved in component manufacture.

Some of these 'Spitfire Girls' have been swept to stardom on documentary television. **Peggy Sugden** from Trowbridge was famously pictured in the *Wiltshire Times* in 1944, proudly showing her engagement ring, and in 2014 she featured in Guy Martin's documentary about Spitfire restoration, but sadly she died just days before the programme was broadcast.

In interviews about life in a Spitfire factory, Peggy would stress the team spirit, which compensated for the long shifts that kept the girls on the production line from 6am to 6pm. Peggy had been conscripted for war work when she left school in 1940 and learned to be a riveter.

Some of the work was truly repetitive. **Megan Rees** (*née* Llewellyn) told BBC West Midlands local radio in 2005 about her experiences at Castle Bromwich's C Block. For the whole of her wartime work at 'Nuffields', as it was known to the workforce, she built Spitfire starboard wings, which were held vertically in jigs. She remembered the noise of the drills and the vibration of the rivet gun – and the occasional injury. 'Once I drilled through my little finger,' she remembered. But there would be no time off, just a visit to first aid and then back on the line.

Another peril for the workforce was an air raid. When on a night shift, workers would prepare their gas masks and outside clothes for the inevitable siren. Each worker had a place pre-selected in a given air raid shelter. 'No one ran, it was all orderly,' one of the Southampton factory girls remembered.

Olive Truscott told the BBC in 2003 how the fitters at the Woolston factory were under such pressure in the summer of 1940 to get Spitfires completed that many would stay at the works for several days and sleep on benches there.

The men and women of the aircraft factories and repair shops were very much the unsung heroes of the Battle of Britain and the subsequent air war.

It was all about team spirit and being prepared to work long hours. The workers here are preparing components to be sprayed in the paint shop, probably in Southampton's former Sunlight Laundry building. Solent Sky

Queen Mary during one of her visits to Trowbridge's Spitfire factories, probably at Bradley Road, seeing how wing structures were fabricated by the female workforce. These visits were made on a Saturday afternoon when the Dowager Queen was staying in the area, at Badminton House. Solent Sky

There were many personalities in the ATA. One of the brightest stars in that firmament was Diana Barnato-Walker, whose claims to fame included taking a Spitfire to Brussels and becoming the first British woman to break the sound barrier. Rex Features (Bill Cross)

assessed after advanced training and progressed to the next class, which included single-engine fighters, among them the Spitfire. Diana adored the Spitfire and spoke of it almost lovingly and certainly was delighted to fly it, probably more than the twin-engine Mosquito or the more powerful Hawker Tempest. In all, she flew 80 different types.

In the period 1943–45 Diana delivered 260 Spitfires, mainly from flight-test facilities such as Eastleigh and Chattis Hill, to Royal Air Force Maintenance Units where armament and radio equipment was installed. Without a radio on delivery flights, navigation was by map and compass. She was the first to fly across the Channel to newly liberated Europe, taking a Spitfire with her then husband, Wing Commander Derek Walker. They departed RAF Northolt on 2 October 1944 and celebrated their delayed honeymoon – they were actually married on 6 May 1944 – in Brussels. On the return flight she became lost mid-Channel because of the weather and only just made RAF Tangmere, low on fuel.

Sadly Derek Walker was killed in November 1945 on a ferry flight in a Mustang. Diana did not marry again but she kept Derek's name despite being delivered of a son in 1947. She went on to become the first British pilot to break the sound barrier, flying the Spitfire's 1960s equivalent, the English Electric Lightning T4, in August 1963. Her strong will and character carried her through to the age of 90 when she died after a long battle with cancer.

Dr Beatrice Shilling OBE
Born 8 March 1909
Died 18 November 1990
Aeronautical engineer and inventor, Royal Aircraft Establishment

Beatrice 'Tilly' Shilling was ahead of her time – and was very significant to the development of the Spitfire. It was through her hard work and intellectual responsiveness that she improved the performance of the Rolls-Royce Merlin engine to allow pilots to carry out the full range of air-combat manoeuvres.

Shilling was also an accomplished motorcycle racer who lapped Brooklands circuit at over 106mph on a Norton she had modified herself, but her greatest contribution to mechanical engineering was her work at the Royal Aircraft Establishment (RAE) at Farnborough.

For most of the 20th century the RAE at Farnborough was at the forefront of aerospace

An engineer with a bent for invention, 'Tilly' Shilling saved many a Spitfire pilot's life with a simple device to keep the Merlin engine performing in negative G. She was also the first woman to exceed 100mph on wheels – on this modified Norton motorcycle at Brooklands in August 1934. TopFoto

engineering not just in Britain but worldwide. The intellectual rigour and the calculated bravery of pilots, flight-test engineers and supporting 'boffins' kept Britain ahead in the technology race with Nazi Germany in the critical periods of the Second World War, and later helped the Allied cause to compete with the Soviet Union in the Cold War.

In the Battle of Britain, Spitfire and Hurricane pilots were unable to 'bunt' away from an enemy fighter by simply pushing the nose down and pulling negative G. The cause of this impediment to combat flying was the floating, direct-feed carburettor of the Rolls-Royce Merlin piston engine. In a bunt, the carburettor flooded – as did the supercharger – due to excess fuel being forced to the top of the float chamber by the opening of the needle valve, the float itself being pulled to the base of the chamber. A rich-mixture cut-out would then cause the engine to lose power or, worse, fail at a critical time of flight. This was described in an official report as 'a serious drawback in combat' – an understatement to say the least.

This shortcoming meant that fighter pilots had to waste valuable time in rolling to the inverted position and then pulling back, whereas the Daimler-Benz fuel-injected engines of the Messerschmitt family were able to deliver power irrespective of the attitude in which the pilot found himself. In fact Daimler had productionised fuel injection in 1937 but had managed to keep its details secret.

Shilling was assigned to study the problem and come up with a solution. She and her team worked tirelessly until late 1940 on the development of an interim solution. Her response was simple and yet effective – a small metal disc with a hole in the middle that was fitted to the SU (Skinners' Union) carburettor of the early Merlin engines. The rectification was completed by Shilling and her team of fitters by March 1941.

According to the late Raymond Kent, chief engineer at SU, the fixes tried by his team did work in theory but a lasting solution did not come until Shilling's fresh approach 'got the geometry right'. For the Merlin 66, which powered the Spitfire Mk IX, a speed-density carburettor system was developed to replace the carburettor venturi with an engine-driven fuel pump that delivered the fuel to either the intake eye of the supercharger or divided it into individual fuel charges that were injected directly into the engine cylinder. Atmospheric pressure and the mass of air passing through the unit combined to control the fuel pump. This was complex technology that needed the ingenuity of both SU and Rolls-Royce and plenty of collaboration between the two companies.

In true fighter-pilot style, the RAE restrictor needed a nickname and it became 'Miss Shilling's Orifice'. The device was only a stop-gap and Rolls-Royce had to work on a production solution in the shape of a Bendix-Stromberg pressure carburettor in 1943, itself partially replaced months later by a patented Rolls-Royce solution.

Even today, fuel management in high-performance engines remains a major technological development area, especially when engineers need to work in the restricted space of a large aero engine in a small aeroplane.

The projects Shilling worked on post-war included the Blue Streak missile and research into aircraft braking on wet runways. She and her husband, George Naylor, also went motor racing with various cars, including an Austin-Healey Sebring Sprite and an Elva Courier.

THEY ALSO SERVED

Lettice Curtis was another ATA pilot who was well known both for her excellent piloting skills and her lust for life. Lettice was the first woman to fly a four-engine bomber and later delivered Avro Lancasters solo as a matter of course. Described by the *Daily Telegraph* in its obituary in July 2014 as 'arguably the most remarkable woman pilot of the Second World War', she was a pilot for the Ordnance Survey before the war and one of the few ATA women who carried on working in aviation after the war in several different roles, including as a flight-test observer. She also continued to fly the Spitfire in several air races after the war and became a qualified helicopter pilot at the age of 77.

First Officer Joy Lofthouse was a renowned ATA pilot who joined the Women's Section in 1943, with her sister Yvonne, and they both quickly moved up the ladder to graduate to the Spitfire by 1944; they were the only sisters to fly the Spitfire. True to her name, Joy describes the Spitfire as 'an absolute joy to fly'. Nowadays Joy is a patron of the aviation support charity, fly2help, which is based at Kemble in Gloucestershire, near where she lives. RAF Kemble, a former maintenance base, was home to the Red Arrows from 1966 to 1983.

Lettice Curtis was a commercial pilot before joining the ATA in 1940 and she became one of the first women to take a single-engine fighter, a Hurricane, on a long cross-country flight. She was also the first to fly a four-engine bomber and she later raced Spitfires in the post-war National Air Races. She died in July 2014 aged 99.
Rex Features

CHAPTER 8
THE NAVAL PILOTS

As early as May 1938, with Spitfire production at Woolston barely under way, the Admiralty showed a distinct interest in acquiring a modern, eight-gun fighter for carrier-borne operations. The Air Ministry had ceded control of the Fleet Air Arm to the Admiralty in the previous year and it was clear that the provision of naval aircraft had been neglected in pursuit of land-based bombers and fighters.

With a close association with naval aviation, Richard Fairey, managing director of Fairey Aviation, which he had founded in 1915, wanted to create a fleet fighter. Fairey was an industrialist of considerable standing, having been twice president of the Royal Aeronautical Society and chairman of the Society of British Aircraft Constructors. With plants at Hayes, where Heathrow now stands, and at Hamble on Southampton Water, he was familiar with both land-based and seaplane construction.

In fact Fairey was intrigued by the idea of designing and building a Spitfire to operate off the Royal Navy's planned new aircraft carriers. He took the idea to the Admiralty in May 1938 but was rebuffed by those who thought the Gloster Sea Gladiator and Blackburn Roc two-seat fighter were sufficient against the German air threat.

One of Neville Chamberlain's first acts on the outbreak of war on 3 September 1939 was to invite Winston Churchill back to the Admiralty as the First Lord – the political head. Churchill engaged in the maritime role with gusto, including support for the need for the Fleet Air Arm to have a state-of-the-art fighter, as championed by Vice Admiral Sir Guy Royle, who commanded the Royal Navy's aircraft carriers and was soon to be appointed Fifth Sea Lord, the professional head of naval aviation.

In late November 1939, Commander A.C.G. Ermen, whose 820 Squadron had landed Swordfish torpedo bombers on the new aircraft carrier HMS *Ark Royal* for the first time earlier in the year, took a Southampton-built Spitfire Mk I for a test flight from the Supermarine airfield at Eastleigh. On landing, he was briefed by Joe Smith, the still-to-be appointed chief designer at Supermarine, about the company's plans to create a 'Hooked' Spitfire. In fact the Admiralty had been briefed on 27 October that a successful test flight in such an aircraft had been undertaken by Jeffrey Quill, Supermarine's chief test pilot (see page 82).

The Admiralty informed the Air Ministry on 29 February 1940 that it required 50 Hooked Spitfires with folding wings to accommodate both the demands of parking aboard ship and the use of aircraft lifts, but Churchill, as the First Lord of the Admiralty, rescinded

Literally a Hooked Spitfire, this Castle Bromwich-built Mk Vb has been modified at Hamble to include not just an arrestor hook but also a tropical filter. Putting Spitfire on aircraft carriers became a priority to combat German reconnaissance aircraft in the Battle of the Atlantic and to provide air cover for future amphibious landings in North Africa and Europe. **Solent Sky**

the request. The relevant correspondence has been lost, but one supposes that Churchill's priority at this time was for all fighter production to be for the Royal Air Force. As a result, naval Spitfires were put on the back burner and the Fleet Air Arm received some more Fairey Fulmar heavy fighters and American Grumman Wildcat fighters.

The matter was raised again by the Admiralty in late 1941 when it was clear that the Sea Hurricane Mk I and even the Wildcat were not effective enough to defend the Fleet against sustained air attack from massed bombers, dive bombers and their fighter escorts. Meanwhile, more work on the Hooked Spitfire had been carried out at Supermarine by Alan Clifton, personal assistant to Joe Smith (as he had been to R.J. Mitchell).

The first deck landings did not happen until December 1941, when Commander Peter Bramwell made a series of them on HMS *Illustrious* in a Spitfire Mk Vb modified with a simple A-frame arrestor gear to catch the transverse steel cables that stop an aeroplane on the deck as it lands.

Later that month 48 Spitfire Mk Vb versions were allocated from the Southampton production line to the nearby Air Training Services Ltd at Hamble to be modified into Hooked Spitfires. The working drawings for the Seafire Mk Ib, as these 48 were eventually designated, show the strengthening that was applied to the lower fuselage, especially to the longerons. Trials were flown at the Service Trials Unit (STU) at Arbroath in Scotland and kept secret for many months.

This first batch of Seafires was effective but not ideal. The STU expressed serious concern about the ability of the design to cope with the rigours of repeated deck landings owing to structural weaknesses. This job of rectifying this shortcoming was given to Eastleigh-based Cunliffe-Owen Aircraft, supported again by Air Training Services Ltd at Hamble.

Converting the Mk Vb into the Seafire Mk Ib was very much within the skill set at Eastleigh and Hamble. The work comprised reinforcement the fuselage, especially around the inspection hatches and along the keel, then adding government-furnished equipment. This equipment included a naval high-frequency radio for beyond-the-horizon communications, naval onboard Identification, Friend or Foe equipment (known as 'Pipsqueak'), and a homing beacon receiver for those rare occasions when a lost Seafire could be brought back to 'Mother' by radio fix. There was provision for a slipper tank of 30 Imperial gallons to be fitted under the fuselage to extend endurance by a claimed 30 minutes. Needless to say, the Seafire had its air speed indicator recalibrated to knots (nautical miles per hour) and its flight reference cards were rewritten accordingly. Like the Spitfire Mk Vb, the Seafire Mk Ib was armed with two 20mm Hispano cannon and four 0.303in Browning guns.

The Seafire Mk Ib was embarked on HMS *Furious* in October 1942 and remained in the front line until September 1944.

Seafire nomenclature can be difficult to follow and the first new variant proves this point. The next Hooked Spitfire – a conversion rather than a 'new build' – was termed the Mk IIc by the Admiralty, but was in fact a navalised Mk Vc. And just to confuse things further, there were three sub-variants: the Merlin 46-powered fighter version Mk F IIc; the camera-equipped fighter-reconnaissance version Mk PR IIc with the same power plant; and the low-level Mk IIc with a Merlin 32 engine, a special version optimised for low-altitude work with supercharger refinements and a four-blade propeller. The naval equipment on the Seafire Mk IIc included catapult spools and a single lifting ring at the centre of gravity, replacing the fore and aft spools of the Mk Ib.

For the Seafire Mk IIc to be embarked on escort carriers – the so-called Woolworth Carriers – trials were flown from the Clyde. On 11 September 1942 Lieutenant Eric Brown landed a Mk IIc on HMS *Biter* without the benefit of batsmen or raised arrestor gear on the flight deck. On launching again, Brown felt that some inexperienced naval pilots might require assistance on what was a very short run for a heavy fighter with fuel and armaments. No immediate action was taken but it was clear that a system to assist take-off might be needed. Brown was also concerned about the consequences of a Seafire running off the flight deck into the sea: 'It ditched like a submarine – very few ditchings were successful, even when semi-controlled, and we lost many pilots that way.'

In February 1943 Brown was given the task of flying trials with rocket-assisted take-off at Boscombe Down and Farnborough. Joe Smith, by then chief designer at Supermarine, attended many of the trials at Farnborough and Jeffrey Quill, the chief test pilot, flew each type and sub-variant of the Seafire.

The trials were a success and thereafter all models of Seafire were built to suit rocket-assisted take-off. Contracts were placed with Supermarine to build 262 Mk IIc Seafires at Southampton and Salisbury, while Westland at Yeovil contributed a further 110, including an additional 30 Mk IIIh (h for hybrid) variants.

The Seafire Mk XV was modified with folding wings so that it could operate on a Light Fleet Carrier and be stored below decks in the hangar. This clever design, which was created by Alan Clifton's team at Hursley Park, gave a stance that was likened to that of a Balinese dancer. Solent Sky

The Seafire Mk IIc was embarked on most of the Royal Navy's aircraft carriers and proved a remarkable success. The first aerial victory for a Seafire is credited to Sub-Lieutenant (A) George Baldwin RNVR flying a Seafire Mk IIc of 807 Naval Air Squadron from the aged aircraft carrier HMS *Furious* during the Operation Torch landings in North Africa.

During this time Alan Clifton was busy at Supermarine's new design office at Hursley Park, where the experiment shop was also based. Using the Mk IIc as his baseline, he developed the Seafire design into a purpose-built naval fighter with folding wings for hangar stowage and to allow more fighters to be accommodated on the flight deck. The wing folds were at the tip and just outboard of the undercarriage wheels, giving the Mk F III a stance that some sailors thought reminiscent of a Balinese dancer.

The Mk III turned out to be a real winner and was built in greater numbers than any other mark of Seafire. Rolls-Royce produced two Merlin engine types for the design: the Merlin 55 for the fighter and fighter-reconnaissance versions and a supercharged Merlin 55M for the low-altitude fighter variant. Lightweight cannon and slipper tank fittings completed the design, which rolled off the Cunliffe-Owen and Westland lines for two years. The final versions were eventually sold to the Union of Burma Air Force and the Irish Air Corps with the naval equipment removed.

By now the Royal Air Force was receiving the Griffon-powered Spitfire and the Admiralty rightly wanted to have the benefits of the Griffon married to the proven design of the Mk III. Clifton again led the design team, under Smith's guidance, to satisfy the Ministry of Aircraft Production's Specification N4/43. The Seafire Mk XV prototype was a modified Spitfire Mk VII with the Griffon VI engine with a single-stage supercharger. More fuel needed to be carried internally and the increased torque of the Griffon power plant with its larger Rotol airscrew required a larger, more pointed fin and rudder.

To bring a Mk XV to a halt on the flight deck, Cunliffe-Owen was tasked with improving the arrestor hook, which was initially just beefed up with more steel but eventually a new 'sting'-type fitting was introduced in the rear fuselage adjacent to the retractable tail wheel arrangement with its retractable wire guard.

Six Mk XV prototypes were commissioned from Supermarine, using both Salisbury and Southampton with flying at High Post and Eastleigh respectively. The Royal Aircraft Establishment at Farnborough was also informed, allowing Lieutenant Brown to become involved – and he was not that impressed. He reasoned that a novice pilot on a take-off run might not cope with the Mk XV's tendency to lurch across the deck to the right (towards the island superstructure) because of the Griffon's torque, and in fact there were collisions with deck superstructure, especially with the use of rocket-assisted take-off – which made the aircraft uncontrollable. The Mk XV did not endear itself to naval aviators.

Only 390 of the Mk XV – now the mark numbers were in sequence with the Spitfire – were built but after the Second World War several air forces bought them, or were gifted them, for use on land, where the longer extent of a runway caused few problems for the pilot, even if the stall was still regarded as 'vicious'.

During 1943 and 1944, Smith's team at Hursley Park reworked the Spitfire into a completely new aeroplane to take the Griffon engine and to become an air-superiority fighter with the rear fuselage stripped down and a tear-drop bubble canopy fitted. Taking this innovation and improving the main undercarriage system, the Achilles' heel of the Mk XV, Supermarine came up with the Seafire Mk XVII, which was a real winner, remaining in service with the Royal Naval Reserve's air wing until the 1950s. The Cunliffe-Owen company assembled the first 20 Mk XVIIs as concept-proof airframes, many without the bubble canopy, and Westland built 212 examples.

The Mk XVII is regarded as the best wartime Seafire but it was still a compromise with its narrow-track undercarriage and relatively short range, even with an extra 33 Imperial gallon fuel tank, giving an endurance approaching two hours. In the Pacific, the Seafire proved to be a better combat air-patrol aircraft than the US Navy's fleet fighters, even if they lacked the stores-carrying capabilities for giving close air support to the troops and marines ashore. Seafires provided the Royal Navy with a fleet fighter of the same calibre as shore-based equivalents, retaining the same tactical Mach numbers as Spitfires in dogfights.

The Royal Navy's top-scoring Seafire pilot was Sub-Lieutenant R.H. Reynolds DSC RNVR of 894 Naval Air Squadron with four confirmed kills and one shared. On 15 August 1945, HMS *Indefatigable*'s Seafires from 887 and 894 Naval Air Squadrons achieved the

Ranged on HMS Indomitable's *flight deck in 1943 are Seafire Mk L IIc fighters from 880 Naval Air Squadron during a work-up captured by Charles Brown's camera.* Getty Images (Hulton Archive)

type's best day in combat with 22 confirmed kills in defence of US warships targeted by Japanese *kamikaze* attacks.

By the time the Seafire Mk 45 was ready for service the Second World War had ended, even in the Pacific. This variant was a straight 'navalisation' of the Spitfire Mk 21 prototype built at Salisbury and then modified at Eastleigh by Cunliffe-Owen to carry a single or 'sting'-type arrestor hook with new fuselage fuel tanks and 'bowser'-type wing leading edges, another Supermarine Salisbury innovation that was originally used for the photo-reconnaissance versions of the Spitfire. The Mk 45 entered service in two versions of fighter and fighter-reconnaissance with the same F24 camera mountings as the Mk III. Fifty Mk 45s were built at Castle Bromwich – some of the last Spitfires to leave the Birmingham plant.

The Griffon 60-series Seafire Mk 46 was a naval version of the Spitfire Mk 22, optimised for land-based operations with solid wings, like the Mk 45. Some were modified with a Rotol contra-rotating airscrew and the powerful Griffon 80-series power plant. Only four were built but the design work on this mark paved the way for the ultimate Seafire – the Mk 47.

Seeing operational service in two further wars, in Malaya in 1949 and the more serious East/West conflict of the Cold War on the Korean peninsula in 1950, the Seafire Mk 47 was the culmination of the development of all other Seafires. It was the sum of the work by Clifton at Supermarine and by test pilots like Brown, as well as the workforces at Supermarine and

The pilot of this Seafire Mk XVII is believed to be Lieutenant Commander Charles Lamb DSO DSC, probably at HMS Daedalus, *the Royal Naval Air Station Lee-on-Solent, in 1949. Lamb served on the staff of Flag Officer (Air) (Home) at the time.* Solent Sky

its sub-contractors such as Cunliffe-Owen and Westland. Brown describes the Mk 47 as the culmination of all the hard work that Joe Smith had put into the Mitchell design to make it a true thoroughbred fighter and describes it as 'thunderous'.

Brown further describes the Mk 47's undercarriage as 'substantial', an improvement that stopped the propensity of earlier marks to float over the arrestor wires and crash into the steel safety barrier or, worse, bounce over the barrier into the deck park beyond. It must be remembered that these operations were in the days before the Royal Navy introduced the angled deck, which allowed the dangerous barrier to be removed. 'The Mk 47 would jump on the deck and hop across it as the power was applied, sometimes making collision with the island [superstructure] seem almost inevitable,' recalls Brown, who was responsible for catapult trials first at Farnborough and then in sea-acceptance trials.

Jeffrey Quill, the Supermarine chief test pilot, reminds us in his autobiography that the Mk 47's weight was the equivalent of a fully loaded Spitfire Mk I carrying 32 airline passengers with 40lb of baggage each. In other words, the last of the line was a completely different aeroplane from Mitchell's little fighter of 1936.

On 28 January 1949 the last Supermarine Seafire Mk 47 left the production line at Southampton and headed for the Royal Naval Air Station at Yeovilton. The Seafire series had been flown by 12 front-line squadrons and served the Royal Canadian Navy and the emerging French Naval Air Arm for three and five years respectively.

During its active service in Korea, when the Royal Navy provided the only British units equipped with fighters, the Seafire Mk 47 flew 360 sorties from HMS *Triumph*, the Light Fleet Carrier, and suffered only two fatalities – one to the guns of a US Air Force B-29 Superfortress and the other to a deck-landing accident. This is testament indeed to aircrew, groundcrew and the aeroplane itself through the drawing pens of Smith, Clifton and their teams at Supermarine.

Lieutenant Commander Eric Brown DSC AFC
Born 21 January 1919
Naval test pilot

Captain Eric Melrose Brown is not only the greatest living test pilot but the Fleet Air Arm's most decorated pilot. No man alive has flown more variants of Spitfire and Seafire. No man has flown so many aeroplane types nor carried out so many deck landings on an aircraft carrier.

Eric Brown was the son of a First World War pilot and so flying was in his blood, especially after being flown on his father's knee in a Gloster Gauntlet in 1929. During a visit with his father to the Berlin Olympics in 1936 he met former First World War ace Ernst Udet, who took him up in a two-seat Bücker Jungmann and threw it around. Udet, who rose to become chief of staff in the Luftwaffe, urged Brown to take up flying, telling him that he had the temperament to be a fighter pilot. While at Edinburgh University studying modern languages with an emphasis on German, Brown received his first formal flying instruction with the University's Air Squadron. His course required a spell in Germany as an exchange student and he found himself there when war broke out but was able to get home via Switzerland.

He joined the Royal Naval Volunteer Reserve as the quickest way of getting into flying training and his initial operational flying was aboard the escort carrier HMS *Audacity*, from which he flew Grumman Martlet (Wildcat) fighters with 802 Naval Air Squadron on convoy-protection duties. In the course of these duties he had two successful combats with Focke-Wulf Fw 200 Condor long-range bombers that resulted in both aircraft being downed. When HMS *Audacity* was sunk Brown was one of only two 802 NAS pilots to survive.

He was transferred to test flying to develop deck-landing techniques for the conversion of land-based fighters to naval use and sent north to Arbroath to join the Service Trials Unit, where he worked with the still-secret Hooked Spitfire. When returning there from successful deck landing trials aboard HMS *Biter* in the Moray Firth, the young naval test pilot thought he might take the opportunity of 'checking out the handling of the Seafire' by looping under the three main spans of the Forth railway bridge, an event captured for posterity by aviation artist Michael Turner. The resultant fuss led to the grounding of all Spitfire units in the area until the miscreant owned up.

No man has more aircraft carrier landings than Eric Brown. Many of those landings were flown with the Seafire from the Service Trials Unit at Arbroath in Scotland. Known to many as 'Winkle' on account of his stature, he is a giant of the test-flying world and probably the only man living who has flown German wartime jets. He remains an inspiration to a new generation of naval pilots.

Brown studied the needs of a landing pilot recovering to the deck of an aircraft carrier and concluded that a curved approach to landing suited most, if not all, flying conditions. The Fifth Sea Lord of the time, Admiral Denis Boyd, was concerned that Brown was a novice on the Spitfire compared with the Supermarine test pilots and asked Jeffrey Quill to check out Brown's theories. So started a 50-year friendship between Brown and Quill.

Quill took the Hooked Spitfire to sea and tried Brown's approach technique of 'skidding in sideways' and approved of it. To please the Admiral, who was the *de facto* head of the Fleet Air Arm, Quill wrote a report and as a result the technique was universally adopted for carrier landings, and subsequently by the US Navy and Marine Corps as well.

Among the 14 types of Spitfire and Seafire recorded in Brown's logbook is the Mk LF XII, which he says was 'the best I have ever flown' at low level. His experience also includes the Mk IX, which he flew with the Canadians on operations from RAF Kenley for a few days. He judged that the Mk IX had an advantage over other fighters in that its tactical Mach number, at 0.80, was higher than contemporary fighters such as the Fw 190 (0.75) and even the Merlin-engined Mustang (0.78) with its laminar-flow wings. For a fighter pilot, the tactical Mach number was critical in a dogfight and made the Mk IX the best-handling Spitfire: 'It was the yardstick by which others were measured.'

Brown's favourite Spitfire was the Mk XIV, which he describes as the best in which to go to war. He undertook the Mk XIV's trials after Quill had flown the prototype and tested its long-range performance. 'I was delighted with the harmony of the controls in the Mk XIV... that's the quality that binds the pilot to the machine. It had better lateral control than the Fw 190 and even the Mustang.'

Brown's Mk XII experience included a low-level flight from Scotland to Hampshire to gather data on extended navigation and low-level characteristics. Departing Arbroath, he ran into bad weather and diverted to RAF Topcliffe, where the Canadians based there were keen to see the new Spitfire. After the weather cleared, Brown flew on to Chattis Hill in Hampshire. 'It was the most exciting Spitfire flying of my career.'

Exciting Spitfire flying also included taking to high altitude a specially modified Mk PR XI with smoothed-off wings and without the weight of guns and ammunition. 'It handled beautifully at 45,000ft, even though the usual ceiling was little more than 30,000ft – that's the same altitude as the early jets reached.' The main purpose of these flights, which Brown shared with Squadron Leader Tony Martindale (see page 177), was to explore the transonic zone of flight as the aeroplane approached the speed of the sound – which some called the 'sound barrier'.

Brown also worked closely with Joe Smith, who often attended Seafire trails at Farnborough, and with Alan Clifton, Smith's personal assistant and the man behind many of the structural changes to the Spitfire and Seafire as it was improved and then redesigned. 'You could always tell Smith was a Geordie and that his apprenticeship had given him an attention to detail. He was determined to get the Seafire to the standard demanded by the Royal Navy.'

The 'thunderous' Seafire Mk 47 prototype was Brown's last flight in a Spitfire at RAE Farnborough. Before it, he was able to interview General Adolf Galland, the former Luftwaffe fighter chief, about the Spitfire and was told that Germany's test pilots rated the Spitfire Mk IX above the Bf 109E/F and even the 109G. Brown believes that much could have been done earlier had Supermarine had the benefit of a wind tunnel of the capability of those found by the British in Germany in 1945, but that is all he can think of.

Like all those who flew the Spitfire and its naval version, the Seafire, Brown was smitten for life. 'Superb,' he says, 'simply superb.'

Captain George Baldwin CBE DSC* RN

Born 17 January 1921
Died 11 November 2005
Seafire pilot and Naval Fighter Wing commander

A veteran of the Norway campaign in 1940, George Baldwin was a dedicated naval aviator throughout his life after flying training on Tiger Moths and early operational experience in the Blackburn Skua with 801 Naval Air Squadron.

In July 1942 Baldwin was posted to 807 Naval Air Squadron as the first senior pilot of a Seafire unit, flying the Mk L IIc. A born leader with a ready smile but with no time for fools and inter-service manoeuvring, he brought the Seafire into service aboard the small carrier HMS *Furious*. On combat operations during Operation Torch from the carrier, Baldwin became the first Seafire pilot to destroy an enemy fighter in air-to-air combat against Vichy French Air Force Dewoitine D520 fighters; 807 NAS claimed four kills and a further 20 Vichy aeroplanes destroyed on the ground.

This group of newly qualified Seafire pilots is seen at RNAS Yeovilton, Somerset, on an unusually sunny day in January 1943, about to take delivery of at least 11 new Seafires built at nearby Westland in Yeovil. In the group are future Squadron commanders Stuart Jewers and R. 'Mike' Crosley. Imperial War Museum

By the Salerno landings on 9 September 1943, Baldwin had mastered the art of aerial fighting. His squadron embarked in HMS *Battler*, a 9,000-tonne escort carrier with a flight deck only 480ft in length and 70ft at its widest, but Baldwin was comfortable with landing the high-powered, skittish Seafire on such a small deck at a time when more Seafires were being written off in deck accidents than to enemy fire.

When 807 NAS disembarked for a forward airfield near Paestrum, the Seafire had to cope with small strips and primitive servicing provision in olive groves and tomato patches. The Fleet Air Arm provided air cover for the Allied force and later, as the Germans withdrew, dive-bombed retreating transport.

Baldwin was a born fighter pilot who instinctively understood the need for speed. He is recorded as having waxed his Seafire wings and had his propellers trimmed to attain better performance. His leadership led to his promotion to squadron commander in October 1943. The following year, still in the Mediterranean, he took 807 NAS against German forces in southern France and then against the Axis powers in the Greek islands, winning a bar to his Distinguished Service Cross, the third highest British gallantry award.

Disembarking to Egypt, 807 NAS, now part of 4th Naval Fighter Wing and commanded by Baldwin at the age of only 24, was allocated to the British East Indies fleet and embarked in the escort carriers HMS *Hunter* and HMS *Stalker*. The Seafire Wing was rated one of the nation's finest fighter groups by the time it engaged Japanese forces in the Andaman Sea and witnessed the surrender of Singapore on 12 September 1945.

Although Baldwin accepted a regular commission as a Lieutenant Commander in the Royal Navy in 1945, it always rankled that he would not command a warship, having been placed on the 'dry list'. He did, however, qualify at the Empire Test Pilots' School, test-flew with the Carrier Trials Unit, including on jets, and commanded the first naval jet squadron, 802 NAS, which operated the Supermarine Attacker. The Attacker was another design from Joe Smith and Alan Clifton, whose respective pedigrees, like that of Baldwin, derived from the Hooked Spitfire and Seafire.

Lieutenant Commander Stuart Jewers DSC RNVR(A)
Born 9 June 1915
Died 12 February 2011
Seafire Squadron Commander

Like so many of his contemporaries, Stuart Jewers trained on obsolete fighters like the Sea Gladiator and Fulmar before converting to the Seafire. By July 1944 Jewers was commanding 801 Naval Air Squadron protecting the Fleet Air Arm's successful operation to fix and attack the German battleship KMS *Tirpitz* in Kåjord Alta, Norway.

Doubling the size of the squadron to 25 Seafires, he led them aboard HMS *Implacable* to join 30 Naval Air Wing and the British Pacific Fleet. Jewers was also an accomplished test pilot and conducted trials with the Focke-Wulf Fw 190 fighter.

Commander R. 'Mike' Crosley DSC* QCVS RNVR(A)
Born 24 February 1920
Died 20 June 2010
Seafire Squadron Commander and author

With a distinguished reputation during Operation Torch and later in the Mediterranean, where he won his first Distinguished Service Cross, Mike Crosley came into his own with operations in support of D-Day. Like so many Fleet Air Arm pilots, he was a skilled practitioner at directing naval gunfire support.

Flying with 886 Naval Air Squadron in June, Crosley's leadership and aggressive spirit against the Luftwaffe was recognised with a mention in despatches and his bar to the DSC came after he had command of 880 Naval Air Squadron in the Norway operations and then with the British Pacific Fleet. He wrote a most entertaining autobiography called *They gave me a Seafire*.

APPENDIX I
POST-WAR SERVICE

The first jet fighters flew in the Second World War. The Messerschmitt Me 262 twin-jet was encountered and engaged by both Spitfires and American Mustangs; Spitfires were both the victim of the jet and the victor over it. The Meteor also entered Royal Air Force service in the latter stages of the war, although no jet-versus-jet combat occurred.

By contrast, in May 1945 there were over 5,850 Spitfires in service with the Royal Air Force and Commonwealth air units. Although the days of the Spitfire were numbered, the cessation of its military operations in Royal Air Force service was still a decade away. Post-war, the Spitfire would rarely see fighter action but it still had a host of useful functions to perform for the Royal Air Force at home and overseas.

The final sorties of the Second World War were flown by No 273 and No 607 Squadrons (the latter being from the Auxiliary Air Force) when both were operating Spitfire Mk VIII fighter-bombers armed with 500lb bombs to entrap Imperial Japanese forces at Sittang Bend in early August 1945 in support of South East Asia Command.

Immediately after the war ended, Spitfires were spread around the globe. The earlier marks were inspected and usually scrapped as having no further use – after six years of active service they were outclassed, worn-out and irrelevant to modern combat.

There have been persistent reports of buried Spitfires left in place after the war, some still in their packing cases. The highly publicised mystery surrounding the Burmese Spitfires continues: if they are there, they are probably Mk VIIIs, not Castle Bromwich-built versions as the local media in Birmingham would have everyone believe. Similar reports of long-lost Spitfires have come from Australia, India and Syria – proof perhaps of the Spitfire's enduring fame and iconic status.

From May 1945 Spitfires were also operating over Germany and patrolling the borders of central Europe against possible incursions by the Soviet Union, Britain's former ally. Newly formed and reforming air forces of recently liberated air forces were given Spitfires, especially Mk IX fighters, for their fledgling air forces. An example was the Royal Norwegian Air Force, which was formed as an independent force during the course of the war and received 71 Spitfires as its first equipment in 1945.

In Greece, where a civil war raged after the German and Italian Axis forces had departed, the Royal Air Force and Spitfire squadrons of the South African Air Force were in combat against communist forces and their role was taken over by the reformed Royal Hellenic Air

The last aerial combat missions flown by Spitfires were against other Spitfires. In the complex days after Israel's Declaration of Independence, there were air battles between Egypt, Israel and the Royal Air Force. On this Mediterranean beach lie the remains of two Royal Egyptian Air Force Spitfire Mk IX fighters that are being salvaged. Getty Images (Life Picture Collection)

Force in 1946. Between 1946 and 1949, the Greek government received 242 Spitfires.

When Italy surrendered in September 1943, plans were put in place to equip an Italian Co-belligerent Air Force on the Allied side. In 1944 Spitfire Mk V fighters flown by a mixture of Royal Air Force and Royal Yugoslav Air Force pilots were delivered across the Adriatic to Italy. These flew on, fighting the Luftwaffe until the arrival of Mk IXs, which were used for post-war training and air operations. The Italians were so delighted with their Spitfires that in 1948 they instituted air races between Spitfires and Mustangs for the Zerbinati Trophy.

Italian Spitfires were passed on to the nascent Israel Defence Force and the Union of Burma Air Force in the period 1952–55. Both of these air forces used these secondhand Spitfires for operations on the borders of their respective countries until the late 1950s. Israel and Egypt also received surplus Spitfires: Israel purchased 59 from the Czech government (without the agreement of London) and Egypt acquired 37 from retired Royal Air Force stocks.

The Spitfire saw service in the first Arab/Israeli War in 1948 with former Royal Air Force-trained pilots, including **Ezer Weizman** (who later became Israel's president), as well as Canadians, Britons and other nationals who found peacetime too dull after the adrenalin rush of combat. This conflict produced the only documented instances of Spitfire-versus-Spitfire engagements in combat.

On 22 May 1948 there was an engagement between a Royal Egyptian Air Force Spitfire Mk IX and Royal Air Force Spitfire Mk XVIII fighters over Ramat David, which was still a Royal Air Force station but had been mistakenly identified as Israeli by the Egyptians. British Spitfires were destroyed on the ground and later avenged by No 32 and No 208 Squadrons, only themselves to be jumped by Israel Defence Force Spitfires with the loss of the aircraft of Flight Lieutenant **Geoff Cooper,** who survived and rose to the rank of Air Commodore.

Israel's first confirmed aerial engagement was by former Royal Canadian Air Force Spitfire pilot **Jack Doyle** flying a Mk IX against the Egyptian aircraft on 21 October 1948. In another less-than-professional engagement, on 7 January 1949, Israel Defence Force Spitfires attacked British Spitfires and Tempest fighters over the Sinai (even though only one of the British fighters was armed), killing two of the British pilots. There is more than a little mistrust between the two air forces to this day despite Weizman's attendance at RAF Staff College and the sale of Meteor jet fighters to Israel almost immediately after the country's independence.

Syria was the last Middle Eastern nation to fly Spitfires, and probably the last nation to use them in active service. The Syrian Arab Air Force kept its Spitfire Mk F 22 fighters in service until 1953, by which time some Gloster Meteor jet fighters had arrived. Later, when Syria 'united' with Egypt, it also received Russian MiG-15s.

Turkey operated Spitfires, with some Turkish pilots being trained in Egypt during the war on redundant Mk Is. Later, as part of Churchill's plan to keep Turkey in the Western camp, some Mk IXs were also delivered.

Malaya's fight against communist insurgency, which began with the murder of three British rubber plantation workers on 16 June 1948, also saw the Spitfire in combat, but this time in a ground-attack role with rockets. Spitfire Mk XVIIIs from No 81 Squadron were used in the first punitive reaction, and military operations continued through into late 1949. In all, Spitfires undertook 1,800 sorties during the 'Emergency'. The last offensive Royal Air Force Spitfire operation was by No 60 Squadron from Singapore on 1 January 1951, but the Spitfire continued to serve after that date.

Back in Europe, the Swedish Air Force took delivery of 50 photo-reconnaissance Mk PR XIX Spitfires modified by Supermarine at RAF Chilbolton, then a Supermarine test airfield. Rather unglamorously, Sweden designated its Spitfires S31 and operated them over Soviet Karelia and the archipelago from Finland to Estonia until Soviet air-defence fighters started to pose a threat in August 1955. Despite Sweden's apparent neutrality, photographs brought back of Soviet nuclear facilities and submarines around Murmansk proved priceless to NATO.

Spitfires were also flown in the colours of a variety of other air forces, including Belgium, the Netherlands, France, Thailand, India and South Africa, where they were used to train Mustang pilots for the Korean War of 1950–53.

In the early 1950s Spitfires were operated in Hong Kong in the air-defence role and for local weather reconnaissance by the Royal Hong Kong Auxiliary Air Force. On 5 February 1952 a Kai Tak-based Spitfire Mk PR XIX flew to an indicated 50,000ft (actually 51,550ft by calculation) before the pilot, **Flight Lieutenant Ted Powles,** noticed that cabin altitude in the pressurised aircraft had dramatically fallen and he had to take the Spitfire down quickly

A major export success for Vickers was selling Spitfire Mk PR 19s to Sweden. This picture was taken at Chilbolton in 1948 and shows the four Swedish Air Force ferry pilots flanked by (from left) Conrad Mann (chief inspector), Wilf Elliott OBE (general manager), Len Gooch (production manager), Guy Morgan (Vickers test pilot) and Denis Le Penn Webb. Solent Sky

or risk passing out. The Spitfire entered an uncontrolled dive to 3,000ft, during which time the Air Speed Indicator (ASI) jammed at 690mph; it could be that the ASI was faulty but this speed, Mach 0.96 (just 0.04 short of the speed of sound), is the fastest *indicated* air speed ever recorded for a propeller-driven aeroplane. If true, it is a remarkable testament to the Spitfire's design, build quality and longevity. Jeffrey Quill, the chief test pilot at Vickers Supermarine, described it as 'extraordinary' – but it is not an official record.

It was from Kai Tak that the last front-line Spitfire flight was made on 1 April 1954 by No 81 Squadron's PS888, now flying with the Battle of Britain Memorial Flight. The Spitfire Mk PR XIXs in Hong Kong were then replaced by Gloster Meteor FR10s. A last Spitfire Mk F 24 sortie in Hong Kong took place on 21 April 1955 when the Royal Hong Kong Auxiliary Air Force participated in The Queen's Birthday flypast.

Spitfires performed usefully in second-line service until June 1957, when twin-engined Mosquitoes replaced them. These non-operational roles included weather reporting and anti-aircraft artillery cooperation with the British Army. In six years over 4,000 meteorological flights were completed without loss – a fitting tribute to a fine aeroplane. The last three Spitfire Mk PR XIXs were flown by the Temperature and Humidity Monitoring Flight.

The post-war use of Spitfires by foreign air forces brought another advantage. Long after British Spitfires were scrapped, there remained a bounty of surviving examples ripe for restoration to flying condition in more recent times.

APPENDIX II
SPITFIRE HERITAGE

There are 54 flying Spitfires in the world. Unsurprisingly, the biggest proportion is in Britain but there are also sizeable numbers in the United States and New Zealand, and other examples in France, Germany, South Africa, Sweden and Switzerland.

Restoration of these marvellous flying machines started after the Second World War when redundant examples became available to buy, including a number of Irish Air Corps machines that had been converted as trainers. Restoration techniques have improved to the extent that completely new Spitfires can be built but the charm and value is in keeping as much of the original as possible while balancing provenance with flight safety.

In recent years the Royal Air Force Battle of Britain Memorial Flight has been at the forefront in honouring the Spitfire and the gallant men and women who flew, built and supported these aeroplanes. The Flight traces its origins to 1957 when the decision was taken to create an Historic Aircraft Flight at RAF Biggin Hill, perhaps the most famous of all Battle of Britain airfields and then still in Crown service. Spitfires were centre-stage from the beginning, with at least one flying Mk XVI and three newly retired Mk PR XIXs joining the last production Hurricane. With the acquisition, in 1973, of the last flying Lancaster in Britain, the name changed to the Battle of Britain Memorial Flight (BBMF), a title that was in keeping with the Air Force Board's ruling that the Flight would commemorate all aircrew who served in the Second World War while also reflecting the Royal Air Force's greatest battle honour.

The BBMF's home since 1976 has been RAF Coningsby in Lincolnshire – 'Bomber County' – and this former Bomber Command station now has a visitors' centre that is a mecca for aviation enthusiasts. A training scheme for pilots to operate the BBMF's historic and valuable aircraft has been developed: Spitfire pilots are trained and converted to tailwheel aeroplanes on one of two Chipmunk trainers and then progress to the Hurricane, a more benign aeroplane than the Spitfire for the novice 'warbird' pilot, before finally being ready to fly a Spitfire. This training pattern allows first-tour Spitfire pilots to progress though the fleet to the nirvana of flying the 'little Spits', including the highly prized Mk IIa that flew in the Battle of Britain and the mighty Mk PR XIX with its 'thunderous' Griffon engine.

In the private sector few have done more to promote the rebuilding of the Spitfire than **John Romain** at the Aircraft Restoration Company based at Duxford, which is also home to the Imperial War Museum's collection of static aircraft. Other companies operating from Duxford are The Fighter Collection of **Stephen Grey** and The Old Flying Machine Company

When it comes to the perfect job in aviation, Squadron Leader Andy Millikin rates in the top ten: Royal Air Force Typhoon pilot as his day job and Battle of Britain Memorial Flight Spitfire pilot in his spare time. He comes from a family of pilots: grandfather was a Pathfinder and his father displayed the Vulcan. BBMF

Norway has turned out some great fighter pilots. Major Eskil Amdal is a test pilot who also serves as a Spitfire instructor at the Boultbee Flight Academy when the opportunity arises. Author's collection

Every inch a fighter pilot, Cliff Spink completes his post-flight shutdown with a glass of champagne handed over by Spitfire student pilot Cate Pye. Spink had just finished displaying in honour of the Canadian Avro Lancaster's visit to Humberside Airport in August 2014.
John Goodman

Carolyn Grace is the world's only female Spitfire owner/pilot. With her son, Richard, she flies this particular two-seat Mk IX from Duxford. During the Second World War it served with a New Zealand squadron and is credited with the first confirmed victory on D-Day.
Author's collection

The world's first training course to take an ab initio *pilot through to the Spitfire was set up at Goodwood (the former RAF Westhampnett) in 2012 and is run by Matt Jones, one of a growing new generation of young Spitfire pilots keen to carry on the tradition.*
Andy Annable

started by **Ray Hanna**, the first leader of the Red Arrows display team, and his son, Mark. With their passing, Sarah Hanna is now in charge.

The world's first female owner/pilot of a Spitfire, **Carolyn Grace**, is also based in East Anglia with the Grace Spitfire, which is a converted Mk IX that saw service over the D-Day beaches. This Spitfire was originally flown by her husband, Nick, and Carolyn took over the mantle when he died in a car crash, and nowadays she is joined by her son Richard.

Rolls-Royce, makers of the Merlin and Griffon engines, keep a superb example of the Spitfire Mk PR XIX in operation throughout the summer season in Britain. Under the management of **Phill O'Dell,** the chief test pilot, this Spitfire has just been rebuilt and now has another 30 years of life ahead of it. The Biggin Hill Heritage Hangar looks after a growing fleet of Spitfires and makes them available for displays in Britain and nearby parts of mainland Europe. **Cliff Spink** is a retired Air Marshal who has been flying Spitfires for more than 20 years and in 1998 he put on an emotional public display near Warsaw, Poland, with a Mk IX that was named 'Maid of Warsaw' for the event and marked as a Polish aircraft in the Royal Air Force.

At Goodwood, the Boultbee Flight Academy is the world's only aviation training school to allow students to make the transition from the Tiger Moth, through the Harvard and on to the Spitfire in a recreation of Second World War training. The Academy has developed an international reputation for engaging with the international aviation community, with students attending its courses from around the world. **Matt Jones**, the managing director, has recently linked to the Royal Foundation of the Duke and Duchess of Cambridge and Prince Harry to promote flying for disabled students in one of the Academy's Spitfire TR9 two-seat training conversions, G-ILDA, which has also been to Norway to fly Spitfire veterans of the Royal Norwegian Air Force.

APPENDIX III
SPITFIRE VARIANTS

In the ten years from its first flight to service after the Second World War, the Spitfire doubled in weight and changed wing shape and cockpit arrangement. Midway through its development it received an improved power plant and its armament was upgraded five-fold. The Spitfire was a fighter, fighter-bomber, naval fighter, strike aircraft, trainer and unarmed, high-speed photographic reconnaissance aircraft. Today, surviving aircraft are treasured warbirds, preserved with loving care.

Merlin-engined fighters

Mk I

The first production type entered service in September 1938 and it was first shown to the public on 4 May 1939. It was the Spitfire version that fought until September 1940 in the Battle of Britain. It was armed with eight 0.303in machine guns as standard with a small number modified to carry cannon. The main power plant was the Merlin III and 1,577 were built (50 by Westland in 1941); several were converted to later marks.

Mk II

Although first flown in April 1939, this improved fighter did not enter service until September 1940. It was powered by a Merlin XII and saw service until 1944. It was developed from and was generally similar to the Mk I, and 920 were built. There was a long-range variant created with a fuel tank built into the port wing, making it, pilots said, 'clumsier' to fly than the standard Mk IIa or IIb. There was a limited number of long-range versions with a slipper tank on the port wing.

Mk III

A development version that did not enter production, the Mk III reached 400mph in trials with clipped wings; only two were completed. It was designed as a replacement for the Mk II but it proved too complex for speedy production and the Merlin XX engines were needed elsewhere, so the Mk II was re-engined with the Merlin 45 instead – creating the Mk V. The Mk III prototype also acted as the prototype for the Mk IX.

Mk IV

Two were built; one converted into the prototype Mk VII (October 1940) and the second as a Griffon-engined prototype for the F 21. This was the most expensive single Spitfire built with the prototype contract agreed at more than £51,000.

Mk V

Created as an interim type by taking the Mk I and II airframes and fitting the new and improved Merlin 45 engine, it was eventually built in the greatest numbers, with 6,787 rolling off the production or modification lines at Vickers (Castle Bromwich), Supermarine (Southampton, Salisbury and Trowbridge) and Westland (Yeovil). It arrived in squadron service in February 1941 and immediately gave advantage for Fighter Command over the Bf 109F. There were three major sub-variants, including the Vb and Vc, which saw extensive service in Malta but were less successful in Australia.

Mk VI

Powered by the Merlin 47, 97 of this specialist high-altitude interceptor (with a pressurised cabin and extra-long wings) were built for entry to service in April 1942 to combat high-flying Junkers Ju 86R reconnaissance bombers overflying Egypt and Britain.

Mk VII

A pressurised version of the Mk VI with a Merlin 61 (later a 64) that entered service in March 1943. Production ran to 140.

Mk VIII

A development of the Mk VI, this Merlin-engined fighter served in the Far East and the Mediterranean theatres. With a two-stage supercharger, this Spitfire's overall length was increased by seven inches to accommodate the extra length; 1,654 were built as interceptor-fighters.

Mk IX

First flown in October 1941 and entering service in June 1942, 5,665 were built, mainly at the Castle Bromwich with five different wing types, carrying various arrangements of cannon and machine gun. It was in widespread service in 1944–45 and formed the backbone of newly created air forces after the end of the Second World War. Flight Lieutenant John Boyle of No 411 Squadron Royal Canadian Air Force downed a Me 262 on 25 December 1944 in a diving pass at 500mph.

Mk X

All 16 built with long-range wing tanks, retractable undercarriage and pressurised cockpit for long-range photographic reconnaissance.

Mk XI

Described by Captain Eric Brown as a 'delight at low level; smooth and fast'. The PR XI was instrumental in finding the V2 rocket launch pads at Peenemünde aided by the specially built structure and added fuel capacity. It was the main PR Spitfire from 1944 and could achieve 417mph at 24,200ft.

Mk XIII

Some 26 were rebuilt from Mk Va airframes as fighter-reconnaissance fighter for the Fleet Air Arm from August 1942.

Mk XVI

Powered by a Packard Merlin 266, this version entered service in September 1944 and 1,053 were built, most with a bubble canopy and cut-down rear fuselage and some with clipped wings.

Griffon-engined fighters

Mk VIII

The G variant, six of which were developed from the Mk VIII for Griffon engine trials as prototypes for the Mk XIV.

Mk XII

This was the first operational Griffon-powered Spitfire; best known for its extensive sorties against V-weapons, this mark first flew in September 1941 and 100 were built.

Mk XIV

Fighter and fighter-reconnaissance Spitfire powered by a Griffon 61 with a two-stage supercharger that entered service in February 1944; it was described by legendary test pilot Captain Eric Brown as the best Spitfire ever built and the best piston-engined fighter of all time. Some completed with a bubble canopy. Led by Squadron Leader R.I.A. Smith, Spitfire Mk XIVs from No 401 Squadron Royal Canadian Air Force were the first piston-engine fighters to destroy a jet in aerial combat on 5 October 1944 near Nijmegen.

Mk XVIII

Best described as a fighter-bomber, the Mk XVIII first flew in December 1942 and owes much of its development to the success of the Mk XIV, with bubble canopy fitted to all. Some were later converted as a fighter-reconnaissance variant and used in Malaya.

Mk F 20

Only two were built and one (DP851) was immediately used as the prototype F 21. Also sometimes designated Mk XX.

Mk F 21

Entering service just as the war in Europe ended, the F 21, with five-blade propeller, had first been developed in 1942 for the Griffon 61 engine and subsequently a contra-rotating prop version with a Griffon 85 was built, sometimes called the Victor. It saw limited service and was admired for the redesigned, strengthened wing. Post-war, the F 21 was used for the regenerated King's Cup air race; 121 were built at South Marston.

Mk F 22

Introduced after the war, in 1946, 264 F 22s were built with enlarged tail surfaces and cut-down fuselage, serving with Royal Auxiliary Air Force squadrons until 1951; many were sold on overseas.

Mk F 23

A single example built to the Mk 23 design on an existing Mk 21 airframe. It was to be named Supermarine Valiant.

Mk F 24

Not leaving service until 1955 (with the Royal Hong Kong Auxiliary Air Force), this was the last mark of land-based fighter, with 78 built with extra fuel and under-wing hard points for rockets and a Spitfire-style tail.

Photo-reconnaissance variants

Mk I

Several PR variants (A to G) were created for the highly skilled and dangerous mission of overflying enemy territory without self-defence weapons and only equipped with cameras. The most numerous version was the PR ID of which 220 were built with D-type 'bowser wing' and many later converted to Mk IV. A PR IB variant was one of the first Spitfires to be captured by the Germans in 1940.

Note on numbering: from 1941, the Air Ministry renumbered remaining Mk PR Is as Mk PR III (Mk IC), Mk PR IV (Mk ID), Mk PR V (Mk IE), Mk PR VI (Mk IF) and Mk PR VI (Mk IG). In 1942, Roman numerals were replaced with Arabic numerals for all new types.

Mk VIII

Seventy of this version were built, many converted on the production line from fighter variants; its first flight was in April 1942.

Mk X

Sixteen pressurised reconnaissance versions were built to enter service in May 1944. Development of the Mk X took longer than anticipated because of issues with fitting a pressurised cockpit.

Mk XI

An unpressurised photo-reconnaissance version with an excellent reputation for finding such exotic targets as the V2 rocket test facilities at Peenemünde research centre on the Baltic coast of Germany. It entered service in December 1942 more than a year ahead of the Mk X. Also used by the US Army Air Force, these Spitfires were reasonably frequent overhead visitors to Berlin.

Mk XIII

These were all converted from other marks and only 26 were completed. It was a fighter-reconnaissance aircraft rather than a straight PR machine, retaining four machine guns.

Mk XIX

First flew in June 1943 but did not enter service until April 1945; 225 built and served on the front line for a further 10 years. The Mk PR XIX was the first historic fighter to be flown by the Battle of Britain Memorial Flight. This was a hugely popular and effective PR aircraft that was also exported, most notably to Sweden, where it succeeded in photographing the Soviet nuclear submarine facility for the first time.

Naval Spitfires

Mark Ib

The original Hooked Spitfire that was secretly tested at Arbroath by the Service Trials Unit; 166 were converted from Mk Vb Spitfires for early delivery to the Fleet Air Arm.

Mk IIc

A developed version of the Mk Ib with its ancestry in the Mk Vc land-based fighter. Sub-contractors converted 262 and Westland built a further 110 for Fleet fighter service in three sub-variants.

Seafires

Mk III

The first purpose-built Seafire served across the British and French navies into 1948. This was based on the Spitfire Mk Vc but with the added practicality of folding wings; except for 30 built by Westland without!

Mk XV

Built as landplanes with Griffon engines and converted to the naval version by Cunliffe-Owen and Westland, the Mk XV first flew in March 1943 and 455 were built. It did not see war service in the Fleet Air Arm but did see active service as landplanes with the Union of Burma Air Force.

Mk XVII

Designed and built as a carrier-borne fighter with a robust undercarriage; 233 were completed for the Royal Navy, seeing service between 1945 and 1954. The main physical identification feature was the bubble canopy.

Mk 45

Fifty of these naval versions of the Griffon-powered Spitfire F 21 were built, giving the Royal Navy its first 450mph fighter. It was also exported for naval and land-based use.

Mk 46

Used for trials and training, this Seafire was a very rare bird with just 24 being built. The main recognition features were two three-blade Rotol contra-rotating propellers and the use of the Supermarine Seafang tail for trials at High Post.

Mk 47

Used by the Royal Navy in the opening stages of the Korean War, with some success, this was a powerful aeroplane with some tricky handling aspects for aircraft carrier use. It can be accurately described as a big Spitfire with an arrestor hook for carrier operations. Captain Eric Brown calls it 'thunderous'. It served from 1946 to 1954; it had a limited production run of 89.

Type 300

K5054, flown from Eastleigh,
January 1938

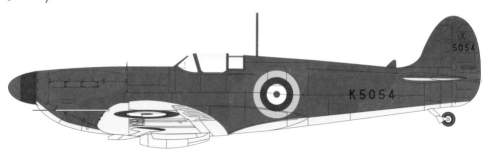

Speed Spitfire

K9834, 'N-17' flown from Eastleigh,
January 1938

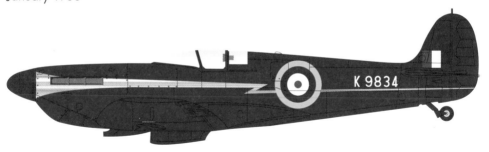

Spitfire Mk I

K9906, 'FZ.L' flown by Flight Lieutenant Robert Stanford Tuck
of No 65 (East India) Squadron, RAF based
at RAF Hornchurch, August 1939

Spitfire Mk IA

P9398, 'KL.B' flown by Pilot Officer Al Deere
of No 54 Squadron, RAF based at RAF
Hornchurch, 9 July 1940

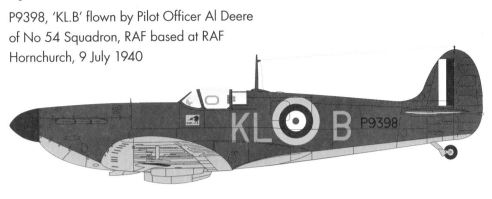

Spitfire Mk PR IA

N3071, flown by Flight Lieutenant Maurice 'Shorty' Longbottom of
No 2 Camouflage Unit, based at Lile-Seclin, France, 18 November 1939

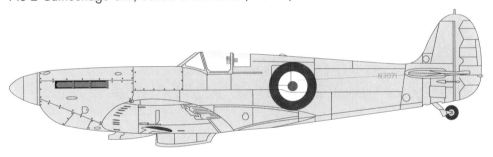

Spitfire Mk PR IB

P9931 of No 212 Squadron, RAF based
at Lille-Seclin, France, spring 1940

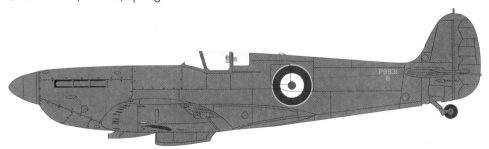

Spitfire Mk IB

R6776, 'QV.H' flown by Flight Sergeant George 'Grumpy' Unwin
of No 19 Squadron, RAF based at RAF Fowlmere, August 1940

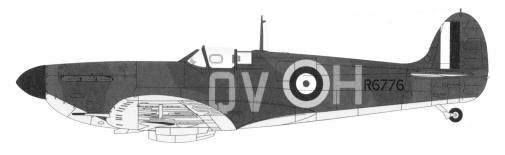

Spitfire Mk PR IC

R6903, 'LY' flown by Pilot Officer Gordon
Green of PRU, RAF St Eval, February 1941

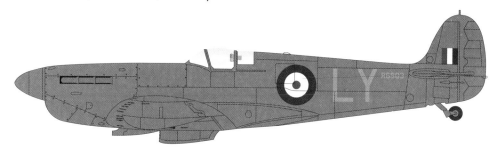

Spitfire Mk IIa

P7895, 'RN.N' flown by Flight Lieutenant R. Deacon Elliot
of No 72 (Basutoland) Squadron, RAF based
at RAF Acklington, April 1941

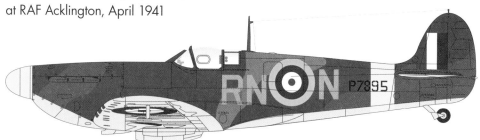

Spitfire Mk LR II

P8388, 'UM.R' flown by Flight Sergeant Walt 'Johnnie'
Johnston of No 151 Squadron RAF, August 1941

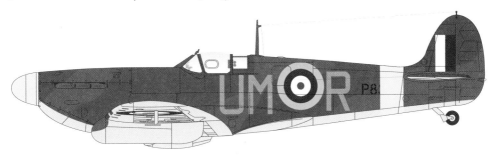

Spitfire Mk IIb

P8932, 'ZD.L' of No 222 (Natal) Squadron,
RAF based at RAF Hornchurch, 1941

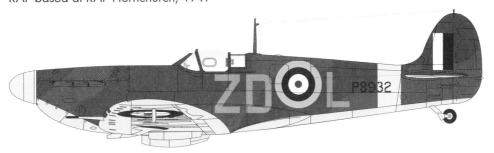

Spitfire Mk PR IF

X4498, 'LY-E', flown by Squadron Leader R.P. Elliott
of PDU, based at RAF Oakington, July 1941

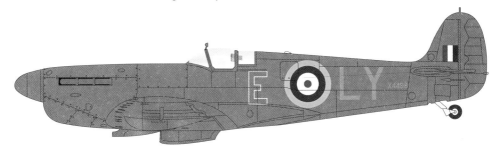

Spitfire Mk PR IG

R7143 of 13 Photographic Survey Squadron, Royal Canadian
Air Force based at Rockcliffe, Ontario, Canada, 1943

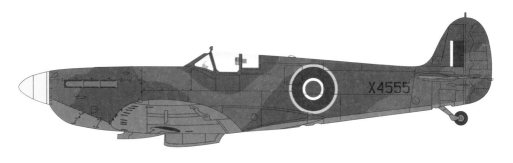

Spitfire Mk PR IE

N3317/3, 'LY', flown by Flight Officer Alistair
Taylor of PDU, based at RAF Heston, 7 July 1940

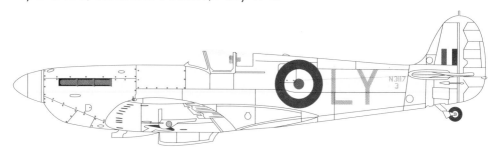

Spitfire Mk Va

W3185, 'DB', flown by Wing Commander Douglas Bader
of the Tangmere Wing, RAF based
at RAF Tangmere, 1941

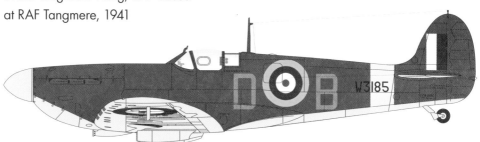

Spitfire Mk Vb

BL292, 'YT.K' flown by Sergeant Vladimir Kopecek of No 65
(East India) Squadron, RAF based at RAF Debden, early 1942

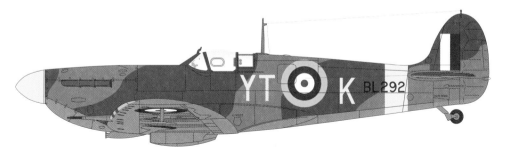

Spitfire Mk LF Vb

BL415, 'AZ.B' flown by Flight Lieutenant Walt 'Johnnie' Johnston
of No 234 (Madras Presidency) Squadron, RAF based
at RAF Deanland, 6 June 1944

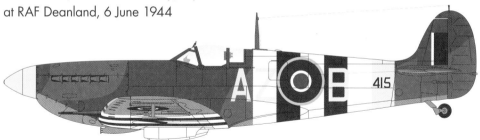

Spitfire Mk PR ID (Trop)

BR416 of No 2 PRU, based at Marble
Arch, Libya, 1942

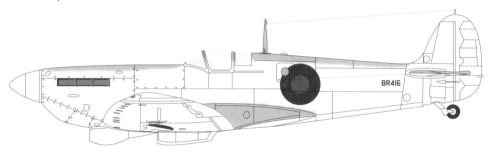

Spitfire Mk PR ID (Trop)

BR416, 'X' of No 74 OTU, RAF, based
in Palestine, Middle East, 1944

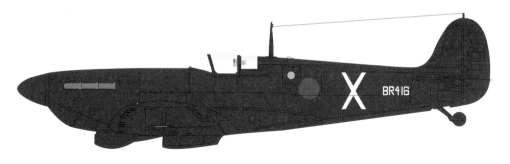

Spitfire Mk PR ID (Trop)

BP880, 'S' flown by Sergeant Ron Monkman
of No 681 Squadron, RAF, based at Comilla,
Bengal, 1944

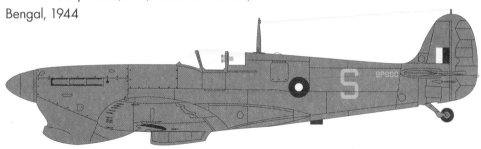

Spitfire Mk PR IV

Serial unknown, of PRU, 1942

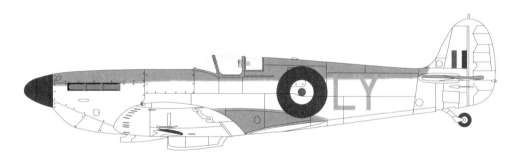

Spitfire Mk PR IV (Trop)

BP880, 'S/The Flying Scotsman' of No 681 Squadron,
RAF, based at Chandina, India, February 1943

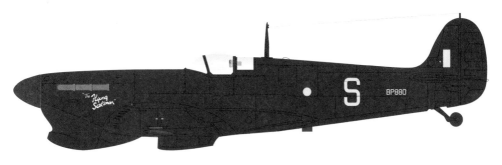

Spitfire Mk Vb (Trop)

ER874, 'AX.N/Cirecooks V' flown by Lieutenant Shalk
Willem van der Merwe of No 1 Squadron, SAAF based
at Goubrine, Tunisia, 17 April 1943

Spitfire Mk Vb (Trop)

ER622, 'WR.D' of No 40 Squadron, SAAF,
based at Gabes, Tunisia, April 1943

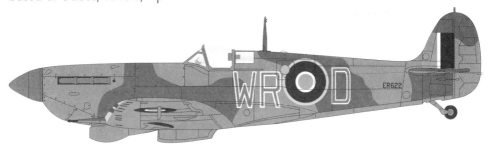

Spitfire Mk Vc

AB216, 'DL.Z' flown by Squadron Leader
Robert Oxspring of No 91 Squadron,
RAF based at RAF Hawkinge, May 1942

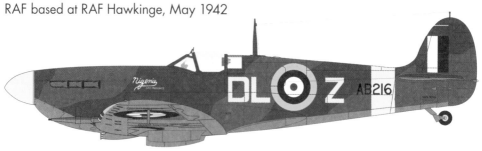

Spitfire Mk Vc (Trop)

BR323, 'S', flown by Sergeant George 'Buzz'
Beurling of No 249 Squadron, RAF,
based in Malta, July 1942

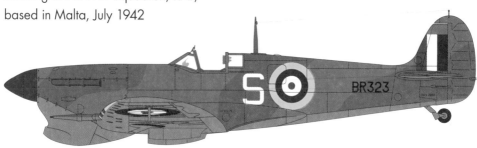

Spitfire Mk VI

BR579, 'ON.H' of No 124 (Baroda) Squadron,
RAF based at RAF Northolt, July 1943

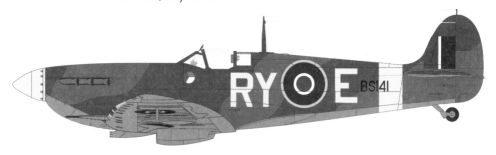

Spitfire Mk HF VII

MD172, 'NX.L' of No 133 Squadron,
RAF, RAF Harrowbeer, June 1944

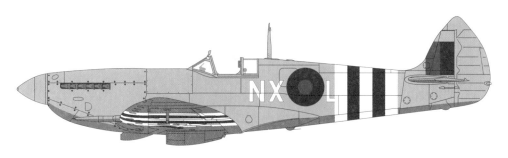

Spitfire Mk VIII

A58-528, 'CRC' flown by Wing Commander Clive 'Killer'
Caldwell of No 80 Fighter Wing, RAAF, based at Morotai,
Dutch East Indies, March 1945

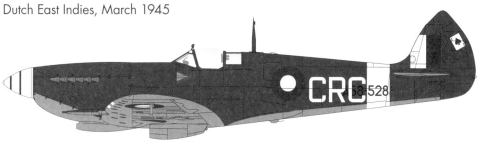

Spitfire Mk VIII

JF472, ZX.J' flown by Squadron Leader Lance
'Wildcat' Wade of No 145 Squadron, RAF
based at San Severo, Italy, 1943

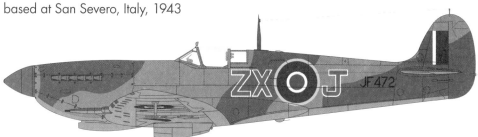

Spitfire Mk VIII

JF470, 'HL.R' of 308th Fighter Squadron,
USAAF, based in Italy, 1945

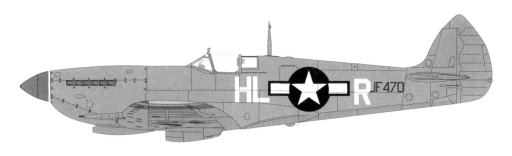

Spitfire Mk F IX

BF273 of Aeroplane and Armament Experimental
Establishment, Boscombe Down, October 1942

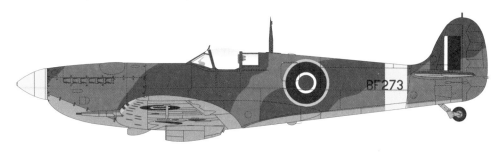

Spitfire Mk IXb

MK892, 'ZD.C' of No 222 Squadron,
RAF based at RAF Coolham, June 1944

Spitfire Mk IXc

MJ586, 'LO.D' flown by Sous Lieutenant P.H. Clostermann of No
602 Squadron, RAF, based at B11, Longues, France, July 1944

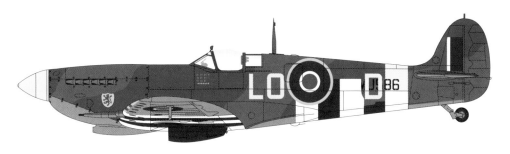

Spitfire Mk FR IXc

MK915, 'V' of No 16 Squadron, No 34
(Reconnaisance) Wing, RAF based at A12 Balleroy,
France, September 1944

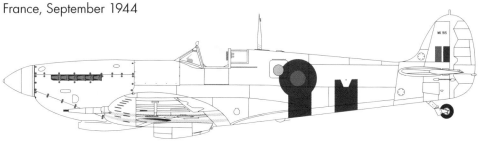

Spitfire Mk IXe

MK392, 'JE.J' flown by Wing Commander J.E. 'Johnnie'
Johnson, Officer Commanding 144 Wing, RAF based
at RAF Ford, June 1944

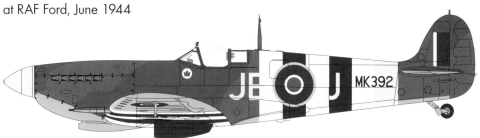

Spitfire Mk PR X

SR396 of No 541 (PR) Squadron, RAF
based at RAF Benson, January 1944

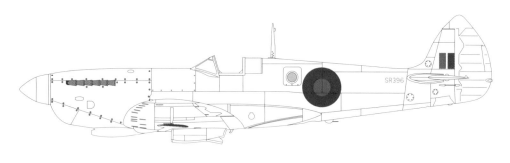

Spitfire Mk PR XI

Registration 'LV-NMZ', Argentina, 1947

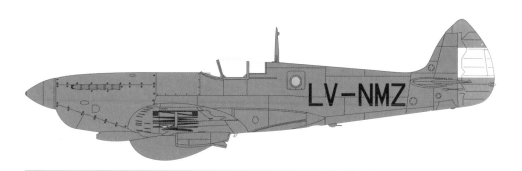

Spitfire Mk XII

MB882, 'EB-B' flown by Flight Lieutenant
Don Smith RAAF, RAF based at RAF
West Malling, 12 April 1944

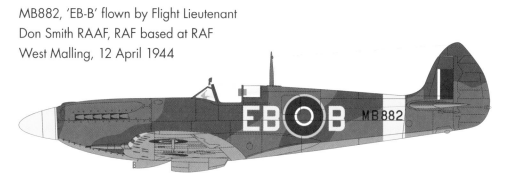

Spitfire Mk PR XIII

R7335, 'G3.K' of 718 Naval Air Squadron, Fleet
Air Air Arm, based at RNAS Henstridge, 1943

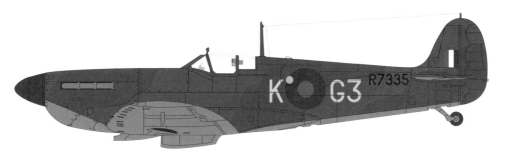

Spitfire Mk F XIVc

RN135 flown by Squadron Leader James 'Ginger' Lacey of
No 17 Squadron, RAF, based at Miho, Japan, May 1946

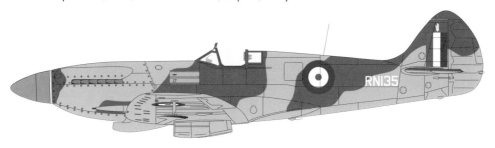

Spitfire Mk FR XIVe

NH869, 'H' of No 28 Squadron, RAF,
based at Kuala Lumpur, 1946

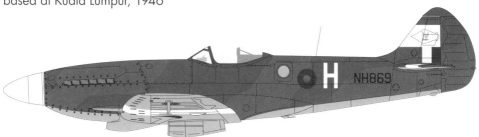

Spitfire Mk LF XVIe

SL727 'HT.L' of No 601 (County of London) Squadron,
RAF, based at RAF North Weald, late 1949

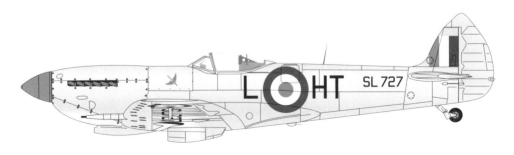

Spitfire Mk FR XVIIIe

TZ203 'J' of No 208 Squadron, RAF,
based at Fayid, Egypt, 1949

Spitfire Mk PR XIX (Type 390)

PM660, 'OI.X' of 2 Squadron, Royal Air Force
based at Furstenfeldbuck, Germany, 1946

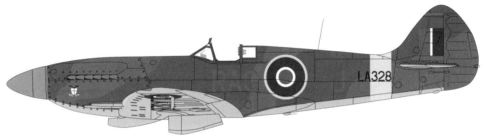

Spitfire Mk 21

LA329, 'RAG.J' of No 600 (City of London)
Squadron, RAuxAF, RAF Biggin Hill, 1945

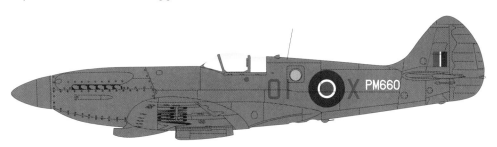

Spitfire Mk F 22

PK599, 'RAT.K' of No 613 (City of Manchester)
Squadron, RAuxAF, RAF Ringway, 1949

Spitfire Mk F 24

VN489, 'W2.A' of No 80 Squadron,
RAF, RAF Kai Tak, Hong Kong, 1950

Spitfire Mk Vb Floatplane

EP754, RAF, Great Bitter Lake, Egypt,
December 1943

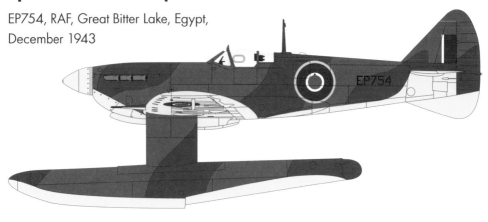

Seafire Mk Ib

PA103, 'AC.B' of 736 NAS based at
RNAS St Merryn, September 1943

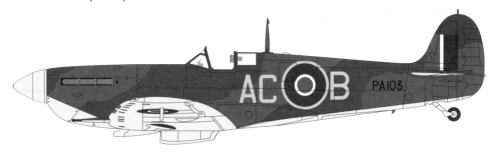

Seafire Mk Ib (Trop)

MB366, 'K' of 801 NAS aboard HMS *Furious*,
during Operation Torch, November 1942

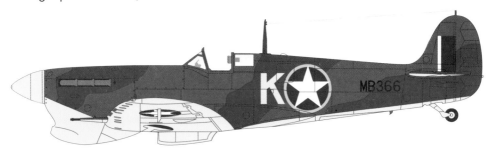

Seafire Mk IIc

MB183, '7.T' of 880 NAS aboard HMS
Argus, Home Fleet, October 1942

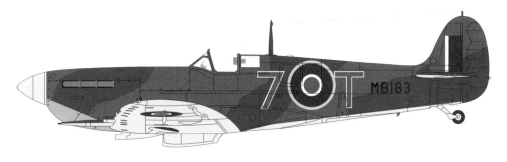

Seafire Mk L IIc

LR755 of The Fighter Flight, 843 NAS
based at Puttalam, Ceylon, March 1944

Seafire Mk IIc (Hybrid)

LR792, 'K/Betty' flown by Lieutenant D.A.E. Holbrook of
834 NAS aboard HMS *Battler*, British East Indies
Fleet, Indian Ocean, June 1944

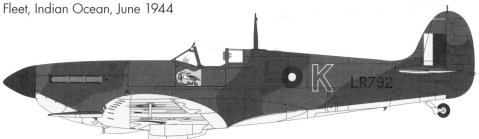

Seafire Mk III

PP979, 'D.5X' of 807 NAS aboard HMS *Hunter*, British
East Indies Fleet, Andaman Sea, May 1945

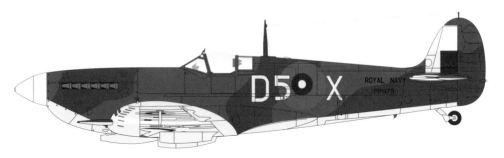

Seafire Mk L III

PR189, 'P7.N' of 801 NAS aboard HMS
Implacable, British Pacific Fleet, 8th Carrier
Air Group, circa May 1945

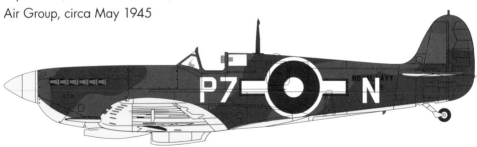

Seafire Mk FR III

NN621, '115/N' flown by Lieutenant Commander R. 'Mike' Crosley,
DSC of 880 NAS aboard HMS *Implacable*, British Pacific Fleet,
8th Carrier Air Group, May 1945

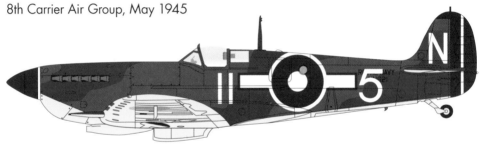

Seafire Mk XV

Serial unknown, '122' of 806 NAS aboard
HMS *Glory*, 16th Carrier Air Group, September 1946

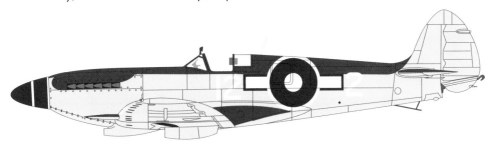

Seafire Mk XV

SR530, 'AA.K' of 883 Squadron, RCN based
at RCNAS Dartmouth, June 1948

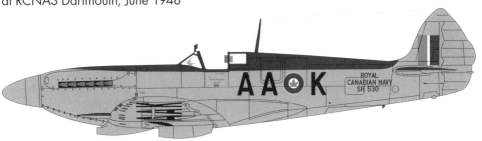

Seafire Mk XVII

SX273, 'S5.0' of 741 NAS, Operational Flying Training Unit, Air
Warfare School based at RNAS St Merryn, early 1947

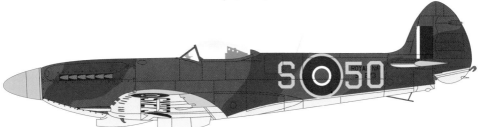

Seafire Mk 45

LA486, '583/LP' of 771 NAS, 51st Miscellaneous Air
Group, RNAS Lee-on-Solent, summer 1950

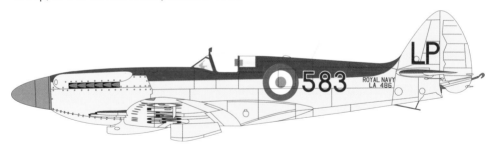

Seafire Mk 46

LA546, '900/LM' flown by Captain (Later Admiral) Caspar
John of the Station Flight, RNAS Lossiemouth, early 1948

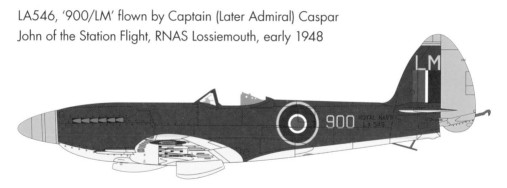

Seafire Mk 47

VP461, '178/P' of 800 NAS, 13th Carrier Air Group
aboard HMS *Triumph* off North Korea, August 1950

INDEX

254